FEARON'S

American
Literature

Globe Fearon Educational Publisher
A Division of Pearson Education
Upper Saddle River, New Jersey
www.globefearon.com

Executive Editor: Joan Carrafiello
Project Editor: Carol Schneider
Editors: Renée Beach and Kirsten Richert
Product Development: Mary Ansaldo, Lucy Jane Bledsoe, Margarete Wright Pruce, and Alyssa Robbins
Adaptations: Janice Greene and Tony Napoli
Permissions: Elsa Peterson Ltd.
Art Direction and Photo Research: Jenifer Hixson
Production Director: Penny Gibson
Production Supervisors: Linda Greenberg and Alan Dalgleish
Production Editors: Nicole Cypher and Alan Dalgleish
Marketing Manager: Margaret Rakus
Electronic Page Production: Margarita Linnartz, José López, and Mimi Raihl
Cover Design: Pat Smythe

ISBN 0-8359-1381-3

Printed in the United States of America
6 7 8 9 10   03 02 01 00

Globe Fearon Educational Publisher
A Division of Pearson Education
Upper Saddle River, New Jersey
www.globefearon.com

Contents

A Note to the Student   ix

Unit One: Suspense   1

   Chapter 1   2

      La Llorona: The Weeping Woman   3
        retold by Joe Hayes

      The Tell-Tale Heart   8
        an adapted story by Edgar Allan Poe

      The Pepper Tree   16
        an adapted story by Alfred Avila

      Chapter Review   22

   Chapter 2   24

      The Raven   25
        by Edgar Allan Poe

      The Cremation of Sam McGee   36
        by Robert W. Service

      Hist, Whist   43
        by e.e. cummings

      Chapter Review   46
      Unit Review   48

Unit Two: Childhood   49

   Chapter 3   50

      Dust Tracks on a Road   51
        adapted from the autobiography
        by Zora Neale Hurston

      Lame Deer Remembers His Childhood   60
        adapted from the autobiography
        by John Fire/Lame Deer and Richard Erdoes

      Prisoner of My Country   68
        adapted from the autobiography by Yoshiko Uchida

      Chapter Review   77

Chapter 4   **79**

The Circuit   80
an adapted story by Francisco Jiménez

The Jacket   91
an adapted story by Gary Soto

Chapter Review   98
Unit Review   100

Unit Three: Heroes   **101**

Chapter 5   **102**

The Ballad of John Henry   103
an anonymous poem

Harriet Tubman   107
by Eloise Greenfield

A Chant of Darkness   110
from the poem by Helen Keller

The Unsung Heroes   114
by Paul Laurence Dunbar

Paul Revere's Ride   117
by Henry Wadsworth Longfellow

Chapter Review   124

Chapter 6   **126**

Behind the Waterfall   127
an adapted story retold by Marion Wood

Paul Bunyan, the Mightiest Logger of Them All   133
an adapted story by Mary Pope Osborne

Thank You, M'am   139
by Langston Hughes

Chapter Review   145

Chapter 7   **147**

   Rosa Parks   148
     from the biography by Eloise Greenfield

   Roberto Clemente: A Bittersweet Memoir   156
     adapted from the article by Jerry Izenberg

   Chapter Review   164
   Unit Review   166

Unit Four: Nature   **167**

   Chapter 8   **168**

     A Visit to the Clerk of the Weather   169
       an adapted story by Nathaniel Hawthorne

     The First Tornado   177
       by C. J. Taylor

     River Man   181
       by Teresa Pijoan de Van Etten

     Chapter Review   187

   Chapter 9   **189**

     Winter Animals   190
       adapted from the essay by Henry David Thoreau

     Shipwreck of the Whaleship Essex   194
       adapted from the essay by Owen Chase

     A Taste of Snow   204
       an adapted essay by Jeanne Wakatsuki Houston

     Chapter Review   209

   Chapter 10   **211**

     Winter   212
       by Nikki Giovanni

     The Sky Is Low   215
       by Emily Dickinson

Birdfoot's Grampa   218
by Joseph Bruchac

In Hardwood Groves   221
by Robert Frost

Sierra   224
by Diane Siebert

Big Yellow Taxi   231
by Joni Mitchell

Chapter Review   234
Unit Review   236

Unit Five: Conflict   **237**

Chapter 11   **238**

Narrative of the Life of Frederick Douglass   239
adapted from the autobiography
by Frederick Douglass

Little Things Are Big   249
an adapted essay by Jesus Colon

Chief Seattle's Oration   253
adapted from the speech by Chief Seattle

Chapter Review   260

Chapter 12   **262**

Ribbons   263
an adapted story by Laurence Yep

Amigo Brothers   276
an adapted story by Piri Thomas

Chapter Review   284

Chapter 13   **286**

Ballad of Birmingham   287
by Dudley Randall

Taught Me Purple   290
by Evelyn Tooley Hunt

Simple-song 293
by Marge Piercy

War Is Kind 296
by Stephen Crane

Chapter Review 299
Unit Review 301

Unit Six: Family 302

Chapter 14 303

from Childtimes 304
by Eloise Greenfield and Lessie Jones Little

The Medicine Bag 312
an adapted story by Virginia Driving Hawk Sneve

Abuela 326
by Rosa Elena Yzquierdo

Chapter Review 329

Chapter 15 331

I Ask My Mother to Sing 333
by Li-Young Lee

Mother to Son 335
by Langston Hughes

My Father's Song 338
by Simon Ortiz

Lineage 341
by Margaret Walker

Abuela 344
by Denise Alcalá

Grandma Ling 347
by Amy Ling

Aunt Sue's Stories 350
by Langston Hughes

Bailando 353
by Pat Mora

To My Dear and Loving Husband   356
by Anne Bradstreet

Chapter Review   359
Unit Review   361

Unit Seven: Adventure   **362**

Chapter 16   **363**

Escape: A Slave Narrative   364
adapted from the autobiography by James W. C. Pennington

At Last I Kill a Buffalo   375
adapted from the autobiography by Luther Standing Bear

Chapter Review   386

Chapter 17   **388**

The Secret Life of Walter Mitty   389
an adapted story by James Thurber

The Invalid's Story   399
an adapted story by Mark Twain

Chapter Review   409
Unit Review   411

Appendix Opener   412
Glossary   414
Handbook of Literary Terms   424
Index of Authors and Titles   429
Acknowledgments   431
Art and Photo Credits   434
Index of Fine Art   437

A Note to the Student

Have you ever wanted to take a trip to a different place? Have you ever thought of yourself living in a different century? Perhaps you wondered what it would be like to live a different lifestyle. Imagine having the chance to just go away and explore. . . .

Incredible as it may sound, you can start your exploration with this literature book. Through literature you will learn about your cultural heritage and the cultures of others. You will experience the meaning of life as others see it. You will respond to their sorrows, joys, and struggles. As your knowledge of other lives increases, you will also become aware of yourself as a growing person. You will begin to ask questions about yourself. You will begin to ask questions about your own sorrows, joys, and struggles.

As you explore the pages of *Fearon's American Literature,* you will read the stories and poems of different authors, both past and present. The selections represent the experiences of people from different cultures and backgrounds. You will also come across language that is very powerful and beautiful. Learning to appreciate language as a way of communicating is part of studying literature as well.

As you read each chapter of this book, you will find several study aids. At the beginning of each chapter, you'll find **Learning Objectives.** Take a moment to study these goals. They will help you focus on the important points covered in that chapter. **Words to Know** will give you a preview of words you may not already know. The first time you see one of the **Words to Know** in the chapter, it will appear in dark type. A **Chapter Review** at the end will give you a quick summary of what you have just read.

In addition, special features throughout the book explore topics of interest that are related in some way, whether culturally or historically to the selection. If you are just looking for interesting information about the selection, these features provide that as well.

Finally, look for the notes printed in color in the margins of the pages. These friendly notes are there to make you stop and think. Sometimes they comment on the material you are learning or they ask you questions that make you think about the selection in a new or different way. Sometimes they give examples. Sometimes they remind you of something you already know.

We hope you enjoy reading this collection of American literature. Everyone who put this book together worked hard to make it interesting as well as useful. The rest is up to you. We wish you well in your studies. Our success is in your accomplishment.

SUSPENSE

Chapter 1

La Llorona: The Weeping Woman
retold by Joe Hayes
The Tell-Tale Heart
an adapted story by Edgar Allan Poe
The Pepper Tree
an adapted story by Alfred Avila

Chapter 2

The Raven
by Edgar Allan Poe
The Cremation of Sam McGee
by Robert W. Service
Hist, Whist
by e.e. cummings

Chapter 1

Somewhere between what you see and what you can imagine is the dark world of mystery and suspense. There are mysteries all around us. Get ready for strange things to happen as you enter a world just beyond the possible.

Chapter Learning Objectives

- Learn about the use of cause and effect in stories
- Learn about imagery
- Learn about the first-person point of view
- Learn about setting
- Learn about an author's use of foreshadowing to create suspense
- Learn about the mood of a story

La Llorona: The Weeping Woman
retold by Joe Hayes

Words to Know

LITERARY TERM

cause and effect any event or action that leads to a certain result

SELECTION VOCABULARY

humble not proud

increased became greater in degree

dashing very stylish

serenade sing below someone's window to get his or her attention

haughty proud acting, stuck up

engaged planning to get married

ignored did not pay attention to

pitifully very sadly

burial burying the dead

This is a story that the old ones have been telling to children for hundreds of years. It is a sad tale, but it lives strong in the memories of the people, and there are many who swear that it is true.

Long years ago in a **humble** little village there lived a fine looking girl named María. Some say she was the most beautiful girl in the world! And because she was so beautiful, María thought she was better than everyone else.

As María grew older, her beauty **increased**. And her pride in her beauty grew too. When she was a young woman, she would not even look at the young men from her village. They weren't good enough for her!

María is very beautiful, *but* she thinks she's better than anyone else. What problems do you think her self-image might cause?

"When I marry," María would say, "I will marry the most handsome man in the world."

And then one day, into María's village rode a man who seemed to be just the one she had been talking about. He was a **dashing** young ranchero—the son of a wealthy rancher from the southern plains.

He could ride like a Comanche! In fact, if he owned a horse, and it grew tame, he would give it away and go rope a wild horse from the plains. He thought it wasn't manly to ride a horse if it wasn't half wild.

He was handsome! And he could play the guitar and sing beautifully. María made up her mind—that was the man for her! She knew just the tricks to win his attention.

If the ranchero spoke when they met on the pathway, she would turn her head away. When he came to her house in the evening to play his guitar

This dashing young ranchero sounds like everything María could ever want. However, there are hints that he may not be the perfect husband for her after all. What are these hints?

and **serenade** her, she wouldn't even come to the window. She refused all his costly gifts.

The young man fell for her tricks. "That **haughty** girl, María!" he said to himself. "I know I can win her heart. I swear I'll marry that girl."

And so everything turned out as María planned. Before long, she and the ranchero became **engaged** and soon they were married.

At first, things were fine. They had two children and they seemed to be a happy family together.

But after a few years, the ranchero went back to the wild life of the prairies. He would leave town and be gone for months at a time. And when he returned home, it was only to visit his children. He seemed to care nothing for the beautiful María. He even talked of setting María aside and marrying a woman of his own wealthy class.

As proud as María was, of course she became very angry with the ranchero. She also began to feel anger toward her children, because he paid attention to them, but just **ignored** her.

One evening, as María was strolling with her two children on the shady pathway near the river, the ranchero came by in a carriage. An elegant lady sat on the seat beside him. He stopped and spoke to his children, but he didn't even look at María. He whipped the horses on up the street.

When she saw that, a terrible rage filled María, and it all turned against her children. And although it is sad to tell, the story says that in her anger María seized her two children and threw them into the river!

But as they disappeared down the stream, she realized what she had done! She ran down the bank of the river, reaching out her arms to them. But they were long gone.

On and on ran María, driven by the fear that filled her heart, until finally she sank to the ground and lay still.

What do you think of María's tricks to win the ranchero's attention? Is she wise or foolish in using the approach she uses?

The ranchero loses interest in María. His new feelings will begin a chain of unhappy events. As you read, notice the effects his behavior has on María.

Extreme anger can make people do terrible things. Why do you think María turns against her children?

The next morning, a traveler brought word to the villagers that a beautiful woman lay dead on the bank of the river. That is where they found María, and they laid her to rest where she had fallen.

But the first night María was in the grave, the villagers heard the sound of crying down by the river. At first they thought it was only the wind they were hearing. But when they listened more carefully, they heard words. "Aaaaiiiii . . . my children," a voice sobbed **pitifully**. "Where are my children?"

And they saw a woman walking up and down the bank of the river, dressed in a long white robe, the way they had dressed María for **burial**.

On many a dark night they saw her walk the river bank. But more often they would hear her cry for her children. And so they no longer spoke of her as María. They called her La Llorona—the weeping woman. And by that name she is known to this day.

There are many names the people could have given María. Why do you think they chose La Llorona, or the Weeping Woman?

And they still warn the young ones, "When it grows dark, get inside the house. La Llorona may be about, looking for her children. Be careful! She might mistake you for one of her own."

They tell of many children down through the years who have been chased by the crying ghost— and of some who have even been caught!

Is the story really true? Who knows? Some claim that it is. Others say that it isn't. But the old ones still tell it to the children, just as they heard it themselves when they were young. And in the same way the children who hear it today will some day tell it to their own children and grandchildren.

Literature Practice

Answer these questions on a separate sheet of paper.

1. Write at least three things about the ranchero that impressed María.

2. The story doesn't say why the ranchero loses interest in María. Why do you think he does?

3. How does María's pride finally cause her unhappiness?

4. How do you think the people from María's village feel when she is found dead? Explain your answer.

5. Why do people now call María, La Llorona, or the Weeping Woman?

6. Why do you think people have told this story to children for hundreds of years?

The Tell-Tale Heart
an adapted story by Edgar Allan Poe

Words to Know

LITERARY TERMS

imagery writers use special words or images to make the reader aware of how something in a story looks, sounds, or feels

first-person point of view the main character tells the story, using *I* to refer to himself or herself

SELECTION VOCABULARY

haunted reappeared, often in a scary way

passion a strong or deep feeling

film a thin coat of something

triumph an important success

shutters attached window covers that can be opened

muffled less loud

furious very angry

intense something that is very strong

seized grabbed suddenly

corpse a dead body

foul play dishonest behavior, murder

paced walked back and forth

Nervous—very, very nervous I had been and am. But why do you say that I am mad? The disease had sharpened my senses—not destroyed or dulled them. Especially sharp was the sense of hearing. I heard all things in heaven and on earth. I heard many things in hell. How, then, am I mad? Listen! See how clearly and calmly I can tell you the whole story.

It is impossible to say how the idea first entered my brain. But once it was born, it **haunted** me day

This story is told from the first-person point of view. This means that all the action of the story is seen through the eyes of the narrator. The narrator is the person telling the story.

and night. There was no reason for it. There was no **passion** to it. I loved the old man. He had never wronged me. He had never insulted me. I had no desire for his gold.

I think it was his eye! Yes, it was this! He had the eye of a vulture. It was a pale blue eye with a **film** over it. Whenever it looked at me, my blood ran cold. And so very gradually I made up my mind to take the life of the old man. This way I would be rid of the eye forever.

Now this is the point. You think I am mad. Madmen know nothing. But you should have seen *me*. You should have seen how wisely, how carefully I went to work. I was never kinder to the old man than during the whole week before I killed him. Every night, about midnight, I turned his door knob. I opened his door—oh, so gently.

The opening I made was large enough for my head. I put in a dark lantern, all closed, so that no light shone out. Then I thrust in my head. You would have laughed to see how smartly I thrust it in! I moved it very, very slowly so that I might not disturb the old man's sleep. Ha!—Would a madman have been so wise as this?

Then, when I was in the room, I undid the lantern carefully—oh, so carefully. I undid it just enough so that a single thin ray fell upon the vulture eye. This I did for seven long nights—every night just at midnight. But I found the eye always closed. So it was impossible to do the work. For it was not the old man that annoyed me, but his Evil Eye.

Every morning, when day broke, I went boldly into his room. I spoke bravely to him. I called him by his first name in a friendly tone and asked how he had passed the night. So he would have been a very smart man indeed to suspect what I did every night at midnight.

On the eighth night I was more careful than ever

How does the narrator describe himself? Do you think he can tell his story calmly and clearly? Why or why not?

Notice the imagery Poe uses to describe the old man's eye. It looks like "the eye of a vulture," and it is "a pale blue eye with a film over it." How does this description make you feel about the old man's eye?

The narrator is very careful in describing how he enters the old man's room. For seven nights he has done the same thing. What do you think will happen on the eighth night?

in opening the door. Never before that night had I *felt* the strength of my powers—of my wisdom. I could hardly hold in my feelings of **triumph**. There I had been opening the door little by little each night. He did not even dream of my secret deeds or thoughts.

I almost laughed at the idea, and perhaps he heard me. For he moved on the bed suddenly, as if he were startled. Now you may think that I drew back— but no. His room was pitch black, for the **shutters** were closed. So I knew he could not see the opening of the door. I kept pushing it open steadily, steadily.

I had my head in. I was about to open the lantern, when my thumb slipped on the tin fastening. The old man sprang up in the bed and cried out, "Who's there?"

I kept quite still and said nothing. For a whole hour I did not move a muscle. During that hour I did not hear him lie down. He was sitting up in the bed listening.

Soon, I heard a slight groan. It was not a groan of pain or of grief. Oh, no! It was the low, **muffled** sound that comes up from the soul when it is filled with fear. I knew the sound well. Many a night, just at midnight, it had welled up from my own chest. With its awful echo, it deepened the terrors that disturbed me. I knew what the old man felt, and I pitied him, although I chuckled at heart.

I waited a long time without hearing him lie down. I decided to make a slight opening in the lantern. I did so quietly—you cannot imagine how quietly. Finally, a single dim ray shot out from the opening and fell upon the vulture eye.

The eye was open, wide open. I grew **furious** as I gazed upon it. I saw it perfectly. It was a dull blue, with a disgusting veil over it that chilled my very bones. But I could see nothing else of the old man's body. For I had directed the light right upon the spot.

I have told you that what you mistake for madness is a sharpness of my senses. Now I say *that* what came to my ears was a low, dull, quick sound. It was a sound such as a watch makes when it is covered with cotton. I knew that sound well, too. It was the beating of the old man's heart. It increased my fury, as the beating of the drum stirs the soldier's courage.

Yet, I kept still. I hardly breathed. I did not move the lantern. I tried to hold the ray of light steadily upon the eye. Meantime the horrible beating of the heart continued. It grew quicker and quicker, and louder and louder. The old man's terror **must** have been rather **intense**.

It grew louder, I say, louder every moment! Do you hear me? I told you that I am nervous. So I am. Now at this dead hour of the night, in the awful silence of that old house, this strange noise excited

The narrator insists, for the third time, that he is not mad. He also says his hearing is very sharp. As you continue to read, do you agree that he is not mad? Why or why not?

Poe uses imagery to help you feel and hear the old man's heartbeat. As you read this, do you feel the terror of the old man? How do you think the narrator feels at this moment?

me to great terror. The beating grew louder, louder! I thought the heart would burst.

Now a new worry **seized** me. The sound would soon be heard by a neighbor! The old man's hour had come. With a loud yell, I threw open the lantern and jumped into the room.

He cried out once—only once. In an instant, I dragged him to the floor and pulled the heavy bed over him. I then smiled happily to find the deed done. But for many minutes the heart beat on with a muffled sound. This, however, did not bother me. It would not be heard through the wall. Finally it stopped. The old man was dead.

I removed the bed and examined the **corpse**. Yes, he was stone dead. I placed my hand upon the heart and held it there for many minutes. There was no pulse. He was dead. His eye would trouble me no more.

Do you still think me mad? You will think so no longer when I describe how I hid the body. I worked quickly, but in silence. I took up three planks from the floor. Then I placed the body under the boards and replaced them. I did this so cleverly that no human eye—not even his—could have found anything wrong.

When I had finished, it was four o'clock, still dark as midnight. There came a knocking at the street door. I went down to open it with a light heart. For what had I *now* to fear?

Three men entered. They introduced themselves as officers of the police. A cry had been heard by a neighbor during the night. Someone suspected **foul play**. The police had been called, and these men were ordered to search the house.

I smiled, for *what* had I to fear? The cry, I said, was my own in a dream. The old man, I said, was away in the country. I took my visitors all over the house. I told them to search—search well.

Finally, I led them to *his* room. I showed them his treasures, safe and secure. I brought chairs into the

---

Note the use of short sentences. This helps the reader understand how frightened the narrator now feels.

The narrator tells the reader the old man is dead three times. Why do you think the narrator needs to repeat this?

Who is the narrator referring to when he says, "not even *his*"?

room and told them to rest *here*. I placed myself in a chair above the very spot where the victim was buried!

The officers were satisfied. I was at ease. They sat and talked of familiar things. But before long, I felt myself getting pale and wished them gone. My head ached, and I thought I heard a ringing in my ears. The ringing became clearer. I talked more freely to get rid of the sound. But it continued. Finally, I found that the noise was not within my ears.

The sound increased—and what could I do? It was *a low, dull, quick sound, much like a watch makes when it is covered with cotton.* I gasped for breath—yet the officers did not hear it. I talked more quickly, more forcefully. But the noise steadily increased.

I **paced** the floor. But the noise steadily increased. Oh, God! What could I do? I swung the chair upon which I had been sitting and scraped it upon the boards. But the noise continued.

It grew louder—louder—*louder*! And still the men talked pleasantly. Was it possible they did not hear it? No! They heard. They suspected. They *knew*. They were making a fool of me.

Anything was better than this agony! I could bear those awful smiles no longer. I felt I must scream or die! And now again, listen! louder! louder! *louder*!

"Villains!" I cried. "Search no more! I admit the deed. Tear up the planks! Here—here! It is the beating of his awful heart!"

As the story closes, Poe uses punctuation to show the reader how upset the narrator has become. It also helps the reader to see how calm the police officers are. This difference helps the reader to feel the mood of the characters.

Seeing is Believing

It is 1962. You are sitting in a movie theater watching *Tales of Terror*. The movie is based on the horror stories of Edgar Allan Poe. The popcorn you are eating reaches your mouth much more slowly as the scenes flash by. In one, you watch a man being buried alive behind a brick wall. In another, you hear the horrible screams of a man being tortured. Do you ever wonder how these scenes are done? The magic is done with special effects. The screams you hear are from a sound track that is added to the film after the action is done. Shadowy background lights add to the creepy feeling you get while watching a horror movie. Those weird, twisted faces can be done with special make-up. Huge hairy spiders, ghosts flying through the air, or madmen screaming in terror—all are skillfully done to make you really believe what you see!

Literature Practice

Answer these questions on a separate sheet of paper.

1. Does the narrator think he is mad? Explain your answer.
2. What does the narrator do in the old man's room each night?
3. Why does the narrator murder the old man?
4. Why do you think the narrator tells the police that he has killed the old man?

The Pepper Tree

an adapted story by Alfred Avila

Words to Know

LITERARY TERMS

setting where a story takes place

foreshadowing clues in a story about what is going to happen next

mood the feeling one gets from reading a story

SELECTION VOCABULARY

hardship trouble; pain and suffering

exile forced away from one's country or home

grove a small group of trees

numbed deadened; unable to feel as a result of the cold

utter speak

overcome defeat or beat; master

shroud a cloth used to wrap a dead body

craze drive

possessed took hold of; owned

silhouette a dark shape or outline seen against a light background

---

The old man lived in a weather-beaten shack on the road that led to the river. He had seen many good times as well as bad times. The fires of life had made him hard and wrinkled. The old man had one dream. That dream was to return to his home, a small town named Meoqui in Chihuahua, Mexico. But the old man was poor. And so, he had to accept a life of **hardship** and **exile**.

"What a life I have! One of these days I'll go back home," he would mutter to himself.

Sometimes the old man would sit on a stool in front of his shack. He would look toward the **grove** of cottonwoods and watch the crows crackling and flying among the trees. Here and there, like lonely guards, grew the old pepper trees. These trees had old, twisted branches and trunks. They looked like old men begging the clouds to release them from standing in the fields under a double curse. In summer they were burned by the hot sun. In winter they were **numbed** by frosty winds. The ground beneath the trees was covered with messy piles of small leaves and berries.

The wind came that night. It whistled and howled around the shack. "It's the Devil himself," the old man mumbled as he lay down to sleep. "He's searching for evildoers to carry away."

Midnight came. The clock on the wall seemed to tick louder than usual. The old man awoke suddenly and was taken with fear. Something was in the room. He strained to see into the darkness. A moan came softly from a shadow on the other side.

"Who is it?" he asked with fear.

"I have gold!" The voice echoed in the room. "I have gold!" it repeated.

The old man stared across the room, trembling. He wanted to say something. But he was so choked with fear that he couldn't **utter** a sound.

"I have gold! I have gold!" the ghost repeated again and again. Then suddenly it disappeared. Only the gentle howling of the wind could be heard.

The old man could feel his heart pounding. He felt faint. His trembling hands could hardly grab the sheets.

The next day, he thought about what had happened the night before. He told himself he had to **overcome** his fear. He had to ask the ghost about the gold and where it was located.

"The ghost must return and tell the secret of the

Notice how Avila writes a good description of the setting for this story. He tells us that the old man's house is a shack. There are old, twisted trees, crows, piles of leaves, and berries all around. Later, Avila describes the wind as whistling and howling. What mood is created by these descriptions of the setting?

The old man says the wind is the devil "searching for evildoers to carry away." What hint does this statement give about what is to come in the story?

gold," he thought. "This way it can find peace in the other world." Silently, he told himself he would find out the location of the treasure that night.

That night, once again at midnight, the ghost returned. "I have gold! I have gold!" it repeated.

The old man tried to overcome his fear. In a frightened, hoarse voice, he asked, "Where is the gold?"

The ghost answered slowly. "In a pepper tree. In a pepper tree." Then once again it disappeared. The lonely hoot of an owl could be heard from the faraway pepper trees. The silence of the night returned to the shadows in the room.

"The gold escaped me again!" the old man muttered. "Well, perhaps tomorrow," he told himself.

The following night the old man was set to learn the secret of the gold. Greed had overcome his fear. "If I find out the secret of the gold, I could return home to Meoqui and Chihuahua, to my homeland. To my country!" he said aloud. He would find out the secret that night.

The ticking of the clock was loud that night. The old man could not sleep. He could only think of the gold.

Suddenly, he heard the low moan and felt the ghost was present. It was standing by the window. It was pointing in the direction of the huge pepper tree that grew beside the large grove of cottonwoods. The old man could not see the features of the ghost. He could only make out its torn **shroud** and its bony fingers pointing in the direction of the tree.

"In the pepper tree. In the pepper tree," the ghost moaned softly. The old man just sat, wide-eyed, across the room.

When the ghost disappeared, the old man raised himself from his bed. He quickly put on his serape and sandals and headed across the room. He looked out in the direction of the tree. "My treasure. My life!" he cried.

Imagine hearing a ghost repeating the same words again and again. The old man is terrified as he hears this constant echo. Getting the reader to "hear" these repeated whispers adds to the scary mood of the story.

The author adds details to his story that make the suspense build. How does the clock create a feeling of excitement?

The old man opened his door. The cold night air hit his face, and a chill ran down his spine. But his mind was made up. The gold was calling to him. Not even the dark of night nor its demons would stop him. The **craze** for gold **possessed** him. It was the driving force that moved him quickly across the grassy field toward the direction of the tree.

The old man could make out the **silhouette** of the pepper tree in the distance. He began almost to run, looking around as he did. It was as if he were

The old man is very afraid of the ghost. Yet, he decides he must talk to it. What strong feeling does he have that makes him overcome his fear?

expecting someone to step out from the darkness and wake him up from a dream.

He got closer to the tree. The sky seemed to get darker and the shadows faded. The remaining light was disappearing. As he got even closer, he could hear the ghostly voice softly repeat, "I have gold!" The words increased his desire to move on.

Now he could make out a figure standing near the tree. "It's the ghost waiting to show me where the gold is." When he got near the figure, he said out loud, "Where's the gold?"

The shroud slipped off the ghostly head. The old man was terrified by what he saw. A white skull shone in the darkness. "The Bald One, the Bald One!" he screamed into the darkness. His eyes were fixed on

Do you think the old man is going to get what he wants? How can you tell?

Here the author describes what Death looks like.

the talking skull of Death as the ground opened up beneath his feet.

"Your treasure is death," the ghost said. Then the old man plunged downward into the bottomless pit of death. His final screams pierced the stillness of the night.

Do not be like the old man. Don't let the lust for gold blind you. Don't let greed be your guide. Remember the saying that gold and greed go hand in hand. If you do not know when to walk away from them, you could well meet their master, the Bald One—in the shade of the pepper tree.

In this last paragraph of the story, the author tells you the meaning of the story. Why do you think he ends the story this way?

Literature Practice

Answer these questions on a separate sheet of paper.

1. What does the old man want to do with the gold if he could get it?

2. The setting of a story sets the mood. Find and write two sentences from the story that set a scary mood.

3. What do the following sentences from the story foreshadow?

   "The old man opened his door. The cold night air hit his face, and a chill ran down his spine."

4. In your own words, what does the saying "gold and greed go hand in hand" mean? Do you believe the saying? Why or why not?

Chapter Review

Summaries

- **La Llorona: The Weeping Woman**—There is a very beautiful woman named María. But she is too proud. María marries a rich ranchero, and they have two children. But the ranchero soon loses interest in his wife. One day, María sees him with an elegant lady. She becomes very angry and jealous. In her anger, María throws her children in the river, killing them. Then María realizes what she has done. She runs along the river, crying, until she dies. Ever since María's death, the villagers say that they can hear her weeping at night. They also say that they can see María's ghost walking along the river.

- **The Tell-Tale Heart**—The narrator says that an old man has an evil eye. Because he hates the evil eye, the narrator kills the old man and hides the body under the floorboards. The police come and search the house. Then the man thinks he hears the old man's heart beating. The sound drives him crazy. He tears up the floorboards and tells the police that he killed the old man.

- **The Pepper Tree**—This is a story about an old man who wants to return to his hometown, Meoqui. One night a ghost visits his bedroom. The ghost tells the man about buried gold. The old man is frightened, but he wants the gold so he can go back home. The ghost tells the man that the gold is in the pepper tree. When the old man goes to the tree to get the gold, the ghost is waiting for him. The ghost turns out to be Death. The story ends with a warning: Do not let greed guide you.

Chapter Quiz

Choose the letter of the correct answer. Rewrite the sentences on a separate sheet of paper.

1. The old man in "The Pepper Tree" forgets his fear of the ghost because of
   a. the ghost's appearance.   c. his love of gold.
   b. his love of ghosts.   d. his love of the pepper tree.

2. In "The Pepper Tree," what does the old man find at the pepper tree?
   a. gold and riches
   b. his hometown
   c. his own death
   d. a long-lost love

3. The narrator in "The Tell-Tale Heart" hates the old man because he
   a. has a scary-looking eye.
   b. is mean.
   c. doesn't pay him well.
   d. hates everyone.

4. In "The Tell-Tale Heart," the police find out who murdered the old man because
   a. they find the body.
   b. they see the evil eye.
   c. they hear the heartbeat.
   d. the narrator tells them.

5. In "La Llorona: The Weeping Woman," María does not marry a man from her village because
   a. there are none her age.
   b. no one will marry her.
   c. her mother will not let her.
   d. she thinks she is too good for them.

Thinking and Writing

Answer the following questions on a separate sheet of paper. Write one or two paragraphs for each one.

1. Ghosts appear in two of the stories in this chapter. Write a description of both ghosts, showing how they are alike and different.

2. The old man in "The Pepper Tree" has two feelings that are in conflict: fear and desire for gold. Explain how this conflict adds to the suspense in the story.

3. Describe the setting of either "The Tell-Tale Heart" or "The Pepper Tree." How does the setting make the story scary?

Chapter 2

Poetry, like music, draws out people's feelings. Sometimes, poetry can be even more scary and suspenseful than stories.

Chapter Learning Objectives

- Learn about rhyme in poetry
- Learn about stanzas in poetry
- Learn about meter in poetry
- Learn what it means to coin a word

The Raven
by Edgar Allan Poe

Words to Know

LITERARY TERMS

rhyme words that sound alike

stanza a group of lines in a poem set apart from other groups of lines

SELECTION VOCABULARY

dreary gloomy and dull

quaint old-fashioned, out of date

bleak cheerless, unhappy

surcease stop

entreating asking

implore to beg for

mortals humans

token sign

obeisance a bow or another sign of respect

pallid pale

In the poem, a man sits alone at midnight. He is trying not to feel so sad about his lost love, Lenore. The man hears a tapping noise. He thinks it is a visitor. He opens the window, and a raven comes into the room.

The raven says its name is "Nevermore." The man asks the bird if he will ever be free from the sadness of losing Lenore. He asks if he will see Lenore in heaven. The bird says nothing but "Nevermore."

The man tells the bird to leave. The bird is making him feel sadder than ever. But the bird says: "Nevermore."

As the poem ends, the bird is still in the man's room.
The man will never be free from the spell of the raven—
or from his own sadness.

———— ❦ ————

As you read the poem,
note the words that
rhyme within a line. In the
opening line, *weary* and
dreary rhyme. Can you
find other words that
rhyme within each line?

Once upon a midnight **dreary**, while I pondered,
    weak and weary,
Over many a **quaint** and curious volume of forgotten
    lore—
5 While I nodded, nearly napping, suddenly there came
    a tapping,
As of someone gently rapping, rapping at my
    chamber door.
"'Tis some visitor," I muttered, "tapping at my
10   chamber door—
              Only this, and nothing more."

This stanza ends with the
word *more*. Find all the
other words in this
stanza that rhyme with
more. How does the
rhyming give the poem a
musical feel?

Ah, distinctly I remember it was in the **bleak**
    December,
And each separate dying ember wrought its ghost
15   upon the floor.
Eagerly I wished the morrow;—vainly I had tried to
    borrow
From my books **surcease** of sorrow—sorrow for the
    lost Lenore—
20 For the rare and radiant maiden whom the angels
    name Lenore—
              Nameless here for evermore.

How does the narrator of
this poem try to calm his
fear about the tapping?
What does he say it is?

And the silken sad uncertain rustling of each purple
    curtain
25 Thrilled me—filled me with fantastic terrors never felt
    before;
So that now, to still the beating of my heart, I stood
    repeating:

"'Tis some visitor **entreating** entrance at my
30   chamber door—
Some late visitor entreating entrance at my chamber
    door;
           This it is and nothing more."

The narrator doesn't open the door until this fourth stanza. How does that build suspense in the poem?

35 Presently my soul grew stronger; hesitating then no
        longer,
    "Sir," said I, "or Madam, truly your forgiveness I
        implore;
    But the fact is I was napping, and so gently you came
        rapping,
40 And so faintly you came tapping, tapping at my
        chamber door,
    That I scarce was sure I heard you"—here I opened
        wide the door;—
                            Darkness there and nothing more.

Note how the last line in each stanza is a variation of the same idea. How does this repetition add to the poem?

45 Deep into that darkness peering, long I stood there
        wondering, fearing,
    Doubting, dreaming dreams no **mortals** ever dared
        to dream before;
    But the silence was unbroken, and the stillness gave
50   no **token**,
    And the only word there spoken was the whispered
        word, "Lenore!"
    This I whispered, and an echo murmured back the
        word, "Lenore!"—
55   Merely this and nothing more.

    Back into the chamber turning, all my soul within me
        burning,
    Soon again I heard a tapping something louder than
        before.
60 "Surely," said I, "surely that is something at my
        window lattice;
    Let me see, then, what thereat is, and this mystery
        explore—
    Let my heart be still a moment, and this mystery
        explore;—
65   'Tis the wind, and nothing more."

    Open here I flung the shutter, when, with many a flirt
        and flutter,

70 In there stepped a stately Raven of the saintly days of
        yore.
    Not the least **obeisance** made he; not a minute
        stopped or stayed he,
    But, with mien of lord or lady, perched above my
        chamber door—
75 Perched upon a bust of Pallas just above my chamber
        door—
                    Perched, and sat, and nothing more.

    Then this ebony bird beguiling my sad fancy into
        smiling,

80 By the grave and stern decorum of the countenance it wore,
"Though thy crest be shorn and shaven, thou," I said, "art sure no craven,
Ghastly grim and ancient Raven wandering from the
85 Nightly shore—
Tell me what thy lordly name is on the Night's Plutonian shore!"
                    Quoth the Raven, "Nevermore."

Much I marveled this ungainly fowl to hear discourse
90 so plainly,
Though its answer little meaning—little relevancy bore;
For we cannot help agreeing that no living human being
95 Ever yet was blessed with seeing bird above his chamber door—
Bird or beast upon the sculptured bust above his chamber door,
                    With such name as "Nevermore."

100 But the Raven, sitting lonely on that placid bust, spoke only
That one word, as if his soul in that one word he did outpour.
Nothing farther then he uttered; not a feather then he
105 fluttered—
Till I scarcely more than muttered: "Other friends have flown before—
On the morrow *he* will leave me as my Hopes have flown before."
110   Then the bird said, "Nevermore."

Startled at the stillness broken by reply so aptly spoken,

"Doubtless," said I, "what it utters is its only stock
    and store,
115 Caught from some unhappy master whom unmerciful
    Disaster
Followed fast and followed faster till his songs one
    burden bore—
Till the dirges of his Hope that melancholy burden
120   bore
           Of 'Never—nevermore.'"

But the Raven still beguiling all my sad soul into
    smiling,
Straight I wheeled a cushioned seat in front of bird
125   and bust and door;
Then, upon the velvet sinking, I betook myself to
    linking
Fancy unto fancy, thinking what this ominous bird of
    yore—
130 What this grim, ungainly, ghastly, gaunt, and ominous
    bird of yore
           Meant in croaking "Nevermore."

This I sat engaged in guessing, but no syllable
    expressing
135 To the fowl whose fiery eyes now burned into my
    bosom's core;
This and more I sat divining, with my head at ease
    reclining
On the cushion's velvet lining that the lamp-light
140   gloated o'er,
But whose velvet violet lining with the lamp-light
    gloating o'er
           She shall press, ah, nevermore!

Then, methought, the air grew denser, perfumed
145   from an unseen censer

Swung by angels whose foot-falls tinkled on the tufted
    floor.
"Wretch," I cried, "thy God hath lent thee—by these
    angels he hath sent thee
150 Respite—respite and nepenthe from thy memories of
    Lenore!
Quaff, oh quaff this kind nepenthe and forget this lost
    Lenore!"
            Quoth the Raven, "Nevermore."

155 "Prophet!" said I, "thing of evil!—prophet still, if bird
    or devil!—
Whether Tempter sent, or whether tempest tossed
    thee here ashore,
Desolate, yet all undaunted, on this desert land
160   enchanted—
On this home by Horror haunted,—tell me truly,
    I implore—
Is there—*is* there balm in Gilead?—tell me—tell me,
    I implore!"
165   Quoth the Raven, "Nevermore."

"Prophet!" said I, "thing of evil!—prophet still, if bird
    or devil!
By that heaven that bends above us—by that God we
    both adore—
170 Tell this soul with sorrow laden if, within the distant
    Aidenn,
It shall clasp a sainted maiden whom the angels name
    Lenore—
Clasp a rare and radiant maiden whom the angels
175   name Lenore."
            Quoth the Raven, "Nevermore."

"Be that word our sign of parting, bird or fiend!"
    I shrieked, upstarting—
"Get thee back into the tempest and the Night's

180   Plutonian shore!
Leave no black plume as a token of that lie thy soul
        hath spoken!
Leave my loneliness unbroken!—quit the bust above
        my door!
185 Take thy beak from out my heart, and take thy form
        from off my door!"
                    Quoth the Raven, "Nevermore."

Pallas is another name
for Athena, the Greek
goddess of wisdom.

And the Raven, never flitting, still is sitting, still is
        sitting
190 On the **pallid** bust of Pallas just above my chamber
        door;
And his eyes have all the seeming of a demon's that is
        dreaming,
And the lamp-light o'er him streaming throws his
195   shadow on the floor;
And my soul from out that shadow that lies floating
        on the floor
                    Shall be lifted—nevermore!

Literature Practice

Answer these questions on a separate sheet of paper.

1. Why is the narrator of this poem sad in the second
   stanza?

2. Why doesn't the narrator open his door right away
   when he hears tapping?

3. What does the narrator find when he opens the
   door?

4. Why do you think Poe named this poem "The
   Raven"?

5. What sound ends the last lines in each stanza of
   the poem?

The Raven's Tale

The raven has been an important symbol for many centuries in the myths of many cultures. When Poe wrote "The Raven" in 1845, he drew from one tradition that viewed the bird as a carrier of misfortune, disease, war, and death. The tradition of the raven as a symbol has many stories. Here are several:

- According to Greek myths, the raven originally had white feathers. The feathers were blackened as a punishment by Apollo, a Greek god, because the raven talked too much. He told everyone's secrets.

- During the Middle Ages, alchemists—people who tried to make gold from simple metals—respected the raven as having great wisdom. The raven was shown with a white head to honor its great wisdom and dignity.

- In ancient China, the three-legged raven was the Sun God's companion. The symbol of the Chou Dynasty, which identified with the sun, was a raven.

- Children growing up in Iceland were warned against using raven quills as drinking straws. One sip from it and a child was destined to become a thief.

- Raven is also an important figure in many Native American stories. Raven is responsible for bringing fire and light to the world. He is often seen as a trickster character—a character who plays tricks on people and other animals.

- The raven was respected as a worthy symbol to represent rulers and important families. Throughout Europe, from the Middle Ages on, the raven appeared on many coat of arms, or shields. The coat of arms displayed special symbols used to represent important families, rulers, or countries.

The Cremation of Sam McGee
by Robert W. Service

Words to Know

LITERARY TERM

meter the rhythm, or beat, in poetry

SELECTION VOCABULARY

moil work hard for

marge edge

cremated burned a dead body

mushing traveling on a sled pulled by dogs

whimper whine or cry

heed pay attention to

ghastly awfully

brawn strength

loathed hated

grub food

harkened answered

derelict something thrown away

trice a very short time, a moment

grisly terrible

Sam cannot leave the Arctic. He cannot stop looking for gold even though he hates the cold weather.

On Christmas night, Sam tells his friend Cap that the cold is going to kill him. He isn't afraid of dying. But he doesn't want to lie in a cold grave. He asks Cap to cremate him. The next morning, Sam dies.

Cap ties Sam's body to a sled. He drives along for days. He wants to stop and bury the body, but cannot. He has promised to cremate his friend.

*Finally, at the edge of Lake Lebarge, Cap sees an empty
cabin. He puts Sam's body inside. He makes a fire
inside the boat's cabin. Then Cap takes a walk. When
he comes back and looks inside the cabin, Sam tells him
that he is warm at last.*

—⟨⟨⟨⟨—

There are strange things done
        in the midnight sun
  By the men who **moil** for gold;
The Arctic trails have their secret tales
    That would make your blood run cold;
5 The Northern Lights have seen queer sights,
    But the queerest they ever did see
Was that night on the **marge** of Lake Lebarge
      I **cremated** Sam McGee.

This story takes place in
the Arctic. There, in the
summertime, the sun
shines twenty-four hours
a day. In the 1890s,
there was a gold rush in
this region.

Try reading this poem out loud to yourself. Notice how the words have a "beat" or rhythm, just like music. In poetry, this rhythm is called meter.

10 Now Sam McGee was from Tennessee,
    where the cotton blooms and blows.
Why he left his home in the South to roam 'round the
    Pole, God only knows.
He was always cold, but the land of gold seemed to
15   hold him like a spell;
Though he'd often say in his homely way that
    "he'd sooner live in hell."

On a Christmas Day
    we were **mushing** our way over the Dawson trail.
20 Talk of your cold! through the parka's fold
    it stabbed like a driven nail.
If our eyes we'd close, then the lashes froze till
    sometimes we couldn't see;
It wasn't much fun, but the only one to **whimper**
25   was Sam McGee.

At the time this poem takes place, the easiest way to get around in the Arctic was by dog sled. Try to imagine how cold it was on Christmas Day in the Arctic!

And that very night, as we lay packed tight
    in our robes beneath the snow,
And the dogs were fed, and the stars o'erhead were
    dancing heel and toe,
30 He turned to me, and "Cap," says he,
    "I'll cash in this trip, I guess;
And if I do, I'm asking that you won't refuse
    my last request."

Well, he seemed so low that I couldn't say no;
35   then he says with a sort of moan:
"It's the cursèd cold, and it's got right hold till
    I'm chilled clean through to the bone.
Yet 'tain't being dead—
    it's my awful dread of the icy grave that pains;
40 So I want you to swear that, foul or fair,
    you'll cremate my last remains."

Sam McGee thinks being buried in this icy ground would be awful. He asks his friend to cremate, or burn, his body if he dies so that he can be warm.

A pal's last need is a thing to **heed**,
    so I swore I would not fail;
And we started on at the streak of dawn; but God!
45   he looked **ghastly** pale.
He crouched on the sleigh, and he raved all day
    of his home in Tennessee;
And before nightfall a corpse was all that was left
    of Sam McGee.

50 There wasn't a breath in that land of death,
    and I hurried, horror driven,
With a corpse half hid that I couldn't get rid,
    because of a promise given;
It was lashed to the sleigh, and it seemed to say:
55   "You may tax your **brawn** and brains,
But you promised true, and it's up to you to
    cremate those last remains."

During the gold rush, thousands of people came to the Yukon. There were few lawmakers at the time and people had to make their own rules to live by. This is what Service means when he writes "the trail has its own stern code."

Now a promise made is a debt unpaid,
    and the trail has its own stern code.
60 In the days to come, though my lips were dumb,
    in my heart how I cursed that load.

In the long, long night,
    by the lone firelight, while the huskies,
    round in a ring,
Howled out their woes to the homeless snows—
65   O God! how I **loathed** the thing.

And every day that quiet clay
    seemed to heavy and heavier grow;
And on I went, though the dogs were spent
    and the **grub** was getting low;
70 The trail was bad,
    and I felt half mad, but I swore I would not give in;
And I'd often sing to the hateful thing, and
    it **harkened** with a grin.

Till I came to the marge of Lake Lebarge,
75   and a **derelict** there lay;
It was jammed in the ice,
    but I saw in a **trice** it was called the "Alice May."
And I looked at it, and I thought a bit, and
    I looked at my frozen chum;
80 Then "Here," said I, with a sudden cry,
    "is my cre-ma-tor-eum."

The poem's narrator sees a cast off boat, called "Alice May," on the edge of Lake Lebarge. What does he decide to use this boat for?

Some planks I tore from the cabin floor,
    and I lit the boiler fire;
Some coal I found
85   that was lying around, and I heaped the fuel higher;
The flames just soared, and the furnace roared—
    such a blaze you seldom see;
And I burrowed a hole in the glowing coal,
    and I stuffed in Sam McGee.

90　Then I made a hike,
　　　　for I didn't like to hear him sizzle so;
　　And the heavens scowled, and the huskies howled,
　　　　and the wind began to blow.
　　It was icy cold, but the hot sweat rolled down my cheeks,
95　　　and I don't know why;
　　And the greasy smoke in an inky cloak
　　　　went streaking down the sky.

　　I do not know how long in the snow
　　　　I wrestled with **grisly** fear;
100　But the stars came out
　　　　and they danced about ere again I ventured near;
　　I was sick with dread, but I bravely said:
　　　　"I'll just take a peep inside.
　　I guess he's cooked, and it's time I looked,"
105　　. . . then the door I opened wide.

　　And there sat Sam,
　　　　looking cool and calm, in the heart of the furnace roar;
　　And he wore a smile you could see a mile, and he said:
　　　　"Please close that door.
110　It's fine in here,
　　　　but I greatly fear you'll let in the cold and storm—
　　Since I left Plumtree, down in Tennessee,
　　　　it's the first time I've been warm."

　　There are strange things done
115　　　　　in the midnight sun
　　　　By the men who moil for gold;
　　The Arctic trails have their secret tales
　　　　That would make your blood run cold;
　　The Northern Lights
120　　　　　have seen queer sights,
　　　　But the queerest they ever did see
　　Was that night on the marge of Lake Lebarge
　　　　　I cremated Sam McGee.

Service tells a pretty horrible story in this poem. Yet, the way he words the poem makes it almost funny. How do you think he achieves this effect?

Why is Sam McGee happy at last?

Yukon Gold

It is a warm summer day in 1897. You are standing around the docks of Seattle, Washington. A big ship comes in. A group of dirty, grisly men gets off, pulling heavy bags. The bags, you soon learn, are full of gold!

This really happened. These men were returning from the gold fields of the Yukon Territory in Canada. They announced to the world that the rivers up there were filled with gold.

Thousands of men and women all over the country quit their jobs and went to Canada. They also wanted to return home with heavy bags of gold.

Unfortunately, by the time the crowds of gold-seekers made it to the north country, most of the land was already claimed. Many people suffered—like Sam McGee—because they weren't prepared for life in the far north.

Robert Service went north during the gold rush. But he did not dig for gold. Instead, he wrote poems about the people he met there.

Literature Practice

Answer these questions on a separate sheet of paper.

1. How is Sam McGee different from the others who are mushing over the Dawson trail on Christmas Day?

2. Why does the poem's narrator keep his promise to Sam McGee?

3. For what purpose does the narrator use the "Alice May"?

4. What does the poem's narrator find when he looks in the furnace?

5. How does the rhythm, or beat, create a suspenseful feeling in the poem?

Hist, Whist

by e. e. cummings

Words to Know

LITERARY TERM

coin words   make up words

SELECTION VOCABULARY

hist hush, silence

whist hush, silence

tweeds wool cloth with a rough surface

scuttling running or moving quickly

hist whist

little ghostthings
tip-toe
twinkle-toe

little twitchy
5   witches and tingling
goblins

hob-a-nob   hob-a-nob

little hoppy happy
toad in **tweeds**
10   tweeds
little itchy mousies
with **scuttling**
eyes   rustle and run   and
hidehidehide
15   whisk

Cummings liked to experiment with words. He often paid no attention to the rules of spelling and did not like to use capital letters, even in his name.

Have you ever seen the word "ghostthings"? Probably not. Cummings liked to coin, or make up, his own words.

whisk   look out for
the old woman
with the wart on her nose
what she'll do to yer
20   nobody knows

How does cummings use
humor to talk about
scary things?

for she knows the devil   ooch
the devil   ouch
the devil
ach   the great

25   green
dancing

devil
devil
devil
30   devil
           wheeEEE

Literature Practice

Answer these questions on a separate sheet of paper.

1. Cummings coined the word "ghostthings." What do you think this word means?

2. What other words does cummings coin in this poem?

3. Name the different creatures cummings describes in this poem.

4. What do you think is the setting for this poem? Use your imagination and describe it in detail.

5. This poem is about ghosts, witches, and the devil. Why do you think cummings ends the poem with the word "wheeEEE?

Chapter Review

Summaries

- **The Raven**—A man is falling asleep late one night while reading. He hears a tapping at his door. He tells himself it is only a late night visitor. He has been trying not to think about a woman named Lenore whom he misses. Finally, he speaks up and says he is coming to the door. He opens it and finds no one. He whispers the name "Lenore." Then he notices the raven that sits above his door. The raven's eyes are like a demon's, and they make a shadow on the floor. He is frightened.

- **The Cremation of Sam McGee**—The narrator is in the Arctic looking for gold. Another man, named Sam McGee, is with him. McGee hates the cold weather and makes the narrator promise that he will cremate him if he dies so that he can be eternally warm. McGee dies on the journey. The narrator ties the body onto his sled and pulls it a long way. Finally, he comes to Lake Lebarge where he finds an abandoned boat. There, he cremates McGee in the furnace of the boat. When he goes to see how the cremation is coming along, McGee smiles from out of the fire at him and says that he is warm at last.

- **Hist, Whist**—Cummings tells a tale of little creatures, such as "ghostthings," "twitchy witches," and "itchy mousies." He tells the creatures to hide and "whisk" because an old woman with a wart on her nose knows the devil.

Chapter Quiz

Choose the letter of the correct answer. Rewrite the sentences on a separate sheet of paper.

1. The man in "The Raven" is afraid because
   a. there is a tapping at his door.
   b. it is very dark.
   c. a ghost appears in his chamber.
   d. a woman appears outside his door.

2. When the man in "The Raven" opens his door, he sees
   a. a skeleton.
   c. Lenore.
   b. nothing.
   d. his father.

3. "The Cremation of Sam McGee" takes place in
   a. a very cold place.
   c. the wintertime.
   b. the far north.
   d. all of the above.

4. In the end, Sam McGee is happy because he
   a. has finally cooled off.
   c. is finally warm.
   b. is with his family again.
   d. loves the Yukon.

5. Which creatures appear in the poem "Hist, Whist?"
   a. skeletons and vampires
   c. kittens and rats
   b. goblins and mousies
   d. fairies and wolves

6. Why should the creatures in "Hist, Whist" look out for the old woman with the wart on her nose?
   a. She knows the devil.
   c. She wears tweeds.
   b. She hates toads.
   d. She hides.

Thinking and Writing

Answer the following questions on a separate sheet of paper. Write one or two paragraphs for each one.

1. In "The Raven," the narrator keeps saying that there is "nothing more" outside his door. What do you think he is afraid of finding there? Use lines from the poem to explain your answer.

2. Did you find "The Cremation of Sam McGee" mostly funny or mostly scary? Give examples from the poem to explain your answer.

3. What story do you think the poem "Hist, Whist" tells? Using your own words, rewrite the poem's story in paragraph form.

Unit One Review

The following questions are from the selections you have read in this unit. Write your answers on a separate sheet of paper.

A. Which story or poem is the quotation from?

1. "There are strange things done in the midnight sun."
2. "On many a dark night they saw her walk the river bank."
3. "'Tis some visitor," I muttered, "tapping at my chamber door—Only this, and nothing more."
4. "He had the eye of a vulture. It was a pale blue eye with a film over it."
5. "little hoppy happy toad in tweeds"

B. Write one or two sentences for each of the following questions. Look back at the selections if you need to.

1. Which story or poem in this unit did you find the most suspenseful? Explain your answer.
2. The stories "The Pepper Tree" and "La Llorona: The Weeping Woman" both have lessons or messages. What is the lesson or message in each of these two stories? How are the messages alike or different?
3. Do you think e.e. cummings's poem "Hist, Whist" is just plain silly, or is there a message in it? Explain your answer.
4. Explain at least two ways that poems are different from stories. Use examples from this unit.

Childhood

Chapter 3

Dust Tracks on a Road
> *adapted from the autobiography by Zora Neale Hurston*

Lame Deer Remembers His Childhood
> *adapted from the autobiography by John Fire/Lame Deer*
> *and Richard Erdoes*

Prisoner of My Country
> *adapted from the autobiography by Yoshiko Uchida*

Chapter 4

The Circuit
> *an adapted story by Francisco Jiménez*

The Jacket
> *an adapted story by Gary Soto*

Chapter 3

The authors in this chapter all write about their childhoods. Their childhood experiences taught them important lessons. They also influenced who they became as adults.

Chapter Learning Objectives

- Learn about autobiography
- Learn how authors use the first-person point of view
- Learn to identify clues to character
- Learn to draw conclusions about what you read

Dust Tracks on a Road

adapted from the autobiography by
Zora Neale Hurston

Words to Know

LITERARY TERMS

autobiography a true story about a person, told by that person

first-person point of view when the writer tells the story with the pronoun *I*

SELECTION VOCABULARY

bold without fear or shame

curious eager to learn or know

spiritual a religious song, first created by African Americans living in the South during the 18th and 19th centuries, which combined elements of European and African music

mark a written line or check used in a book to show where a person should begin reading

chariot a two-wheeled, horse-drawn cart used in battles, races, or parades during ancient times

pause to stop briefly

preserved food prepared in a special way, such as drying, cooking, or canning, so it can be saved for a long time

cylinder a long, round tube

I used to take a seat on top of our gate and watch the world go by. One of the roads to Orlando ran past my house. Carriages and cars would often pass by me. I liked to see them go by. Often the white travelers would call to me. But more often I called to them. I would say, "Don't you want me to go part of the way with you?"

They always did. I know now that they must have thought I was pretty funny. But I was so sure of myself;

In an autobiography, the writer uses the first-person point of view. This means that the writer uses the word *I* and is part of the story. What do you know so far about this writer?

they never said no. I would ride up the road for about half a mile and then walk back. I didn't ask my parents if I could do this. When they found out later, I was usually whipped. My grandmother worried about my being so **bold**. She had known slavery, and she could not believe I dared to act the way I did.

She would say, "Git down offa dat gate! Git down! Sitting up dere looking dem white folks right in de face! They's going to hang you, yet. And don't stand in dat doorway looking out at 'em. You too bold to live long."

But I kept right on looking at them and getting a ride with them whenever I could. My little town seemed dull to me most of the time. If that town had a song to sing, I must have missed the tune.

One day I met two white people in a different way. They were women.

It came about this way. The whites who came down from the North often came to visit our school. A Negro school was something strange to them. The white visitors were always kind. But they must have been **curious**, too. They came and went, came and went. When they came, the school room was put in order quickly. The teachers promised us a quick and bloody death if we fooled around while the visitors were here. We always sang a **spiritual**, led by Mr. Calhoun himself. Mrs. Calhoun always stood in the back of the room with a switch in her hand. We were all angels when visitors were there, because we'd better be. Mrs. Calhoun would give us a look that meant trouble. Then she would turn her face and smile at the visitors as if to say it was wonderful to teach such lovely children. The visitors couldn't see that switch in her hand. But we knew where our good manners were coming from.

Usually, the visitors let us know the day before they were coming. We would be told to put on shoes, comb our hair, and clean our ears and fingernails. Then the teachers checked us over before we marched in that morning. Anyone who had hair with knots in it, or dirty ears or fingernails got pulled out of line and whipped. Then that child would be sent home to be whipped all over again.

But on this afternoon, two young ladies just came without warning. Mr. Calhoun didn't know what to do, but he put on the best show he could. He was teaching one of the classes at the front of the room. He had them sit down. Then he called the fifth grade class to come up and read. That was my class.

So we took our readers and went up front. We stood in the usual line and opened our books to the lesson. It was the story of Pluto and Persephone. It was new and most of the class found it hard. Mr. Calhoun was not happy as he listened to the readers slowly spell out words with their lips.

Then it came to me. I was fifth or sixth down the line. The story was not new to me. I had read my reader from front to back the first week that Papa had bought it for me.

That is why my eyes were not on the book, figuring out which paragraph I would read. I was watching our visitors. They held a book between them, following the lesson. They had shiny hair, mostly brownish. One had a gold chain around her neck. The other one was dressed all in black and white with a pretty ring on her left hand. But the thing that held my eyes were their fingers. They were long and thin, and very white, except near the tips. The tips were baby pink. I had never seen such hands. I wondered how they felt. I would have looked at those hands longer, but the child next to me was almost through. My turn next, so I got on my **mark** and made sure of my place. Some of the stories I had read several times. This one was one of my favorites. I loved it, and that is the way I read my paragraph.

Why does Mr. Calhoun put on a show for the visitors? What does he do to show off for the visitors?

In mythology, Pluto is the god of the dead. He is also the king of the underworld. Persephone is his wife and the queen of the underworld.

What else do you know about the writer now? How would you describe her to a friend?

I read: "Yes, Jupiter had seen her (Persephone). He had seen the maiden picking flowers in the field. He had seen the **chariot** of the dark king **pause** by the maiden's side. He had seen him when he grabbed Persephone. He had seen the black horses leap down Mount Aetna's fiery throat. Persephone was now in Pluto's dark kingdom, and he had made her his wife."

The two women looked at each other and then back to me. Mr. Calhoun broke out with a proud smile under his mustache. Instead of having the next child read, he nodded to me to go on. So I read the story to the end. I read how Mercury, the messenger of the Gods, had brought Persephone back to earth, back to the arms of her mother, Ceres. With Persephone back on earth, the world had spring, and summer with its flowers, and fall. But Persephone had bitten a pomegranate while she was with Pluto. This meant she must go back to him for three months every year, and be his queen. While Persephone was with Pluto, the earth had winter, until she came back to earth.

Then the reading was over. The visitors went to talk in low voices with Mr. Calhoun for a few minutes. They looked my way once or twice. I began to worry. I had no shoes, and my feet and legs were dusty. My hair was not combed, and my nails were not shiny clean. I thought, oh, I'm going to get it now. Those ladies noticed how dirty I am. Mr. Calhoun is promising them he's going to whip me. So I thought.

Then Mr. Calhoun called me up to the front of the room. I went up, thinking how awful it was going to be to get a whipping in front of visitors. I heard a low laugh. Hennie Clark and Stell Brazzle laughed loud, so I would be sure to hear them. They thought, now the smart-aleck was going to get it. I slipped one hand behind me and switched my dress tail at them. I had to show them I didn't care.

Pomegranate is a fruit about the size of an orange with thick, reddish skin and many seeds.

For each pomegranate seed she ate, Persephone has to spend one month in the underworld. According to this myth, how does she affect the seasons?

What more do you know about Zora Neale now?

"Come here, Zora Neale," said Mr. Calhoun in a sweet voice as I reached the desk. He put his hand on my shoulder and gave me little pats. The ladies smiled and held out those flower-like fingers to me. I took a good look.

Mr. Calhoun said, "Shake hands with the ladies, Zora Neale." They took my hand one after the other and smiled. They asked if I loved school. I lied that I did. There was *some* truth in it. I liked geography and reading, and I liked to play at recess time. But whoever thought up writing and math got no thanks from me. And I didn't like having a teacher who could sit up there with a switch and whip me whenever he liked. I hated things I couldn't do anything about. But I knew better than to say so right there. So I said yes, I *loved* school.

The woman in the brown dress smiled. "I can tell you do," she said. She patted my head. She was lucky she didn't get sandspurs in her hand. Children who play in the grass in Florida often get sandspurs in their hair. They shook hands with me again, and I went back to my seat.

Sandspurs, or sandburs, are small, round plants with spikes.

When school let out at three o'clock, Mr. Calhoun told me to wait. He told me I was to go to the Park House hotel the next day to visit the two women, Mrs. Johnstone and Miss Hurd. Mama must make sure that I was clean and brushed from head to foot. I must wear shoes and socks. The ladies liked me, he said, and my manners must be perfect.

The next day I was let out of school an hour early. I went home and was stood up in a tub full of suds. I was scrubbed and had my ears dug into. I had a red ribbon in my hair to match my red and white dress. The dress was so full of starch that it could stand up by itself. Mama made sure my shoes were on the right feet, because I was careless about right and left. I was given a handkerchief to carry and told again to watch my manners. My big brother John went with me as far as the hotel gate.

Why might John have to accompany Zora Neale to the hotel?

First thing, the ladies gave me strange things like stuffed dates and **preserved** ginger. They told me to eat as much as I wanted. Then they showed me their Japanese dolls and just talked. They gave me a copy of *Scribner's Magazine* and asked me to read to them. After a paragraph or two, they smiled and told me that would do.

I was led out to the grounds, and they took my picture under a palm tree. They handed me a heavy **cylinder** which was wrapped in fancy paper and tied with a ribbon. They told me good-bye, asking me not to open it until I got home.

My brother was waiting for me down by the lake. We hurried home. We couldn't wait to see what was inside the cylinder. It was too heavy to be candy or anything like that. John said he had to carry it for me.

My mother made John give the cylinder back and let me open it. I think I shall never feel such joy again. The nearest thing to opening that cylinder was the telegram telling me that my first book was going to be published. Out of the cylinder rolled one hundred bright new pennies. Their glow lit up the world. It didn't matter to me that this was money. It was the beauty of the thing. I stood on the mountain. Mama let me play with my pennies for a while then put them away for me to keep.

The author compares seeing the pennies to hearing that her book is going to be published. In what ways do you think her childhood experience is similar to this other event?

Segregated Schools Are Outlawed

For many years, U.S. schools were segregated. Segregation means that people of different races must live apart. White children went to their own schools. African Americans and other groups had to go to separate schools. The white schools had more money for books, buildings, and teachers.

Then in 1954, the U.S. Supreme Court ruled that segregation in public schools was against the law. Some states did not want to let African American students go to all-white schools. In Little Rock, Arkansas, the governor closed the public schools. Then he reopened them as private schools for white students only. The President of the United States had to send in Army troops to make sure that African Americans could go to public schools. It took many years before all of this country's public schools, in the North as well as the South, were integrated, or open to all students.

Literature Practice

Answer these questions on a separate sheet of paper.

1. Why does Zora Neale's grandmother say that she is "too bold to live long"?

2. Why does Mr. Calhoun have Zora Neale keep on reading?

3. How does Zora Neale really feel about school? What are her favorite subjects?

4. When the author tells how she feels about seeing the coins, she says, "I stood on the mountain." What do you think she means by this statement?

5. In what ways does Zora Neale feel special while growing up?

Lame Deer Remembers His Childhood
adapted from the autobiography by John Fire/Lame Deer and Richard Erdoes

Words to Know

LITERARY TERM

character clues thoughts, actions, and words in a story that help the reader find out what a character is like

SELECTION VOCABULARY

prairie a large area of land with rich soil, grass, and very few trees

notch a V-shaped mark cut into a material, such as wood or cloth

ceremonies special events, such as weddings and graduations

pampered treated with a great deal of attention; spoiled

harsh cruel, unpleasant

awl a sharp pointed tool for making holes in leather

gasped the sound heard when a person very loudly and quickly draws in a breath after being shocked or surprised

powwow a meeting or gathering of a tribe

I was born a full-blooded Indian. I was born in a log cabin, twelve feet by twelve feet, between Pine Ridge and Rosebud. *Maka tanhan wicasa wan*—I am a man of the earth, as we say. Our people don't call themselves Sioux or Dakota. That's white man talk. We call ourselves Ikce Wicasa—the natural humans. We are the free, wild, common people. I am happy to be called that.

Pine Ridge and Rosebud are Indian reservations in South Dakota. Reservations are areas of land set aside for Native Americans.

I was brought up by my grandparents—Good Fox and . . . Plenty White Buffalo. This is the way with most Indian children. With our people, the ties to one's grandparents are as strong as the ties to one's parents. We lived in a little hut way out on the **prairie**, in the back country. For the first few years of my life I had nothing to do with the outside world. Of course we had a few white man's things—coffee, iron pots, a shotgun, an old wagon. But I never thought much about where these things came from, or who had made them. . . .

Most of my childhood days weren't very exciting. That was all right with me. We had a good, simple life. One day passed like another. I was different from other Indian kids in only one way. I was never hungry, because my dad had so many horses and cattle. . . .

One of my uncles used to keep a moon-counting stick. This was our own kind of calendar, and a good one. He had a special stick. Every night he cut a **notch** in it until the moon "died"—that is, disappeared. On the other side of this stick, he made a notch for every month. He started a new stick every year in the spring. That way we always knew when it was the right day for one of our **ceremonies**.

Every so often my grandparents would take me to a little celebration down the creek. Grandpa always rode his old red horse. All the tribes knew that horse. We always brought plenty of food for everybody. We had squaw bread, beef, and the kind of dried meat we call *papa*. We also had *wansa*, or pemmican, which was meat pounded together with berries and kidney fat. We also brought a kettle of coffee, wild mint tea, soup, or stuff like that. Grandfather was always the leader of the *owanka osnato*—the rehearsal ground. He prepared the place carefully. Only the real warriors were allowed to dance there—men like Red Fish or Thin Elk, who had fought in the Custer battle. As the years passed, the dancers grew older and older, and

Reading an autobiography helps the reader learn about people. As you read, stop once in a while and ask yourself: What do I know now about the people that I didn't know before?

What have you learned about children, parents, and grandparents in Sioux culture?

Many Native Americans refer to months as moons. A new month begins with every new, or full, moon. Every moon has a name. For example, the Lacota Sioux call December the "Moon of the Popping Trees."

Lame Deer writes about ceremonies and celebrations in these two paragraphs. Readers can conclude that ceremonies are important in Lame Deer's culture.

The Custer battle is also known as Custer's Last Stand, or the Battle at the Little Big Horn. This was a major battle in which the Plains Indians, including the Sioux, fought for their lands. Soon after this battle, the Sioux reluctantly agreed to live on reservations.

What have you learned so far about how children are raised in Lame Deer's culture?

fewer and fewer. Grandfather danced, too. Everybody could see the scars all over his arm where he had been wounded by the white soldiers. . . .

I was the *takoja*—the **pampered** grandson. Like all Indian children, I was spoiled. I was never scolded, never heard a **harsh** word. The worst thing I was ever told was "*Ajustan*," which means "leave it alone." No one ever spanked me. Indian children aren't treated that way. . . .

When I didn't want to go to sleep, my grandma would try to scare me with the *cicye*. This was a kind of bogeyman, or monster. "*Takoja, istima ye,*" she would say. This meant, "Go to sleep, sonny, or the *cicye* will come after you." Nobody knew what the *cicye* was like, but he must have been something terrible. When the *cicye* wouldn't scare me anymore, she would scare me with the *siyoko*—another kind of monster. Nobody knew what the *siyoko* was like either, but he was ten times more terrible than the *cicye*. Grandma did not have much luck. Neither the *cicye* nor the *siyoko* scared me for long. . . .

People said I was not like my grandpa Good Fox, whom I loved. They said I was like my other grandfather, Crazy Heart, whom I never knew. They said I picked up where he left off, because I was so bold and full of the devil. I was told that Crazy Heart had been like that. . . . He had a hot temper, always fighting and on the warpath. At the same time, he saved lots of people. He gave wise advice and urged the people to do what was right. He made good speeches. Everybody who listened to him said that he was a very encouraging man. He always told people to be patient. . . . But he wasn't like that himself. His temper got in the way.

I was like that. Things I was told not to do—I did them. I liked to play rough. We played shinny ball, a kind of hockey game. We made the ball and sticks ourselves. We played the hoop game and shot with a

bow and arrow. We had foot races, horse races, and water races. . . .

I liked to ride on a horse behind my older sister. I held onto her. As I got a little bigger, she would hold onto me. When I was nine years old, I had my own horse to ride. It was a beautiful gray pony. My father had given it to me, along with a fine saddle and a Mexican saddle blanket. That gray was my best friend. I was proud to ride him. But he was not mine for long. I lost him, and it was my own fault.

Nonge Pahloka—the Piercing of Her Ears—is a big event in a little girl's life. By this ceremony, the girl's parents, and especially her grandmother, want to show her how much they love and honor her. They ask a man who is very wise or brave to pierce the ears of their daughter. The grandmother makes food for everybody. The little girl is placed on a blanket. All around her are the many gifts her family will give away in her name. The man who does the piercing gets the best gift. Then everybody gets down to the really important part—the eating.

Well, one day I watched somebody pierce a girl's ears. I saw the fuss they made over it, and the presents he got. I thought I should do this to my little sister. She was about four years old at the time, and I was nine. I don't remember why I wanted to pierce her ears. Maybe I wanted to feel big and important like the man I watched do the piercing. Maybe I wanted to get a big present. Maybe I wanted to make my sister cry. I don't remember what was in my little boy's mind then. I found some wire and made a pair of "earrings" out of it. Then I asked my sister, "Would you like me to put these on you?" She smiled. *"Ohan*—yes." I didn't have the sharp bone used for piercing. I didn't know the prayer that goes with it. I just had an old **awl**. I thought this would do fine. Oh, how my sister yelled. I had to hold her down. But I got that awl through her earlobes,

Throughout this story, Lame Deer has given clues about the kind of person he is. What have you learned so far about what Lame Deer is like? As you read on, look for other clues that tell you more about Lame Deer. Also look for clues that tell you about his father.

Remember that ceremonies are important to the Sioux. Lame Deer has pierced his sister's ears before the correct time. He did not wait for the special ceremony.

Lame Deer's father will not punish him now. Do you think this is a good idea? Why or why not?

To honor a person at a ceremony, the family gives away its valuable possessions. The more valuable the possession, the more the person is honored.

Lame Deer is very hurt about losing his horse. He cannot show his sadness. It would be rude to those who received the horse as a gift. Why do you think Lame Deer's father punishes him this way?

How do you think Lame Deer will feel about the new white horse? Why?

and I put the "earrings" in. I was proud of the neat job I had done.

When my mother came home and saw those wire loops in my sister's ears she **gasped**. But then she went and told my father. That was one of the few times he talked to me. He said, "I should punish you and whip you, but I won't. That's not my way. You'll get your punishment later." Well, some time passed. I forgot all about it. One morning my father told me we were going to a **powwow**. He had the wagon ready. It was piled high with boxes and bundles. At the pow-wow, my father told people he was doing a big *otuhan*—a give-away. He put my sister on a pretty Navaho blanket. Then he laid out things to give away—quilts, food, blankets, a fine shotgun, his own new pair of cowboy boots, a sheepskin coat. It was enough to give a whole family all they needed. Dad was telling the people, "I want to honor my daughter for her ear-piercing. This should have been done in a ceremony, but my son did it at home. I guess he's too small. He didn't know any better." This was a long speech for Dad. He told me to come closer. I was sitting on my pretty gray horse. I thought Dad and I were looking pretty fine. Well, before I knew it, Dad had given my pony away, along with its beautiful saddle and blanket. I had to ride home in the wagon. I cried all the way. Dad said, "You have your punishment now. But you will feel better later on. All her life your sister will tell about how you pierced her ears. She'll brag about you. I bet you are the only small boy who ever did this big ceremony."

Dad's words did not make me feel better. My beautiful gray horse was gone. For three days, my heart was broken. On the fourth morning, I looked out the door. There stood a little white horse with a new saddle and bit. "It's yours," my father told me. "Get on it." I was happy again. . . .

Sioux Medicine Man

Lame Deer grew up to be a very important person to the Sioux. He was a great medicine man. A medicine man has many responsibilities to his people. In addition to healing the sick, he tells people what their visions mean, as well as tells people of his own visions. Visions come to people through special ceremonies. They are like dreams. For boys, one of the most important vision ceremonies, or vision quests, is the first one. After a boy has a vision, he becomes a man and is given a man's name. At the time of this story, Lame Deer still had his childhood name. When he was sixteen, Lame Deer went on his first vision quest. During his vision, Lame Deer saw his great grandfather Lame Deer. Because of this vision, Lame Deer took his great grandfather's name.

Like many Native Americans, Lame Deer has two names—his Sioux name and his white name. Lame Deer is his Sioux name. John Fire is his white name.

Literature Practice

Answer these questions on a separate sheet of paper.

1. What is Lame Deer's relationship with his family?
2. What does the "Piercing of Her Ears" ceremony mean to a young Sioux girl?
3. How does Lame Deer lose his gray horse?
4. What lesson do you think Lame Deer learns from losing the horse?
5. a.) What kind of man is Lame Deer's father?
   b.) What clues in the story led you to your answer?
6. How do you think Lame Deer feels about his childhood years?

Prisoner of My Country
adapted from the autobiography by Yoshiko Uchida

Words to Know

LITERARY TERM

drawing conclusions   forming an opinion based on information

SELECTION VOCABULARY

grounds area of land around a building

bayonets rifles with steel knives attached to the end of the barrel

barracks a group of buildings used for temporary housing

refugee a person who leaves his or her country to seek safety in another country

degrading insulting, embarrassing

civil rights rights which are guaranteed to an individual by the U.S. Constitution

betrayed broke someone's trust; disappointed

Our beautiful garden was now full of holes. Mama had dug up a few favorite plants to give to her friends. Other plants were given to people like the woman who stopped by one day. She asked if she could have some gladiolas. She said, "Since you're leaving any-way . . ." She smiled an embarrassed smile.

Our rented house was now an empty shell, with only three mattresses on the floor. In the corner of Mama's room was a large bag we called our Camp Bundle. We tossed into it all the things we had been told to take with us. There were sheets, blankets, pillows, dishes, and knives, forks, and spoons.

We also put in other things we thought we'd need. These things were boots, umbrellas, flashlights, tea cups, a hot plate, a kettle, and anything else we thought we could use in camp.

Kay said, "You know, we're supposed to bring only what we can carry."

We tried lifting our suitcases. We found we could each carry two. But what were we going to do about the Camp Bundle? Each day it grew and grew, like some living thing. We had no idea how we would ever get it to camp. There was nothing to do but keep filling it up and hope that somehow things would work out.

When you read the word *camp* and the list of things the family is preparing to take, what picture comes to your mind? Why might the family be packing for camp?

What feeling is behind the words, "Or even if we would ever come back"?

Sum up everything you found out about the camp. See if you can draw a conclusion: What do you think is going on? Why?

When Yoshiko sees the soldiers, it becomes clear what is really happening. What *is* happening?

The night before we left, our Swiss neighbors invited us to dinner. Mrs. Harpainter made a wonderful chicken dinner. She served it on her best dishes. It made me think of all the times we'd invited guests to our own house in happier days.

When we got home, Marian and Solveig came from next door to say good-bye. They brought gifts for each of us.

They hugged us, saying, "Come back soon!"

"We will," we answered. But we had no idea when we would come back. Or even if we would ever come back.

The next morning, Mrs. Harpainter brought us breakfast on a tray full of dishes with bright colors. Then she drove us to the First Congregational Church of Berkeley. The church was a Civil Control Station, where we were supposed to report.

We said our good-byes quickly. We couldn't speak many words. Already the **grounds** of the church were filled with hundreds of Japanese Americans. They held bundles with tags that showed their names and their family's number. At the curb were rows of trucks. They were being loaded with large things that people could not carry by hand.

Kay said in a low voice, "I wish they'd told us there would be trucks. We wouldn't have worried so much about our Camp Bundle."

But the army didn't seem to care if we worried or not. To them, we were only prisoners. There were guards all around the church. Their **bayonets** were ready. It wasn't until I saw them that I really knew what was happening to us. I was filled with horror. My knees felt weak, and I almost lost my breakfast.

The First Congregational Church had been good to us. Many of the families in the church had offered to store things for the Japanese Americans while they were gone. Now the church women were serving tea and sandwiches. But none of us could eat.

Soon we were loaded onto waiting buses. We began our one-way trip down streets we knew well. We went across the Bay Bridge and down the Bayshore Highway. Some people were crying quietly, but most of us were silent. We kept our eyes on the window. We watched as sights we knew well slipped away behind us, one by one.

Then we were there—at the Tanforan Racetrack Assembly Center. This was one of the 15 centers at racetracks and fairgrounds along the West Coast where Japanese Americans were held.

From the bus window, I could see a high fence with barbed wire that was around the whole area. At each corner of the camp was a guard tower with soldiers.

The gates swung open to let us in. The guards with their guns closed them behind us. We were now locked in. The guards would be there 24 hours a day.

We had never broken the law. We had done nothing wrong. Yet, we had now become prisoners of our own country.

There was a huge crowd of us. It looked as if there was a horse race that day, except that all the people there were Japanese of all ages, sizes, and shapes.

We looked through the crowd for faces we knew. It felt good to find several friends. They had arrived a few days earlier from Oakland.

They called to us: "Hey, Kay and Yo! Over here!"

Our friends led us through the crowds to a spot where doctors looked down our throats and said we were healthy. Then they helped us find the place we were supposed to be—Barrack 16, Apartment 40.

I asked, "We get apartments?"

My friend said, "Not the kind of apartment you're thinking of, Yo. Wait, you'll see." My friend knew I'd be shocked.

Mama was wearing her hat, gloves, and Sunday

How accurate was your conclusion?

Draw a new conclusion: Why are there barbed wire fences, guards, and locked gates for women and children?

Now make a prediction: What do you think Apartment 40 will look like?

clothes. This was because she would never have thought of leaving home any other way. In her good Sunday shoes, she picked her way over the mud puddles that the rain had left the night before.

The army had quickly built dozens of **barracks** around the track for the eight thousand of us. Each barrack was split into six rooms. Each family got one room. But our barrack was not one of these.

Our barrack turned out to be nothing but an old horse stable. Our "apartment" was a small, dark horse stall, 10 feet by 20 feet. I couldn't believe what I saw.

Dirt, dust, and bits of wood were all over the floor. I could smell that horses had lived there. There were two tiny windows on each side of the door.

Tiny bodies of spiders and bugs had been painted onto the walls by army painters. A single light bulb hung from the ceiling. Three army cots lay on the dirty floor. This was to be our "home" for the next five months.

One of our friends found a broom and swept out our stall. Two of the boys went to pick up our mattresses. They had to fill them up with straw themselves.

Another friend loaned us some dishes and silverware until our bundle was delivered. She said, "We'd better leave soon for the mess hall before the lines for dinner get too long."

For now, all meals were being served in the basement. Holding our plates and silverware, we made our way down the muddy racetrack.

When we got to the mess hall, there were already long lines of people waiting to get in. Soon we were separated from our friends. Mama, Kay, and I took our places at the end of one line. We stood close together to keep warm. A cold, sharp wind had begun to blow as the sun went down. It blew dust in our faces.

I felt like a **refugee** in a strange land. Being here was not only **degrading**, but it did not seem real. It was like an awful dream.

Since we had missed lunch, I was eager for a nice hot meal. But dinner was a piece of bread, a boiled potato, and two sausages from a can. The cooks picked up the food with their fingers and dropped it on our plates.

We ate at picnic tables in the cold, damp basement, along with hundreds of people. Even though I was still hungry, I couldn't wait to get back to our stall.

It was dark now. The north wind was blowing into our stall from all the cracks around the windows and door. We put on our coats and sat on our mattresses, too sad even to talk.

Then we heard a truck outside. A voice called, "Hey, Uchida! Apartment 40!"

How close was your prediction?

Describe how being in such a place would be *degrading*.

Kay and I rushed to the door. "That's us!" we called. We saw two boys trying to get our big Camp Bundle off their truck.

The boys were grinning. They asked us, "What ya got in here, anyways? Did ya bring everything in your whole darn house?"

I was embarrassed. Our bundle was the biggest one in their truck.

I joked, "It's just our pet rhino."

While the boys were still laughing, we dragged our huge bundle into the stall. Quickly, we untied all the knots we'd tied just that morning.

Everything we'd put in the bundle rolled out like old friends.

I grabbed the kettle. "I'll go get some water," I said.

I went quickly to the women's toilets and washroom. It was about 50 yards from our stable. While I was gone, Kay and Mama got our sheets and blankets from the bundle to make up our cots.

When I got back, I had news for them.

"There are no doors for the toilets or showers," I said in horror. "And we have to wash up at long tin sinks. They look like they were used for feeding horses."

I had also taken a look at the laundry barrack. It had rows of tubs for washing. Everything, even sheets and towels, had to be washed by hand. They were still empty, but in the morning there would be long lines of people waiting to use those tubs.

Mama said, "Well, at least we can make some tea now."

We plugged in the hot plate and waited for the water to boil.

Then came a knock at the door. This was the first of many knocks we would hear, as friends found out where we lived.

A voice said, "Hey, Kay and Yo. Are you home?"

How does the condition of the bathrooms add to the degraded feeling?

Four of my college friends had come by to see how we were doing. They had brought along the only snack they could find. It was a box of dried prunes. The day before, I wouldn't have eaten the prunes. But now they were as welcome as a box of the special chocolates Papa used to bring home from San Francisco.

We sat close to the warmth of the hot plate. We sipped the tea Mama had made for us. We wondered how we had come to be in this awful place.

We were angry that our country had taken away our **civil rights.** But we had been raised up to respect and trust the people in power. We never thought to protest, the way people would today. The world was a totally different place then.

Back then, there had been no freedom marches. No one had heard yet of Martin Luther King, Jr. No one knew about pride for one's own people. Most Americans didn't think much of civil rights. They would have given us no support if we had tried to stop the army from taking us away.

We thought that by going along with our government, we were helping our country. We did not know then how badly our leaders **betrayed** us.

They had put us in prison. They knew it was against the Constitution. And they knew there was no need to put us in prison. We were no danger to anyone.

We wondered how America—our own country— could have done this to us? We tried to cheer up. We talked about steaks and hamburgers and hot dogs as we ate the cold dried prunes.

This is the first time Mr. Uchida is mentioned. Draw a conclusion: Where might he be?

Draw another conclusion: If the U.S. government knew these things, why did they intern Japanese Americans?

The Internment of Japanese Americans

After Japan attacked Pearl Harbor in December 1941, the United States declared war against Japan. Some people were afraid that Japanese Americans might betray the United States. Others were jealous of Japanese Americans who had money. As a result, the U.S. government decided to intern Japanese Americans. To intern means to put in prison. More than 100,000 Japanese Americans were put in prison camps. It did not matter how many were born here or had lived in America for many years. It didn't matter what their jobs were.

The war ended in 1946. Japanese Americans were allowed to return home. But many had no homes or businesses when they got back. They had to begin life all over again.

Literature Practice

Answer these questions on a separate sheet of paper.

1. What is the Uchida family like? How do you know?

2. What conclusion can you make about the life of the Uchida family before they went to the internment camp? How do you know?

3. What is Barrack 16, Apartment 40? Describe it.

4. What conclusions can you draw about how the family feels about being in the internment camp?

5. What does the writer mean when she says that the world was "totally different" then?

6. Who does the author say betrayed the family? Explain.

Chapter Review

Summaries

- **Dust Tracks on a Road**—Zora Neale lives in the South during the early 1900s. Like all African American children there, she attends a segregated school. The school often has curious white visitors from the North. One day, two white women visit the school unexpectedly. The schoolteacher wants to show off. He lets Zora Neale read aloud. Zora Neale does a very good job reading. So the women ask her to visit them. She visits them, and they give her gifts. The most exciting gift is one hundred pennies. Zora Neale is happy and is very proud of herself.

- **Lame Deer Remembers His Childhood**—Lame Deer lives on a Sioux reservation in South Dakota. Ceremonies are important in Lame Deer's culture. Piercing a girl's ears is an important ceremony. One day, Lame Deer gets into trouble. He pierces his sister's ears himself. His father punishes him by giving away his favorite pony. Then his father gives him a new horse.

- **Prisoner of My Country**—Yoshiko Uchida lives in California. When the United States enters World War II, Yoshiko's family is forced to leave their homes. They are moved to a prison camp. Her family, without their father, arrives at the camp. Yoshiko describes how she and her family must live while in the camp. She also describes her anger about how her family and other Japanese Americans are being treated.

Chapter Quiz

Choose the letter of the correct answer. Rewrite the sentences on a separate sheet of paper.

1. In "Dust Tracks on a Road," what special gift do the two white women give Zora Neale?
   a. a cyclinder with new pennies in it
   c. shoes and socks
   b. a book about Persephone
   d. candy

2. In "Lame Deer Remembers His Childhood," Lame Deer is punished because he
   a. gives away his gray pony.
   b. does not want to go to sleep.
   c. pierces his sister's ears.
   d. loses his Uncle's moon-counting stick.

3. What happens at the powwow?
   a. The father gives away gifts to honor his daughter.
   b. The father decides not to punish Lame Deer.
   c. Lame Deer's sister takes out her earrings.
   d. Lame Deer's father gives him a new white horse.

4. In "Prisoner of My Country," Yoshiko Uchida realizes what is happening when she
   a. says good-bye to her neighbors.
   b. packs the Camp Bundle.
   c. sees guards with bayonets.
   d. goes to dinner at the Harpainter's house.

5. How does Yo feel about the bathrooms at the Tanforan Racetrack Assembly Center?
   a. horrified
   b. happy
   c. excited
   d. peaceful

Thinking and Writing

Answer the following questions on a separate sheet of paper. Write one or two paragraphs for each one.

1. Imagine that you are Yoshiko Uchida. Write a letter to your neighbors telling them what happened after you left home.

2. In "Dust Tracks on a Road," Zora Neale Hurston receives a special gift. She feels great joy. Have you ever received a gift that made you feel joy? Write a description of your experience.

3. Explain why you think Lame Deer pierces his sister's ears.

Chapter 4

In each story in this chapter, a young person receives a gift. This gift changes how each character feels about himself or herself.

Chapter Learning Objectives

- Learn to make predictions about what you read
- Learn how authors use symbols to show what things mean
- Learn how authors use figurative language

The Circuit

an adapted story by Francisco Jiménez

Words to Know

LITERARY TERM

making predictions using what you know and what you have read to tell what might happen next in a story

SELECTION VOCABULARY

sharecropper someone who works a farm for part of the crop

It was that time of year again. The strawberry **sharecropper**, whose name was Ito, did not smile. The time for picking strawberries was almost over. The workers were not picking as many boxes as they had in June or July.

By the time August was almost over, there were fewer workers than before. On Sunday, only one worker—the best one—came to work. I liked him. Sometimes I talked to him during our half-hour lunch break. That is how I found out he was from Jalisco. Jalisco is the same state in Mexico my family was from. That Sunday was the last time I saw him.

At the end of that day, when the sun had gone down behind the mountains, Ito told us to go home. He yelled, *"Ya esora" (es hora*, meaning it's time, or time's up), in his broken Spanish. Every day at work, those had been the words I had waited to hear. I waited for those words twelve hours a day, every day,

The author is describing the lives of migrant workers. Migrant workers pick crops. They must travel from place to place as the crops are ready to be picked. Moving from one area to the next is called a circuit, which is the title of this story.

seven days a week, week after week. It made me sad to think I would never hear them again.

As we drove home, Papá did not say a word. He drove with both hands on the wheel. He stared at the dirt road. My older brother, Roberto, also said nothing. He leaned his head back and closed his eyes. Once in a while he cleared from his throat the dust that blew in the car window.

Yes, it was that time of year. We had to move on. When I opened the front door to our shack, I stopped. Everything we owned had been put in boxes. Suddenly I thought once more of all those hours, days, weeks, and months of work I had just finished. They seemed like the heavy load I was carrying. I sat down on a box. I thought of moving to Fresno and what was waiting for me there. The thought brought tears to my eyes.

That night I could not sleep. I lay in bed thinking about how I hated this move.

A little before five o'clock in the morning, Papá woke everyone up. A few minutes later, the quiet of the new day was broken by the yelling and screaming of my brothers and sisters. To them, moving was a great adventure. Soon, the barking of the dogs added to the noise.

While we packed the breakfast dishes, Papá went outside to start the "Carcanchita." That was the name Papá gave his old black 1938 Plymouth. He had bought it in a used car lot in Santa Rosa in 1949. Papá was proud of his little car. He had a right to be proud of it. He had spent a lot of time looking at other cars before buying this one. Finally, he chose the "Carcanchita." He checked it very carefully before driving it out of the car lot. He looked over every inch of the car. He listened to the motor, holding his head sideways, like a parrot. He listened for any noises that might mean car trouble. At last, Papá thought the car

Fresno is a city in north central California. Why might the character in the story be so sad at the idea of going to Fresno? Predict what you think might be waiting for him there.

Why would a car be so important to the family?

Listo means "Ready!"

Mi olla means "My pot." Why might the mother be proud of her pot?

Es todo means "That's all."

This is not the first year that the family has gone from place to place working on farms. Why might the young boy be sad about leaving a shack?

looked and sounded all right. But he wanted to know who the original owner was. He never did find out from the car salesman. Papá bought the car anyway. He figured the original owner must have been an important man. This was because he found a blue necktie behind the back seat of the car.

Papá parked the car out in front and left the motor running. "*Listo*," he yelled. Without saying a word, Roberto and I began to carry the boxes out to the car. Roberto carried the two big boxes, and I carried the two smaller ones. Papá then threw the mattress on top of the car roof. Then he tied it with ropes to the front and back bumpers.

Everything was in the car except Mama's pot. It was a large, old pot she had bought at an army surplus store. She bought it in Santa Rosa the year I was born. The pot had many dents and nicks. The more dents and nicks it had gotten, the more Mama liked it. "*Mi olla*," she would say in a proud voice.

I held the front door of the car open. Mama carefully carried out the pot by both handles. The pot was full of cooked beans. She was careful not to spill them. When she got to the car, Papá reached out to help her with the pot. Roberto opened the back door of the car. Papá put the pot gently on the floor behind the front seat. Then all of us climbed in. Papá sighed. He wiped the sweat off his forehead with his sleeve. In a tired voice, he said, "*Es todo*."

We drove away. I felt a lump in my throat. I turned around and looked at our little shack for the last time.

At sunset, we drove into a labor camp near Fresno. Papá did not speak English so Mama talked to the camp boss. She asked if he needed any more workers.

The camp boss scratched his head. He said, "We don't need no more. Check with Sullivan. He lives down the road. You can't miss his house. It's a big white house with a fence around it."

When we got there, Mama walked up to the house. She went through a white gate, past a row of rose bushes, up the stairs to the front door. She rang the doorbell. A light came on, and a tall man came out. Mama and the man talked for a short time. Then the man went back into his house. Mama came back to the car quickly. She said, "We have work! Mr. Sullivan says we can stay over there the whole season." She pointed to an old garage.

From what you have read, describe how a migrant family gets work in different places.

Why might the mother be so excited about what she finds out at the house?

The garage was very old. It had no windows. The walls had been eaten by termites. The roof was full of holes. The dirt floor was the home of many worms. They made the floor look like a gray road map.

That night, by the light of a kerosene lamp, we cleaned our new home. Roberto swept away the loose dirt, so we had a floor of hard ground. Papá plugged the holes in the walls with old newspaper and the tops of tin cans. Mama fed my little brothers and sisters. Then Papá and Roberto brought in the mattress. They put it in the far corner of the garage. Papá said, "Mama, you and the little ones sleep on the mattress. Roberto, Panchito, and I will sleep outside under the trees."

For the first time, readers learn the storyteller's name. His name is Panchito.

Early next morning, Mr. Sullivan showed us where we would be working. After breakfast, Papá, Roberto, and I went out to pick Mr. Sullivan's grapes.

By about nine o'clock, it was very hot. The temperature was almost one hundred degrees. I was wet all over from sweat. My mouth felt like I had been eating cloth. I walked to the end of the row of grapevines. I picked up the jug of water we had brought and began to drink.

Roberto yelled, "Don't drink too much; you'll get sick." As soon as he said that, I felt sick to my stomach. I dropped down to my knees. I let the jug roll off my hands. I didn't move. I fixed my eyes on the hot, sandy ground. All I could hear was the noise of insects. Slowly, I began to feel better. I poured water over my face and neck. I watched the dirty water run down my arms to the ground.

I still felt a little dizzy when we stopped to eat lunch. It was past two o'clock. We sat under a large walnut tree that was on the side of the road. While we ate, Papá wrote down how many boxes we had picked. Roberto drew in the dirt with a stick. Suddenly Papá's face seemed scared as he looked down the road. He whispered loudly, "Here comes the school bus."

Before reading on, make a prediction: Why might the father be scared seeing the school bus?

Roberto and I ran and hid behind the grapevines. We did not want to get in trouble for not going to school. Boys about my age, in nice clothes, got off the bus. They carried books under their arms. After they had crossed the street, the bus drove away. Roberto and I came out from behind the grape vines. Papá told us, *"Tienen que tener cuidado."*

Was your prediction right? How did you know?

After lunch, we went back to work. The sun beat down on us. The buzzing insects, the wet sweat, and the hot dry dust were with us all afternoon. The day seemed to last forever. At last, the sun went down behind the mountains. In an hour, it was too dark to work anymore. The vines covered the grapes like

Tienen que tener cuidado means "Be careful." Why might the father say that?

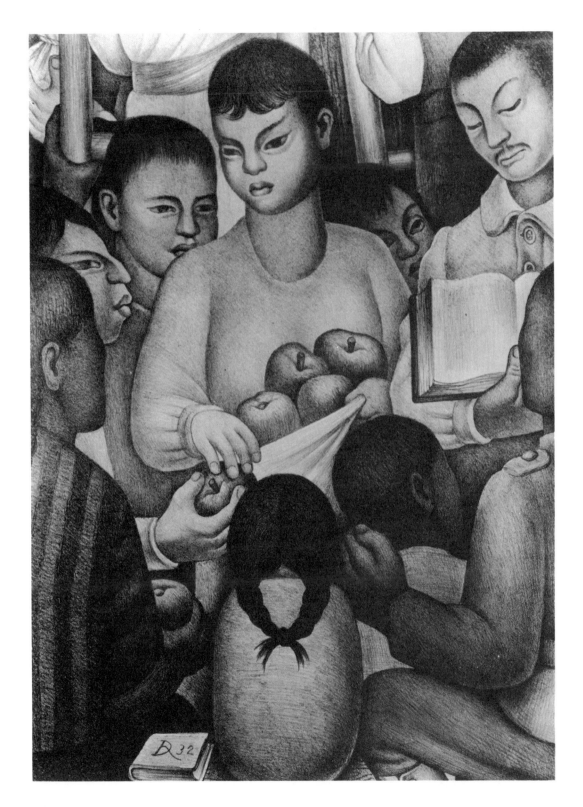

blankets. It was hard to find them. Papá said *"Vámanos."* It was time to quit work. Then Papá took out a pencil. He began to figure out how much money we had made on our first day. He wrote down numbers and crossed some out. Then he wrote down some more. At last, he said, *"Quince,"* in a low voice.

When we got home, we stood under a hose for a cold shower. Then we sat down to eat dinner. We used wooden boxes as a table. Mama had cooked a special dinner for us. We had rice and tortillas with *"carne con chile."* It was my favorite dish.

The next morning, I almost couldn't move. My body hurt all over. My arms and legs wouldn't move the way I wanted them to. I felt this way every morning for days. Then my body finally got used to the work.

It was Monday, the first week in November. Grape picking was finished. Now I could go to school. I woke up early that morning. I lay in bed and looked at the stars. I didn't have to work and that felt good. It also felt good to be starting sixth grade for the first time that year.

Since I couldn't sleep, I had breakfast with Papá and Roberto. I sat at the table across from Roberto. I kept my head down. I did not want to look up and face him. I knew he was sad. He was not going to school today. He was not going tomorrow, or next week, or next month. He would not go until he and Papá had finished picking cotton. That would be sometime in February. I rubbed my hands together. Pieces of my skin, dried out from picking grapes, fell to the floor in little rolls.

I felt better when Papá and Roberto left for work. I walked out to some high ground next to the shack. I watched the "Carcanchita" drive away in a cloud of dust.

Two hours later, around eight o'clock, I stood by the side of the road. I waited for school bus number

Vámanos means "Let's go."

Quince means "fifteen."

Carne con chile means "meat with chili."

When do most schools begin the school year? How old do you think Panchito is?

20. When it stopped, I climbed in. All the kids were busy talking or yelling. I sat in an empty seat in the back.

The bus stopped in front of the school. I felt very nervous. I looked out the bus window. I saw boys and girls carrying books under their arms. I put my hands in my pants' pockets and walked into the principal's office. When I walked in, I heard a woman's voice say, "May I help you?" The voice made me jump. I had not heard English words for months. For a few seconds, I did not speak. I looked at the lady. She was waiting for an answer. My first thought was to answer her in Spanish, but I held back. Finally, I remembered English words. I was able to tell her I wanted to be in the sixth grade. After I answered many questions, I was taken to the classroom.

Mr. Lema was the sixth grade teacher. He said hello and told me which desk to sit at. Then he told the class who I was. Everyone's eyes were on me. I felt so nervous and scared I wished I were with Papá and Roberto picking cotton.

Mr. Lema took attendance. Then he told the class what they would be doing for the first hour. He said, "The first thing we have to do this morning is finish reading the story we began yesterday." His voice was happy and full of energy.

Mr. Lema walked up to me. He handed me an English book and asked me to read. He said in a polite voice, "We are on page 125." When I heard this, I felt my blood rush to my head. I felt dizzy.

Mr. Lema asked, "Would you like to read?" His voice didn't sound very sure. I opened the book to page 125. My mouth was dry. My eyes began to water. I could not begin. Mr. Lema said in a kind voice, "You can read later."

The rest of reading time, I got more and more angry with myself. I thought to myself: I should have read.

Why has Panchito not heard English words for a long time?

Sum up how Panchito feels when Mr. Lema asks him to read. Why might he feel this way?

Why might Panchito feel angry with himself for not reading?

During recess, I went into the restroom. I opened my English book to page 125. I began to read in a low voice. I pretended I was in class. There were many words I did not know. I closed the book and went back to the classroom.

Mr. Lema was sitting at his desk. He was correcting papers. When I came in, he looked up at me and smiled. I felt better. I walked up to Mr. Lema. I asked him if he could help me with the new words. Mr. Lema said, "I would be happy to help you."

The rest of the month I spent my lunch hours working with Mr. Lema. He was my best friend at school.

One Friday during lunch hour, Mr. Lema asked me to walk with him to the music room. As we walked into the building, he asked me, "Do you like music?"

I said, "Yes, I like *corridos*."

Mr. Lema picked up a trumpet. He blew on it and handed it to me. The sound gave me goose bumps. I knew that sound. I had heard it in many *corridos*.

Mr. Lema said, "How would you like to learn how to play the trumpet?" He must have read my face. Before I could answer, he said, "I'll teach you how to play it during our lunch hours."

I could hardly wait to get home. I wanted to tell Papá and Mama the great news. As I got off the bus, my little brothers and sisters ran up to meet me. They were yelling and screaming. I thought they were happy to see me. But when I opened the door to our shack, I saw that everything we owned was packed up in boxes.

Corridos is a kind of Mexican dance music.

Why might trumpet lessons be special for Panchito? Make a prediction: How will the lessons go?

Was your prediction accurate? Why or why not?

Migrant Workers

Migrant workers travel from place to place to pick crops. They work long hours and earn very little pay. Their children must change schools every time they move. It is a difficult life.

In the 1960s, U.S. migrant workers started a union. A union is a group that fights for better working conditions and more pay. César Chávez was an important leader of this union. By 1970, César Chávez got many migrant workers to join the union. Slowly, the union improved living conditions and pay. But even today, the life of migrant workers is still very difficult.

Literature Practice

Answer these questions on a separate sheet of paper.

1. Who is Mr. Sullivan? Why is he important to the family?

2. Why does the family have to move to Fresno?

3. Why does Panchito get nervous when the woman in the office speaks English?

4. How do you think Panchito feels when he realizes the family has to move again?

5. Predict how you think Panchito's experiences as a child influenced how he would become as an adult.

The Jacket
an adapted story by Gary Soto

Words to Know

LITERARY TERMS

symbolism using something to stand for an idea

figurative language words that say one thing but mean another; used by an author to add color and interest to a story

SELECTION VOCABULARY

vinyl a material made of strong plastic

blurry when something cannot be seen clearly

scab the crust that forms on the skin where a sore or cut is healing

grunt a deep, unpleasant sound

My clothes have failed me. I remember the green jacket that I wore in fifth and sixth grades. In those grades, some kids danced like champs. But other kids pressed themselves against a greasy wall, feeling bitter as pennies toward the happy couples.

When I needed a new jacket, my mother asked what kind I wanted. I described something like bikers wear. I wanted a jacket with black leather, silver studs, and enough belts to hold down a small town. Mother and I were in the kitchen. Steam was on the windows from her cooking. She listened for a long time while stirring dinner. I thought for sure she knew the kind of jacket I wanted

The next day when I came home from school, I

Guacamole is made from crushed avocados. When fresh, it is green. When old, it turns an ugly brownish-green color.

When the author compares the new jacket to day-old guacamole, he is using figurative language. After reading the definition of guacamole, why do you think the author does not like the new jacket?

saw a jacket hanging on my bedpost. It was the color of day-old guacamole. I threw my books on the bed. I walked up to the jacket slowly, as if it was a stranger's hand I had to shake. I touched the **vinyl** sleeve, the collar, and looked at the mustard-colored lining.

From my bed, I stared at the jacket. I wanted to cry because it was so ugly. And it was so big that I knew I'd have to wear it a long time. I was a small kid, thin as a young tree. It would be years before I'd have a new one. I stared at the jacket, like an enemy. Then I took off my old jacket, the sleeves of which climbed halfway up to my elbow.

I put the big jacket on. I zipped it up and down several times. I rolled the cuffs up so they didn't cover my hands. I put my hands in the pockets and flapped the jacket like a bird's wings. I stood and

looked in the mirror. Then I combed my hair to see what I would look like doing something natural. I looked ugly. I threw the jacket on my brother's bed and looked at it for a long time.

Then I put the jacket on and went out to the backyard. As I passed the kitchen, I smiled a "thank you" to my mom. Outside, I kicked a ball against a fence. Then I climbed the fence to sit looking into the alley. I threw orange peels at the mouth of an open garbage can. When the peels were gone, I watched the white puffs of my breath thin out to nothing.

I jumped down, hands in my pockets. I stood on my knees and teased my dog, Brownie, by swooping my arms while making bird calls. He jumped at me and missed. He jumped again and again. At last he caught me. One of his teeth sunk deep, making an L-shaped tear in the sleeve. I pushed Brownie away. I looked closely at the tear as if it was a cut on my arm. Darn dog, I thought. I pushed him away hard when he tried to bite again. I got up from my knees and went to my bedroom. I sat with my jacket on my lap, with the lights out.

That was the first afternoon with my new jacket. The next day I wore it to sixth grade and got a D on a math quiz. During the morning recess, Frankie T., the playground terrorist, pushed me to the ground. He told me to stay there until recess was over. My best friend, Steve Negrete, ate an apple while looking at me. The girls turned away to whisper on the monkey bars. The teachers were no help. They looked my way and talked about how foolish I looked in my new jacket. I saw their heads shake with laughter. Their hands half-covered their mouths.

Even though it was cold, I took off the jacket during lunch. I played kickball in a thin shirt. My arms felt like Braille from goose bumps. When I got back to class, I slipped the jacket on. I shook until I was warm. I sat on my hands, heating them up. My

Again, the author uses language that helps the reader to see how unhappy he is with the jacket. The jacket must be very large to flap like a bird's wings.

Why do you think Gary doesn't tell his mother he hates the jacket?

Gary tells readers ways in which the jacket gives him bad luck. Review the ways. Do you think he is serious?

The author is again using figurative language to describe the goose bumps on his arms. Braille is a system that blind people use to read and write. The letters and numbers are formed by patterns of raised dots that are felt with the fingers.

South America is the continent south of Mexico. Gary's family is originally from Mexico, but they now live in California.

The jacket has become a symbol of everything wrong. What does the author now blame on the jacket?

Gary blames his mother, but he never tells her how he feels. Why?

teeth chattered like a cup of crooked dice. When I was finally warm, I slid out of the jacket. But a few minutes later, I put it on when the fire bell rang. We walked out into the yard. We sixth graders had to walk past all the other grades to stand against the back fence. Everybody saw me. Nobody said out loud, "Man, that's ugly." But I heard the buzz-buzz of talk and even laughter that I knew was meant for me.

And so I went, in my guacamole jacket. I was so embarrassed, so hurt, I couldn't even do my homework. I got Cs on quizzes. I forgot the state capitals and the rivers of South America, our friendly neighbor. Even the girls who had been friendly blew away like loose flowers. They followed the boys in neat jackets.

I wore that thing for three years, until the sleeves grew short and my arms stuck out like the necks of turtles. All during that time no love came to me. No little dark girl in a Sunday dress she wore on Monday paid attention to me. At lunch I stayed with the ugly boys. We leaned against the fence and looked around with propellers of grass spinning in our mouths. We saw girls walk by alone. We saw couples walking hand in hand. Their heads were like bookends, pressing the air together. We saw them and spun our propellers so fast our faces were **blurry**.

I blame that jacket for those bad years. I blame my mother for her bad taste and her cheap ways. It was a sad time for the heart. With a friend, I spent my sixth-grade year in a tree in the alley. I was waiting for something good to happen to me in that jacket. It had become the ugly brother who tagged along wherever I went.

It was about that time that I began to grow. My chest puffed up with muscle. I even seemed to get a few more ribs. My fingers were already getting hard for coming fights.

But that L-shaped rip in the sleeve of the jacket

got bigger. Bits of stuffing came out after a hard day of play. I finally closed the rip with scotch tape. But in rain or cold weather, the tape peeled off like a **scab**. More stuffing came out until the sleeve hung like an arm that had shrunk.

That winter the elbows began to crack. Whole pieces of green began to fall off. I showed the cracks to my mother. She always seemed to be at the stove with steamed-up glasses. She said that there were children in Mexico who would love that jacket. I told her that this was America. I yelled that Debbie, my sister, didn't have a jacket like mine. I ran outside, ready to cry. I climbed the tree in the alley to think bad thoughts and watch the white puffs of my breath float into nothing.

But whole pieces still flew off my jacket when I played hard, read quietly, or took awful spelling tests at school. When the jacket become so spotted that my brother called me "camouflage," I threw it over the fence into the alley. Later, though, I picked it up off the ground. I went inside to lay it across my lap and feel low.

I was called to dinner. Steam made my mother's glasses cloudy as she said grace. My brother and sister bowed their heads and made ugly faces at their glasses of powdered milk. I hated it, too. But I was eager to scoop up beans with big pieces of buttered tortilla. When I finished, I went outside with the jacket across my arm. It was a cold sky. The faces of the clouds were piled up, hurting. I climbed the fence and jumped down with a **grunt**. I started up the alley. Soon, I put on my jacket, that green ugly brother that breathed over my shoulder—that day and ever since.

Why does Gary pick up the jacket from the alley?

How do you think the writer's attitude about the jacket has changed? What is the jacket a symbol of?

Literature Practice

Answer these questions on a separate sheet of paper.

1. Why does Gary think that his mother should know what kind of jacket he wants?

2. What kind of jacket does she buy Gary? Why might she have done that?

3. Why doesn't Gary tell his mother he hates the jacket?

4. What symbol does the jacket become for Gary? Why?

5. Do you think Gary ever stops hating the jacket? Why?

6. What value do you think the jacket has for Gary as an adult?

Chapter Review

Summaries

- **The Circuit**—A young Mexican American boy remembers life with his family as migrant workers. He tells about their car— the Carcanchita—and about its importance to the family. He describes how the family lives and what the end of a crop season means. He shares his feelings about always having to move. When he gets to go to school in the sixth grade, one teacher makes a lasting impression on the young boy. But he has to leave the new school because his family moves again.

- **The Jacket**—In this story, a man remembers some terrible years in his pre-teen life. He blames his unhappiness on a green jacket that his mother buys for him. He tells about all the terrible things that happen to him in the fifth and sixth grades. He has bad luck with girls and bad scores on tests. He is embarrassed by the jacket. He always thinks others are talking about it. The boy never tells his mother how much he hates the jacket. He just wears it until he finally outgrows it.

Chapter Quiz

Choose the letter of the correct answer. Rewrite the sentences on a separate sheet of paper.

1. In "The Circuit," why does the family have to move so often?
   a. They are migrant workers.
   b. The father gets sick.
   c. The children need good schools.
   d. They have to move to New York.

2. How does Panchito spend his lunch hours in his new school?
   a. outside playing with other children
   b. picking grapes in the fields
   c. working with Mr. Lema
   d. correcting papers

3. What is the great news that Panchito wants to tell his parents?
   a. He is going to learn to play the trumpet.
   b. He likes school.
   c. He reads aloud in class.
   d. He is moving again.

4. In "The Jacket," why does Gary Soto hate his new jacket?
   a. It is too hot.
   b. It is the kind that bikers wear.
   c. His mother buys it for him.
   d. It is ugly.

5. What does Soto blame on his jacket?
   a. his mother's failure to listen to him
   b. all the girls liking him
   c. all his bad times in fifth and sixth grade
   d. his brother's unhappiness

Thinking and Writing

Answer the following questions on a separate sheet of paper. Write one or two paragraphs for each one.

1. In "The Jacket," Gary Soto feels very unhappy when he wears his green jacket. Think of a piece of clothing you have that you don't like. Explain how wearing it makes you feel.

2. Choose one of the stories in this chapter. Imagine that you are a different character in the story, such as the mother or the teacher. Write your own version of what happened.

3. In "The Circuit," when Panchito comes to Mr. Lema's class, he feels nervous. Why do you think he feels this way?

Unit Two Review

A. The following questions are about the selections you read in this unit. Write one or two sentence answers on a separate sheet of paper.

1. Why does Panchito's family always have to move?
2. In "Lame Deer Remembers His Childhood," why do you think Lame Deer's father punishes him the way he does?
3. Why does Yoshiko Uchida's family leave their home in "Prisoner of My Country"?
4. What does the jacket mean for the boy in "The Jacket"?
5. In "Dust Tracks on a Road," why do the two white women invite Zora Neale to visit them?
6. In "The Circuit," why can't Panchito go to school until November?

B. Choose two of the essay questions below. Answer them on a separate sheet of paper. Write one or two paragraphs for each one.

1. Lame Deer said that in his culture children are never scolded or spanked. How does this help explain the way his father punishes him?
2. In "The Circuit," Panchito starts to enjoy school. He is very excited about learning to play the trumpet. Then he has a terrible disappointment. Why is Panchito so disappointed? Explain your answer with details from the story.
3. Choose one of the selections in this unit. Write a description of the main character in that selection. Tell what he or she is like as a person. Then say whether you would like that person as a friend and why.

HEROES

Chapter 5

The Ballad of John Henry
an anonymous poem
Harriet Tubman
by Eloise Greenfield
A Chant of Darkness
from the poem by Helen Keller
The Unsung Heroes
by Paul Laurence Dunbar
Paul Revere's Ride
by Henry Wadsworth Longfellow

Chapter 6

Behind the Waterfall
an adapted story retold by Marion Wood
Paul Bunyan, the Mightiest Logger of Them All
an adapted story by Mary Pope Osborne
Thank You, M'am
by Langston Hughes

Chapter 7

Rosa Parks
from the biography by Eloise Greenfield
Roberto Clemente: A Bittersweet Memoir
adapted from the article by Jerry Izenberg

Sometimes, when we dare to believe, we really can do the impossible. The poems that follow celebrate heroes who took the challenge and dared to believe in achieving the impossible.

Chapter Learning Objectives

- To understand why ballads are written and sung
- To identify idiomatic expressions
- To learn about stanzas
- To understand rhythm and repetition
- To identify personification
- To understand rhyme
- To identify narrative poetry
- To learn about imagery

The Ballad of John Henry

an anonymous poem

Words to Know

LITERARY TERMS

ballad a song that tells a story

idiom a group of words with a special meaning

stanza a group of lines in a poem

SELECTION VOCABULARY

steel-drivin' using a hammer to pound a pointed piece of metal, or chisel, into rock

drive to force a piece of metal, or a chisel, into rock with a hammer

steam drill a machine that uses steam power and a sharp tool to cut a hole through rock

choke to block or clog

locomotive an engine used to push or pull railroad cars

This song tells the story of John Henry. John Henry says that he would rather die than have a steam drill drive steel faster than he can.

John Henry is able to hammer steel faster than a steam drill. But he works so hard, he dies.

—◦◦◦◦—

John Henry was a little baby boy
You could hold him in the palm of your hand.
He gave a long and lonesome cry,
"Gonna be a **steel-drivin'** man, Lawd, Lawd,
5 Gonna be a steel-drivin' man."

This ballad, or song, begins with the baby John Henry giving a "long and lonesome cry" that he repeats.

Notice that each stanza, or group of lines, has words at the end that are repeated. These repeated words help listeners remember the song. Look for more lines that repeat in the ballad.

They took John Henry to the tunnel,
Put him in the lead to **drive**,
The rock was so tall, John Henry so small,
That he laid down his hammer and he cried,
10   "Lawd, Lawd,"
Laid down his hammer and he cried.

John Henry started on the right hand,
The **steam drill** started on the left,
"Fo' I'd let that steam drill beat me down,
15   I'd hammer my fool self to death, Lawd, Lawd,
Hammer my fool self to death."

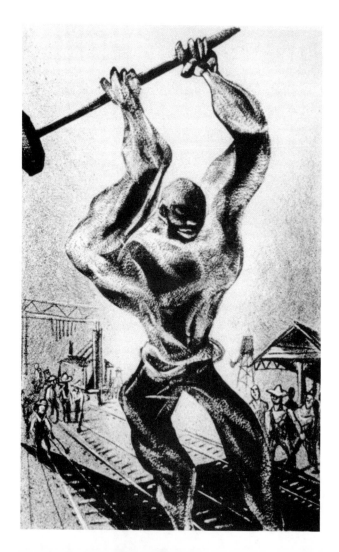

John Henry told his captain,
"A man ain't nothin' but a man,
Fo' I let your steamdrill beat me down
20   I'll die with this hammer in my hand, Lawd,
          Lawd,
Die with this hammer in my hand."
Now the Captain told John Henry,
"I believe my tunnel's sinkin' in."
25   "Stand back, Captain, and doncha be afraid,
That's nothin' but my hammer catchin' wind,
          Lawd, Lawd,
That's nothin' but my hammer catchin' wind."

John Henry told his Cap'n,
30   "Look yonder, boy, what do I see?
Your drill's done broke and your hole's done
          choke,
And you can't drive steel like me, Lawd, Lawd,
You can't drive steel like me."

35   John Henry hammerin' in the mountain,
Til the handle of his hammer caught on fire,
He drove so hard till he broke his po' heart,
Then he laid down his hammer and he died,
          Lawd, Lawd,
40   He laid down his hammer and he died.

They took John Henry to the tunnel,
And they buried him in the sand,
An' every **locomotive** come rollin' by
Say, "There lies a steel-drivin' man, Lawd, Lawd,
45   There lies a steel-drivin' man."

Maybe the Captain hears a loud noise. He tells John Henry he's afraid that his railroad tunnel will fall in. John Henry tells him not to be afraid. He says, "That's nothin' but my hammer catchin' wind." This statement is an example of an idiom. An idiom is a saying that means something different than when each word is used alone. What do you think John Henry means when he makes that statement?

Reread the poem aloud. Notice how the repeated words at the end of each stanza create the rhythm of the swinging hammer.

Who Was John Henry?

Most of what we know about John Henry comes from stories and ballads. No one is sure of the facts about him. Most people agree he was an African American man who lived in West Virginia around 1870. He worked hard with other African American men. They cut holes in mountains to make tunnels for a new railroad. The men had to be very strong to hammer away at the rock all day. It was very tiring work. Around this time, a new machine called a steam drill was invented. It was said to be better at drilling holes than men were! Back then, people had a difficult time believing that a machine could do the same work that a man could do.

Like today, people did not want to believe that a machine could take the place of a person. The ballad says that John Henry did not want to be beaten by a machine. There was a contest to see who could drill holes faster—John Henry or the machine. John Henry beat the machine, but he died the same night. On the day he beat the machine, John Henry became a hero to many people!

Literature Practice

Answer these questions on a separate sheet of paper.

1. In the ballad, what does the baby John Henry say that he will do when he grows up?
2. a.) How does John Henry feel about the steam drill? b.) How do you know?
3. What happens to John Henry after he beats the steam drill?
4. Why do you think people sing this ballad about John Henry?

Harriet Tubman
by Eloise Greenfield

Words to Know

LITERARY TERMS

rhythm a special sound pattern of stressed and unstressed syllables, or beats, in a poem

repetition the use of the same word or words over and over to create a sound or rhythmical pattern

SELECTION VOCABULARY

farewell a way of saying "good-bye"

mighty very; extremely

Harriet Tubman didn't take no stuff
Wasn't scared of nothing neither
Didn't come in this world to be no slave
And wasn't going to stay one either

5 "**Farewell**!" she sang to her friends one night
She was **mighty** sad to leave 'em
But she ran away that dark, hot night
Ran looking for her freedom

She ran to the woods and she ran through the woods
10 With the slave catchers right behind her
And she kept on going till she got to the North
Where those mean men couldn't find her

Nineteen times she went back South
To get three hundred others
15 She ran for her freedom nineteen times
To save black sisters and brothers

Notice that each line has a certain number of strong beats. This makes the rhythm of the poem. If you read the poem aloud, you'll hear the rhythm of the words. Count the number of strong beats in each line.

Slave catchers are people who caught runaway African American slaves and returned them to their slave owners for money.

This stanza is also at the beginning of the poem. The writer uses repetition to make a strong point. What do you think the writer wants the reader to remember about Harriet Tubman?

Harriet Tubman didn't take no stuff
Wasn't scared of nothing neither
Didn't come in this world to be no slave
20 And didn't stay one either

And didn't stay one either

Fearless Harriet Tubman

Harriet Tubman was born in Maryland in 1820. She was born into slavery. At that time, laws in the South said that African Americans could be enslaved. When she was a child, Tubman's owner beat her. One time, he hit her on the head and hurt her very badly. For the rest of her life, Tubman had dizzy spells and sometimes fainted.

In 1849, Tubman was 29 years old. She decided to run away to the North to be free. It was not an easy trip. She had to hide in the daytime and run as far as she could at night. If she had been caught, she would have been punished severely. It was against the law to help slaves escape. But some people, both African American and white, helped her anyway. By hiding in people's houses and farms and in graveyards and cellars, Tubman made her way north. The people who hid runaway slaves were called conductors on the Underground Railroad. Tubman got to Philadelphia safely. She went back to the South many times. She helped her family and more than 300 other slaves escape safely through the Underground Railroad. Because she was so good at helping runaway slaves, many slave owners were angry. They wanted to catch her. But they never did.

Literature Practice

Answer these questions on a separate sheet of paper.

1. In the poem, what does the poet mean when she says that Harriet Tubman "didn't take no stuff"?

2. What does Tubman do that makes the writer think she is brave?

3. Why does Tubman go back to the South so many times?

4. Why does the poet repeat the first stanza at the end of the poem?

5. Which words in the poem tell you that the poet sees Tubman as a strong and determined woman?

A Chant of Darkness
from the poem by Helen Keller

Words to Know

LITERARY TERM

personification giving human characteristics to nonliving things

SELECTION VOCABULARY

void empty

affrighted afraid of

beseeching begging

aflame very warm and alive

sacredness being worthy of deep respect

discerned understood

ecstasy great feeling of joy

evoke bring out

quiver shaking just a little bit

fathomless not understood

balm something that makes someone or something feel better

Helen Keller was deaf and blind. As a child, she could not communicate with anyone. Then a teacher showed her sign language. This is a way of talking with your hands. Keller could finally talk to people. She also began to understand what was happening around her.

In this poem, Keller describes her life. At first, she is afraid because she is deaf and blind. Everything is dark and scary. Then her teacher comes. Keller begins to understand life through her hands. She learns to like the dark. She learns to love her life.

Once in regions **void** of light I wandered;
In blank darkness I stumbled,
And fear led me by the hand;
My feet pressed earthward,
5   Afraid of pitfalls.
By many shapeless terrors of the night
    affrighted,
To the wakeful day
I held out **beseeching** arms.

10 Then came Love, bearing in her hand
The torch that is the light unto my feet,
And softly spoke Love: "Hast thou
Entered into the treasures of darkness?
Hast thou entered into the treasures of the night?
15 Search out thy blindness. It holdeth

Helen Keller writes about what it is like to be blind. She says that she is afraid of the darkness. When she says "fear led me by the hand," she makes fear seem like a person leading her. This technique is called personification.

For Keller, "Love" is her teacher who teaches her sign language. Once Keller learns to speak with her hands, she begins to understand the world around her.

Here, Keller talks about how happy she is to learn new things by using her hands.

Riches past computing."
The words of Love set my spirit **aflame**.
My eager fingers searched out the mysteries,
The splendors, the inmost **sacredness**, of
20   things,
And in the vacancies **discerned**
With spiritual sense the fullness of life;
And the gates of Day stood wide.

I am shaken with gladness;
25 My limbs tremble with joy;
My heart and the earth
Tremble with happiness;
The **ecstasy** of life
Is abroad in the world.

At this point, Keller describes using her hands to talk with others. She also uses her senses of touch and smell to understand things.

30 My hands **evoke** sight and sound out of feeling,
Intershifting the senses endlessly;
Linking motion with sight, odor with sound
They give color to the honeyed breeze,
The measure and passion of a symphony
35 To the beat and **quiver** of unseen wings.
In the secrets of earth and sun and air
My fingers are wise;
They snatch light out of darkness,
They thrill to harmonies breathed in silence.

Here is another example of personification. "Night" is described as a living person. Keller decides she loves "Night." What do you think she means when she talks about "Night"?

40 I walk in the stillness of the night,
And my soul uttereth her gladness.
O Night, still, odorous Night, I love thee!
O wide, spacious Night, I love thee!
O steadfast, glorious Night!
45 I touch thee with my hands;
I lean against thy strength;
I am comforted.

O **fathomless**, soothing Night!
Thou art a **balm** to my restless spirit,
50 I nestle gratefully in thy bosom,
Dark, gracious mother!
Like a dove, I rest in thy bosom.
Out of the uncharted, unthinkable dark we came,
And in a little time shall return again
55 *Into the vast, unanswering dark.*

A balm is something that makes a cut or a burn feel better. When Keller writes "Thou art a balm to my restless spirit," she means that she feels safe and calm with "Night."

Heroes

It is easy to see why Helen Keller is respected by many people. As an adult, Keller traveled around the world and met important leaders. Using sign language, Keller talked with President Franklin D. Roosevelt. He had his own special problem. He could not use his legs. With Keller's help, he worked to have laws passed that helped blind people.

Today, there are many famous Americans who are not stopped by physical problems. Ray Charles and Stevie Wonder are great musicians who are blind. Stephen Hawking is a famous scientist who cannot speak or walk. Jim Abbott is a baseball pitcher who is missing one arm. All of these people have done something very special with their lives. All are heroes.

Literature Practice

Answer these questions on a separate sheet of paper.

1. Why is the poet afraid at the beginning of the poem?

2. Describe two ways that Keller uses personification.

3. How do the writer's feelings change in the poem?

4. What one thing has most changed in Keller's life?

5. Why do you think the poet calls her poem "A Chant of Darkness"?

The Unsung Heroes
by Paul Laurence Dunbar

Words to Know

LITERARY TERM

rhyme words that have the same end sounds

SELECTION VOCABULARY

unsung haven't been praised or spoken well of

threatened in danger

cruel very mean, unfeeling

greed wanting too much

plough a farm tool used to cut and turn over soil

flail a farm tool used to cut seed from a plant

rallied came together

rail railroad, train

humblest most simple

boast brag

sod earth, soil, dirt

This poem was written for the African American soldiers in the Civil War. These men came from working in the fields to fight in the war. Their country needed them, and these heroes fought and died for it.

———— ∞∞∞ ————

A song for the **unsung** heroes who rose in
    the country's need,
When the life of the land was **threatened**
    by the slaver's **cruel greed**,
5 For the men who came from the corn field,
    who came from the **plough** and the **flail**,
Who **rallied** round when they heard the
    sound of the mighty man of the **rail.**

The heroes are "unsung" because they were African American men who often did not receive the credit or fame they deserved.

A song for the unsung heroes who stood
10   the awful test,
When the **humblest** host that the land
       could **boast** went forth to meet the
       best;
A song for the unsung heroes who fell on
15   the bloody **sod**,
Who fought their way from night to day
              and struggled up to God.

In both stanzas, the end words in each line rhyme. To make the poem "sing," Dunbar also rhymes words in the middle of lines. *Round* and *sound* rhyme in lines 7 and 8. Can you find a middle rhyme pattern in lines 9-17?

They Gave Their Lives

The American Civil War lasted five years, from 1861 to 1865. It was fought between the North and the South. People in the North wanted all of the states to stay together. Their army was called the Union. The Union wanted to end slavery. The people in the Southern states wanted to become a separate country from the North. They also wanted to keep their slaves.

At first, African American men were not allowed to be soldiers in the Union Army. Some white leaders said that African Americans were not brave enough. Finally, in 1862, they were allowed to join. Then many African American soldiers fought for the North.

One brave group of African American soldiers was called the 54th Massachusetts Infantry. These men attacked a fort in North Carolina. The fort was guarded by 1,700 Southern soldiers. During the battle, over 100 African American men from the Union Army were killed. After that night, no one could say that the African American soldier was not brave. Many African Americans became heroes in the Civil War. These men gave their lives to unite the country and to end slavery.

Literature Practice

Answer these questions on a separate sheet of paper.

1. What are two words in the poem that rhyme?
2. a.) Who are the "unsung heroes"?

   b.) Where do they come from?
3. What are the heroes fighting for?
4. Why does the writer think that these men are heroes?

Paul Revere's Ride
by Henry Wadsworth Longfellow

Words to Know

LITERARY TERMS

narrative poem a poem that tells a story

imagery vivid words that help the reader to "see" how something looks, sounds, feels, or tastes

SELECTION VOCABULARY

lantern a lamp or light with a cover that can be carried

moorings a place where a boat is tied up

grenadiers soldiers who carried small bombs in their hands

dread great worry or fear

impetuous to act in a sudden way

steep a very high hill

defiance not doing something you're told to do

peril danger

On April 18, 1775, Paul Revere warns Americans that the British are coming to fight them.

Paul Revere's friend learns that the British soldiers will be coming by boat. So he goes to the top of the Old North Church Tower in Boston. He holds up two lanterns. Two lanterns is the signal that the British will be coming by water and not by land.

Then Paul Revere rides off through the night to the town of Concord. Along the way, he tells people that the British are coming and that they must get ready to fight. He passes places where people will soon be fighting and dying.

A narrative poem tells a story. The story in this poem takes place in 1775. It tells the story of a man who spends a night planning, waiting, and then riding his horse to give his friends a message. Read the poem to see why you think the man and the poem became so famous.

The future of our country rode with Paul Revere on that night. History will always remember his famous ride.

—⊷⊶—

The poet uses rhythm to make the words sing like a song. Read the poem out loud. Do you notice the beats?

The writer tells us what Paul Revere says to his friend. This lets us know at the beginning what Paul Revere's plan is. His friend must watch to see if the British will come to fight. Then he must signal Paul Revere by hanging one lantern if the British are coming by land or two lanterns if they are coming by sea.

Listen, my children, and you shall hear
Of the midnight ride of Paul Revere,
On the eighteenth of April, in Seventy-five;
Hardly a man is now alive
5 Who remembers that famous day and year.

He said to his friend, "If the British march
By land or sea from the town tonight,
Hang a **lantern** aloft in the belfry-arch
Of the North Church tower as a signal light,—
10 One, if by land, and two, if by sea;
And I on the opposite shore will be,
Ready to ride and spread the alarm
Through every Middlesex village and farm,
For the country folk to be up and to arm."

15 Then he said, "Good night!" and with muffled oar
Silently rowed to the Charlestown shore,
Just as the moon rose over the bay,
Where swinging wide at her **moorings** lay
The *Somerset,* British man-of-war;
20 A phantom ship, with each mast and spar
Across the moon like a prison bar,
And a huge black hulk, that was magnified
By its own reflection in the tide.

Meanwhile, his friend, through alley and street,
25 Wanders and watches with eager ears,
Till in the silence around him he hears
The muster of men at the barrack door,
The sound of arms, and the tramp of feet,
And the measured tread of the **grenadiers**,
30 Marching down to their boats on the shore.

Then he climbed the tower of the Old North
    Church,
By the wooden stairs, with stealthy tread,
To the belfry-chamber overhead,
35 And startled the pigeons from their perch
On the somber rafters, that round him made
Masses and moving shapes of shade,—
By the trembling ladder, steep and tall,
To the highest window in the wall,
40 Where he paused to listen and look down
A moment on the roofs of the town,
And the moonlight flowing over all.

Here, the writer tells us about the silent graveyard below the church. This is where Paul Revere's friend must wait. How do you think his friend feels?

Beneath, in the churchyard, lay the dead,
In their night-encampment on the hill,
45 Wrapped in silence so deep and still
That he could hear, like a sentinel's tread,
The watchful night-wind, as it went
Creeping along from tent to tent,
And seeming to whisper, "All is well!"
50 A moment only he feels the spell
Of the place and the hour, and the secret **dread**
Of the lonely belfry and the dead;
For suddenly all his thoughts are bent
On a shadowy something far away,
55 Where the river widens to meet the bay,—
A line of black that bends and floats
On the rising tide, like a bridge of boats.

Meanwhile, impatient to mount and ride,
Booted and spurred, with a heavy stride
60 On the opposite shore walked Paul Revere.
Now he patted his horse's side,
Now gazed at the landscape far and near,
Then, **impetuous**, stamped the earth,
And turned and tightened his saddle-girth;
65 But mostly he watched with eager search
The belfry-tower of the Old North Church,
As it rose above the graves on the hill,
Lonely and spectral and somber and still.
And lo! as he looks, on the belfry's height
70 A glimmer, and then a gleam of light!
He springs to the saddle, the bridle he turns,
But lingers and gazes, till full on his sight,
A second lamp in the belfry burns!
A hurry of hoofs in a village street,
75 A shape in the moonlight, a bulk in the dark,
And beneath, from the pebbles, in passing, a
      spark
Struck out by a steed flying fearless and fleet;
That was all! And yet, through the gloom and the
80   light,
The fate of a nation was riding that night;
And the spark struck out by that steed in his
      flight,
Kindled the land into flame with its heat.

85 He has left the village and mounted the **steep**,
And beneath him, tranquil and broad and deep,
Is the Mystic, meeting the ocean tides;
And under the alders that skirt its edge,
Now soft on the sand, now loud on the ledge,
90 Is heard the tramp of his steed as he rides.

The first part of this stanza tells how Paul Revere waits. Then he finally gets the signal from his friend. His friend flashes two lights. This means the British are coming in boats. The writer uses exclamation points (!) in the last part of the stanza to show Paul Revere's excitement. Paul Revere now has to move quickly!

The writer gives readers a sense of time passing. He tells us, "It was one by the village clock." He also uses imagery, or words that paint a picture in the reader's mind. He says that Paul Revere "felt the damp of the river fog that rises after the sun goes down." This is a different way to tell the reader that the night is getting later.

It was twelve by the village clock,
When he crossed the bridge into Medford town.
He heard the crowing of the cock,
And the barking of the farmer's dog,
95 And felt the damp of the river fog,
That rises after the sun goes down.

It was one by the village clock,
When he galloped into Lexington.
He saw the gilded weathercock
100 Swim in the moonlight as he passed,
And the meeting-house windows, blank and bare,
Gaze at him with a spectral glare,
As if they already stood aghast
At the bloody work they would look upon.

105 It was two by the village clock,
When he came to the bridge in Concord town.
He heard the bleating of the flock,
And the twitter of birds among the trees,
And felt the breath of the morning breeze
110 Blowing over the meadows brown.
And one was safe and asleep in his bed
Who at the bridge would be first to fall,
Who that day would be lying dead,
Pierced by a British musket-ball.

Have you noticed that the last words of certain lines in the poem rhyme, or sound the same? Try to match the words that rhyme. Do you see a pattern?

115 You know the rest. In the books you have read,
How the British Regulars fired and fled,—
How the farmers gave them ball for ball,
From behind each fence and farmyard wall,
Chasing the redcoats down the lane,
120 Then crossing the fields to emerge again
Under the trees at the turn of the road,
And only pausing to fire and load.

So through the night rode Paul Revere;
And so through the night went his cry of alarm
125 To every Middlesex village and farm,—
A cry of **defiance** and not of fear,
A voice in the darkness, a knock at the door,
And a word that shall echo forevermore!
For, borne on the night-wind of the Past,
130 Through all our history, to the last,
In the hour of darkness and **peril** and need,
The people will waken and listen to hear
The hurrying hoofbeats of that steed
And the midnight message of Paul Revere.

The colonists hear Paul Revere's cry. They wake up to get ready to fight the British for their independence. What do you think would have happened if Paul Revere had not warned them?

The Revolutionary War

Paul Revere risked his life to warn people that the British were coming. At the time, Great Britain ruled the American colonies. Many colonists were angry with the British. These colonists called themselves Patriots. They wanted to be free from British control. The British soldiers came to stop the Patriots.

In real life, Revere didn't make it to Concord. He was caught by the British. But others carried his message, and because of these riders, the Patriots were ready to fight the British for their freedom.

Literature Practice

Answer these questions on a separate sheet of paper.

1. What is the story that this narrative poem tells?
2. What is the famous date in the poem?
3. Name two images that you remember from the poem.
4. How does Longfellow create rhythm in the poem?
5. Why do you think that Paul Revere is considered a hero?

Chapter Review

Summaries

- **The Ballad of John Henry**—This ballad tells the story of John Henry. According to the legend, Henry drills holes in rock for a living. A new machine called a steam drill is invented. It is said to drill holes faster than any man. Henry refuses to believe it. There is a contest between Henry and the machine. Henry beats the machine, but he dies that same night.

- **Harriet Tubman**—In this poem, Eloise Greenfield uses rhythm and repetition to show Harriet Tubman's great strength and determination. Tubman escapes from slavery. Then she goes back to take other slaves to the North. Slave owners try to stop her. But that does not keep her from going back and helping even more slaves escape to freedom.

- **A Chant of Darkness**—Helen Keller describes how she learns to communicate. She is afraid of being blind at first. Then her teacher teaches her sign language. Keller begins to understand her life. She also uses her other senses to enjoy and learn about life.

- **The Unsung Heroes**—Paul Dunbar's poem celebrates African American soldiers. These soldiers served in the 54th Massachusetts Infantry during the Civil War. The poet calls them "unsung" because they are often forgotten. These brave men died on the battlefields fighting for freedom.

- **Paul Revere's Ride**—This poem tells the story of Paul Revere's famous horseback ride on April 18, 1775. It takes place right before the Revolutionary War. British soldiers are coming to try to capture the Patriots. Paul Revere is a Patriot. His friend sends him a message that the British are coming by sea. He rides very fast on his horse to spread the message to the other Patriots.

Chapter Quiz

Decide whether the statements below are true or false. On a separate sheet of paper, rewrite each incorrect statement correctly.

1. John Henry loses the contest against the steam drill.

2. Helen Keller learns to speak with her hands and feels much better about her life.

3. In the poem "A Chant of Darkness," *Love* is Helen Keller's mother.

4. Harriet Tubman goes to the South to escape slavery.

5. The "unsung heroes" are men who fought during the War of Independence.

6. Many of the "unsung heroes" are killed during the war.

7. Paul Revere made his famous horseback ride in 1876.

8. Paul Revere does not understand his friend's message.

Thinking and Writing

Answer the following questions on a separate sheet of paper. Write one or two paragraphs for each one.

1. Helen Keller talks about being afraid at the beginning of her poem. Choose a hero from another poem and explain how he or she might also have been afraid.

2. John Henry gave his life to beat the steam drill in a contest. Choose another poem where the hero or heroes give their lives to fight for what is right. Explain how the heroes from the two poems are the same or different.

3. Two of the poems tell about a hero who must travel alone and in danger. Name the poems and explain what happens in each of them.

Chapter 6

In these short stories, you will meet several heroes. Can you figure out what makes them heroes?

Chapter Learning Objectives

- To learn how a storyteller creates the setting
- To understand a writer's use of simile
- To identify characteristics of a tall tale
- To understand a writer's use of exaggeration and tone
- To understand character
- To understand a writer's use of metaphor

Behind the Waterfall

an adapted story retold by Marion Wood

Words to Know

LITERARY TERMS

setting where and when the story takes place

simile using the words *like* or *as* to compare one thing to another

SELECTION VOCABULARY

roaring making a huge, loud sound

plain flat land, as in a valley, without trees

customs special habits, traditions, things that people do regularly

buffalo a large furry animal from the oxen family hunted for skin and meat

terror great fear

The Cheyenne had camped in a wide river valley. The sun had just risen, but people were already busy. Fires had been made, and thin curls of smoke rose from the lodges. Women were busy with their cooking pots. Men and boys were bathing in the stream nearby. Two of these men were Sweet Medicine and Standing On The Ground.

"Shall we join the hunt today?" Sweet Medicine asked his friend as he poured icy water over his body.

Standing On The Ground replied "I suppose so. But we have had little luck for many days now. We have caught only a few deer and one or two rabbits."

"That is true," agreed Sweet Medicine. "People are hungry in the camp, and sick, too, I hear."

Here, the storyteller describes the setting. To do this, the storyteller paints a picture with words to make the listener or reader "see" the setting.

This is one of many stories about Sweet Medicine. Sweet Medicine is one of the Cheyenne's greatest heroes.

The two young men got out of the water. They looked across the valley, hoping to see an animal to hunt. But they saw nothing.

Suddenly Sweet Medicine said, "Do you see that hill over there? If we climb to the top, we will see much better than we can from down here. If there are any deer around, we might be able to see them."

They dressed quickly. They got their weapons and went toward the hill. They followed the river. As they came closer to the hill, they heard the sound of thunder. They saw the **roaring** waterfall crash down the rocky face of the hill. Clouds of spray curled like smoke around the waterfall.

"What power the water has!" said Standing On The Ground. "If a man had that power, he could do anything, I think."

Sweet Medicine was quiet for a moment. Then he said, "Maybe that power could be ours. I want to see

what is behind that roaring water. What do you say, my friend? Will you come with me?"

At first Standing On The Ground did not want to. But he wanted to be brave in front of his friend. So at last he let Sweet Medicine talk him into doing it. The young men took deep breaths and together dove into the rushing water.

The water pounded their bodies. It roared in their ears. Several times, the water almost swept them away. But they fought against it. At last, almost tired out, they reached the other side of the waterfall. They wiped the water from their eyes and looked around.

They could not believe what they saw. Instead of wet rocks, they a saw a great grassy **plain** stretched out before them. And they were not alone. Close by, an old woman sat over a fire. She walked toward them.

"Welcome, my grandchildren! Why did you not come sooner! Why have you gone hungry for so long? I have made food for you. Come, sit by the fire with me and eat what I have cooked."

The young men looked at each other in wonder. They thought from the way she acted, the old woman must be one of the Listeners Under The Ground. Those were the spirits who taught the Cheyenne how to follow their ways and **customs**.

The old woman put two dishes in front of the young men. One was filled with meat. The other was filled with yellow mush. "Here is **buffalo** meat," she said, "and here is corn."

The young men ate the food happily. It was good, and they were very hungry. But no matter how much they ate, the dishes stayed as full of food as before they started eating.

When the young men had finished, the old woman stretched her hand out over the fire. She drew out two feathers painted red. She tied the feathers to the young mens' scalplocks. She painted their bodies red. She also drew a yellow sun and moon on their foreheads.

Sweet Medicine is curious about the power of the waterfall. He wants to learn about something unknown that he thinks may be important.

Notice the new setting!

The old woman is a spirit, or a great being. She wants to teach the young men. Many Native Americans call their spirits Grandmother and Grandfather. For this reason, the old woman refers to the two men as her grandchildren.

By describing the dishes that never empty, the storyteller shows that the old woman is from a different world.

Scalplocks are long locks of hair left on a shaven head.

Here, the storyteller compares the sound of the moving corn plants to whispers. She uses the word *like* to compare them. Using the word *like* or *as* to compare two things is called a simile. Can you find another simile in the story?

Then the old woman pointed to the left. She said, "See the buffalo!" The young men looked and saw great animals they had never seen before. They were running across the plain. Clouds of dust rose from under their hoofs.

Again the old woman pointed. This time she pointed to the right. She cried, "See the corn!" And the young men saw fields of growing plants. They moved in the wind and made soft sounds like whispers.

The old woman gave Sweet Medicine a bowl of meat. She said, "When the sun goes down, I will send the buffalo out of the hill. They will live on your plains. You will be able to hunt them, just as you hunt deer and rabbits now. As long as your people eat this meat, they will be strong, and not get sick."

The old woman gave Standing On The Ground a bowl of corn. She said, "If your people plant the seeds and take good care of the corn, they will always have something to eat."

Then the old woman led them back to the waterfall. She told them to go back home. She said, "Tell your people that you have brought them wonderful things. Things that will make them happy."

The people saw Sweet Medicine and Standing On The Ground coming back to camp. They saw the feathers on their heads and the painting on their bodies. They knew the young men brought good news. Standing On The Ground gave the people corn to eat. Sweet Medicine gave them meat. They gave food to everyone, except to one old man and one old woman. They told these two people to wait until last. Finally, when everyone else had eaten, they gave food to the old man and the old woman. When they finished eating, the bowls were empty at last.

Standing On The Ground said, "I gave the old man the corn last. This is because when corn is ripe, it turns pale and old men have white hair. The men shall plant and take care of the corn so it will become ripe in the summer sun."

Sweet Medicine said, "I fed the old woman last. This is because it is the women who will cook the buffalo meat and tan the skins."

At sunset, the buffalo began to come out of the hill. There were so many of them that the ground shook. The people were afraid, and they hid in **terror**. All night the buffalo ran past the camp. In the morning there were buffalo all over the country. The hunters went out with their spears and arrows. They brought back more meat than had ever been seen before.

From that time on, when the buffalo moved to a new place, the people followed them. When spring came, they planted their corn. In fall, they picked the ripe ears of corn. In this way the buffalo and corn came to the Cheyenne. As long as they had buffalo and corn, they were never hungry nor sick, just as the old woman had said.

This story explains how the Cheyenne became hunters of buffalo and planters of corn.

The Cheyenne

The Cheyenne are one of many Native American nations of North America. Long ago, they lived near the Great Lakes in what is now Minnesota. They were mostly farmers. But they also hunted small animals for food. This story begins when the Cheyenne lived in this area.

When Europeans began to settle on their lands, the Cheyenne moved to the Plains into what are now North and South Dakota. They began to hunt buffalo. The buffalo were very important to the Cheyenne. They used the meat for food and the skin for clothing and shelter.

This story most likely gave the Cheyenne hope that they would live happily in this new area once they were pushed off their land by white settlers. The old woman taught Sweet Medicine and Standing On The Ground how to hunt buffalo and grow corn. With this new knowledge, Sweet Medicine and Standing On The Ground helped the Cheyenne live in the Plains.

The Cheyenne lived well in the Plains for many years. But like the other Plains Indians, they were forced to live on reservations once whites settled in the West. The Cheyenne now live mostly in Oklahoma and Montana.

Literature Practice

Answer these questions on a separate sheet of paper.

1. What is the setting at the beginning of the story?
2. In the story, who are Standing On The Ground and Sweet Medicine?
3. What do the two men find on the other side of the waterfall?
4. a.) What does the old woman give the two men to eat?
   b.) What does she tell them to do after they eat?
5. Why are Sweet Medicine and Standing On The Ground heroes to the Cheyenne?
6. List two similes used in the story.

Paul Bunyan,
The Mightiest Logger Of Them All
an adapted story by Mary Pope Osborne

Words to Know

LITERARY TERMS

tall tale a story in which facts and details are exaggerated

exaggeration making something seem more than it really is

tone the mood, or feeling, in a story that is created by using certain words and punctuation

SELECTION VOCABULARY

hauled pulled

civilization area where people live and do business

pioneers early settlers

logging cutting trees down for wood

felled cut down

untamed wild

pickaxe tool with a sharp point

requirements what is needed

gigantic very large

The facts in this story are difficult to believe. The narrator, or the person telling the story, wants you to feel a certain way about Paul Bunyan. He stretches the facts to let you know that Paul Bunyan was a very unusual and special person. This kind of story is called a "tall tale."

———✕✕✕———

It seems an amazing baby was born in the state of Maine. When he was only two weeks old, he weighed more than a hundred pounds. For breakfast every

Exaggeration is used to
make a point about how
special the baby is. Look
for more examples of
exaggeration as you
read.

Why do you think the
story starts with a
description of Paul as a
baby? What do you think
the rest of the story will
be about?

Flint rocks are hard
stones used to make a
fire.

morning he ate five dozen eggs, ten sacks of potatoes, and a half-barrel of mush made from a whole sack of cornmeal. But the baby's strangest feature was his big, curly black beard. It was so big and bushy that every morning his poor mother had to comb it with a pine tree.

Except for that black beard, the big baby wasn't much trouble to anybody until he was about nine months old. That was when he first started to crawl, and since he weighed over five hundred pounds, he caused an earthquake that shook the whole town.

The baby's parents tried putting him in a giant floating cradle off the coast of Maine but every time he rolled over, huge waves drowned all the villages along the coast.

So his parents **hauled** the giant toddler to a cave in the Maine woods far away from **civilization** and said good-bye. His father gave him a fishing pole, a knife, some flint rocks, and an axe. "We'll think of you often, honey," his mother said, weeping. "But you can't come back home—you're just too big."

That's the story of how Paul Bunyan came to take care of himself in the Maine woods. And even though he lived alone for the next twenty years, he got along quite well.

In those times, huge sections of America were filled with dark green forests. It would be nice if those trees could have stayed tall and thick forever. But the **pioneers** needed them to build houses, churches, ships, wagons, bridges, and barns. So one day Paul Bunyan took a good look at all those trees and decided to invent **logging**.

"Tim-ber!" he yelled, and he swung the bright steel axe his father had given him in a wide circle. There was a terrible crash, and when Paul looked around, he saw he'd **felled** ten white pines with a single swing.

After that Paul traveled plenty fast through the **untamed** North Woods. He cut pine, spruce, and red willow in Minnesota, Michigan, and Wisconsin. He

Paul Bunyan became a hero to people because he was so good at his work. Other loggers looked up to him. Whether they really knew him or not, loggers loved to tell a good story about him.

cleared cottonwoods out of Kansas so farmers could plant wheat and oaks out of Iowa so farmers could plant corn.

When next heard of, Paul was headed to Arizona. He dragged his **pickaxe** behind him on that trip, not realizing he was leaving a big ditch in his tracks. Today that ditch is called the Grand Canyon.

When Paul got back from the West, he decided to start a logging camp. Word spread fast. Since all the woodsmen had heard of Paul Bunyan, thousands of them hurried to Paul's headquarters at Big Onion on the Big Onion River in Minnesota to be part of his crew.

"There's only two **requirements**," Paul announced to the men who'd gathered to apply for the job. "All my loggers have to be over ten feet tall and able to pop six buttons off their shirts with one breath."

Well, about a thousand of the lumberjacks met those requirements, and Paul hired them all. Then he built a **gigantic** logging camp with bunkhouses a mile long and bunks ten beds high. The camp's chow table was so long that it took a week to pass the salt and pepper from one end to the other. Paul dug a few ponds to provide drinking water for everyone. Today we call those ponds the Great Lakes.

Things went pretty well at the Big Onion Lumber Company until the Year of the Hard Winter. One day Shot Gunderson, the crew boss, complained to Paul, "Boss, it's so cold that the flames for all the lanterns are freezing. And, Boss, when I give orders to the woods crew, all my words freeze in the air and hang there stiff as icicles."

"Well, haul away your frozen words and store them somewhere next to the lantern flames," Paul advised. "They'll both thaw out in the spring."

Sure enough, they did. The only problem was that, come spring, the melting lantern flames started some mean little brush fires. And when Shot's frozen words thawed, old cries of "Timber!" and "Chow time!" started to echo throughout the woods, causing all sorts of confusion. But other than that, things ran pretty smoothly.

Well, there's stories and stories about Paul Bunyan. For many years, old loggers sat around potbellied stoves and told about the good old times with Paul. Those loggers are all gone now, but many of their stories still hang frozen in the cold forest air of the North Woods, waiting to be told. Come spring, when they start to thaw, some of them might just start telling themselves. It's been known to happen.

The narrator tells us that many other people have told the Paul Bunyan story. Each time a new person tells the story, it changes a little bit. The facts are exaggerated until the story becomes a tall tale.

Tall Tales

Paul Bunyan is a famous American folk hero. Many tall tales have been told and written about him. Tall tales are usually about special people, animals, or events. They are partly true at first, but the details are exaggerated and changed each time someone tells them. Tall tales are often about someone who is very clever, big, strong, or hard working, because these are traits that many people admire.

Paul Bunyan stories have been retold by many people over many years. Some people think that they were started either by French-Canadian loggers in the 1800's or by the Scottish or Irish loggers who moved to the United States a little later. Whoever told the stories first must have done so after a hard day's work in the wilderness. People didn't have television or radio, so telling stories around a campfire was a popular way to relax and have fun. The storyteller would act as though he was telling the simple truth. But he or she often couldn't help adding and exaggerating the details. After all, the more strange and far-out the tale, the more entertaining it was!

Literature Practice

Answer these questions on a separate sheet of paper.

1. What is so "amazing" or exaggerated about the baby at the beginning of the story?
2. Why do Bunyan's parents have to leave him in the woods?
3. What do people need the trees for?
4. What problems does the Year of the Hard Winter cause?
5 Give two examples of exaggeration in this story.

Thank You, M'am
by Langston Hughes

Words to Know

LITERARY TERMS

character a person in a story

metaphor comparing two things without using the words *like* or *as*

SELECTION VOCABULARY

permit allow

frail weak, thin

contact two things or people coming together

jerked to give a quick pull or twist

roomers people who pay money to live in a room or building

whereupon after which

suede soft leather

pause to stop or wait a short time

latching holding tightly

barren empty, dull, not interesting

She was a large woman with a large purse that had everything in it but hammer and nails. It had a long strap and she carried it slung across her shoulder. It was about eleven o'clock at night, and she was walking alone, when a boy ran up behind her and tried to snatch her purse. The strap broke with the single tug the boy gave it from behind. But the boy's weight, and the weight of the purse combined caused him to lose his balance so, instead of taking off full blast as he had hoped, the boy fell on his back on the sidewalk, and his legs flew up. The large woman simply turned around

The writer has created characters, or people in the story, who do things that you might not expect. As you read, you'll see from their actions that these characters are two very special people.

Were you surprised by what the woman did? Why? Do you think that the boy was surprised?

and kicked him right square in his blue-jeaned sitter. Then she reached down, picked the boy up by his shirt front, and shook him until his teeth rattled.

After that the woman said, "Pick up my pocketbook, boy, and give it here."

She still held him. But she bent down enough to **permit** him to stoop and pick up her purse. Then she said, "Now ain't you ashamed of yourself?"

Firmly gripped by his shirt front, the boy said, "Yes'm."

The woman said, "What did you want to do it for?"

The boy said, "I didn't aim to."

She said, "You a lie!"

By that time two or three people passed, stopped, turned to look, and some stood watching.

"If I turn you loose, will you run?" asked the woman.

"Yes'm," said the boy.

"Then I won't turn you loose," said the woman. She did not release him.

"I'm very sorry, lady, I'm sorry," whispered the boy.

"Um-hum! And your face is dirty. I got a great mind to wash your face for you. Ain't you got nobody home to tell you to wash your face?"

"No'm," said the boy.

"Then it will get washed this evening," said the large woman starting up the street, dragging the frightened boy behind her.

He looked as if he were fourteen or fifteen, **frail** and willow-wild, in tennis shoes and blue jeans.

The woman said, "You ought to be my son. I would teach you right from wrong. Least I can do right now is to wash your face. Are you hungry?"

"No'm," said the being-dragged boy. "I just want you to turn me loose."

"Was I bothering *you* when I turned that corner?" asked the woman.

"No'm."

"But you put yourself in **contact** with *me*," said the woman. "If you think that that contact is not going to last awhile, you got another thought coming. When I get through with you, sir, you are going to remember Mrs. Luella Bates Washington Jones."

Sweat popped out on the boy's face and he began to struggle. Mrs. Jones stopped, **jerked** him around in front of her, put a half nelson about his neck, and continued to drag him up the street. When she got to her door, she dragged the boy inside, down a hall, and into a large kitchenette-furnished room at the rear of the house. She switched on the light and left the door open. The boy could hear other **roomers** laughing and talking in the large house. Some of their doors were open, too, so he knew he and the woman were not alone. The woman still had him by the neck in the middle of her room.

She said, "What is your name?"

"Roger," answered the boy.

"Then, Roger, you go to that sink and wash your

The author uses *italics*, or different-looking letters, here. Words in italics tell the reader to make that word sound stronger while reading.

Most people would say that Mrs. Jones has the "right" to be very angry with the boy. What do you think she plans to do to him?

face," said the woman, **whereupon** she turned him loose—at last. Roger looked at the door—looked at the woman—looked at the door—*and went to the sink.*

"Let the water run until it gets warm," she said. "Here's a clean towel."

"You gonna take me to jail?" asked the boy, bending over the sink.

"Not with that face, I would not take you nowhere," said the woman. "Here I am trying to get home to cook me a bite to eat and you snatch my pocketbook! Maybe you ain't been to your supper either, late as it be. Have you?"

"There's nobody home at my house," said the boy.

"Then we'll eat," said the woman. "I believe you're hungry—or been hungry—to try to snatch my pocketbook."

"I wanted a pair of blue **suede** shoes," said the boy.

"Well, you didn't have to snatch *my* pocketbook to get some suede shoes," said Mrs. Luella Bates Washington Jones. "You could of asked me."

"M'am?"

The water dripping from his face, the boy looked at her. There was a long **pause**. A very long pause. After he had dried his face and not knowing what else to do dried it again, the boy turned around, wondering what next. The door was open. He could make a dash for it down the hall. He could run, run, run, run, *run!*

The woman was sitting on the daybed. After awhile she said, "I were young once and I wanted things I could not get."

There was another long pause. The boy's mouth opened. Then he frowned, but not knowing he frowned.

The woman said, "Um-hum! You thought I was going to say *but,* didn't you? You thought I was going to say, *but I didn't snatch people's pocketbooks.* Well, I wasn't going to say that." Pause. Silence. "I have done things, too, which I would not tell you, son—neither

Do you think the boy will run? Why or why not?

tell God, if He didn't already know. So you set down while I fix us something to eat. You might run that comb through your hair so you will look presentable."

In another corner of the room behind a screen was a gas plate and an icebox. Mrs. Jones got up and went behind the screen. The woman did not watch the boy to see if he was going to run now, nor did she watch her purse which she left behind her on the daybed. But the boy took care to sit on the far side of the room where he thought she could easily see him out of the corner of her eye, if she wanted to. He did not trust the woman *not* to trust him. And he did not want to be mistrusted now.

"Do you need somebody to go to the store," asked the boy, "maybe to get some milk or something?"

"Don't believe I do," said the woman, "unless you just want sweet milk yourself. I was going to make cocoa out of this canned milk I got here."

"That will be fine," said the boy.

She heated some lima beans and ham she had in the icebox, made the cocoa, and set the table. The woman did not ask the boy anything about where he lived, or his folks, or anything else that would embarrass him. Instead, as they ate, she told him about her job in a hotel beauty shop that stayed open late, what the work was like, and how all kinds of women came in and out, blondes, redheads, and Spanish. Then she cut him a half of her ten-cent cake.

"Eat some more, son," she said.

When they were finished eating she got up and said, "Now, here, take this ten dollars and buy yourself some blue suede shoes. And next time, do not make the mistake of **latching** onto *my* pocketbook *nor nobody else's*—because shoes come by devilish like that will burn your feet. I got to get my rest now. But I wish you would behave yourself, son, from here on in."

She led him down the hall to the front door and opened it. "Goodnight! Behave yourself, boy!" she said, looking out into the street.

The boy wanted to say something else other than, "Thank you, m'am," to Mrs. Luella Bates Washington Jones, but he couldn't do so as he turned at the **barren** stoop and looked back at the large woman in the door. He barely managed to say, "Thank you," before she shut the door. And he never saw her again.

She doesn't really mean that the boy's feet will burn. She's using a metaphor. A metaphor is when you say something is like something else without using the words *like* or *as*. What do you think she is really saying to the boy?

Literature Practice

Answer these questions on a separate sheet of paper.

1. How do Roger and Mrs. Jones meet?

2. Where does Mrs. Jones take Roger?

3. What is Roger's reason for trying to steal from Mrs. Jones?

4. Why doesn't Roger run out the door when Mrs. Jones is looking away?

5. What special things does Mrs. Jones do for Roger?

6. Why do you think Mrs. Jones is nice to Roger?

Chapter Review

Summaries

- **Behind the Waterfall** — The Cheyenne are hungry. Sweet Medicine and Standing On The Ground go hunting. They see a big waterfall and go behind it. There is another world on the other side. An old woman invites them to eat. She is a spirit. She gives them buffalo meat and corn. They go back to the village and give their people the meat and corn. The buffalo come from out of the hill and spread over the plain. The people plant the corn. The Cheyenne are no longer hungry.

- **Paul Bunyan, The Mightest Logger Of Them All** — Paul Bunyan is a huge baby. He is so big that his parents have to leave him in the woods. When he grows up, he invents logging. He travels through the whole country cutting trees. He starts a logging camp. He hires a thousand giant men. Many stories about Paul Bunyan are still waiting to be told.

- **Thank You, M'am** — A boy tries to steal a woman's purse. She catches him. She drags him home with her. The boy says he wants a pair of blue suede shoes. She says that he does not have to steal. He could have asked her for the shoes. Now he wants her to trust him. She feeds him. She also gives him money for the shoes and tells him not to steal again. Then she says goodbye. He only has time to say thank you.

Chapter Quiz

Decide whether the statements below are true or false. Use a separate sheet of paper to explain your answers. Look back at the stories if you need to. Use details from them to support your answers.

1. The setting at the beginning of "Behind the Waterfall" is a boat at night.
2. In "Behind the Waterfall," two boys find a magic fish that speaks to them.
3. Standing On The Ground and Sweet Medicine return home with their gifts and their people are never hungry again.
4. When Paul Bunyan is a baby, his mother worries about him because he doesn't eat enough.
5. Paul Bunyan travels around the country cutting down trees.
6. The tale of Paul Bunyan includes some parts that are not true.
7. In the story "Thank You, M'am," Mrs. Jones meets Roger at a bus stop.
8. Roger does not run away from Mrs. Jones because she is always watching him.
9. Mrs. Jones gives Roger money to go buy shoes for himself.

Thinking and Writing

Answer the following questions on a separate sheet of paper. Write one or two paragraphs for each one.

1. The heroes in "Behind the Waterfall" and "Paul Bunyan, The Mightiest Logger of Them All" are helpful to many people. Describe what the heroes do for others in both stories.
2. Mrs. Rogers, the woman in "Thank You, M'am," is not especially big or strong. Explain why she is a hero.
3. Which story did you enjoy most? Explain your choice.

The stories in this chapter are true. They are about two people who are heroes for being strong and for helping others to feel strong, too.

Chapter Learning Objectives

- To identify elements of a biographical story
- To identify elements of a nonfiction story
- To understand a writer's use of facts to tell a true story
- To understand a writer's use of quotations to tell a true story

Rosa Parks

from the biography by Eloise Greenfield

Words to Know

LITERARY TERM

biography account of a person's life told by another person

SELECTION VOCABULARY

ached hurt

bond money paid as bail so the accused can be freed from jail

citizens people living in a city or country who have rights under the law

courteously politely; with manners

pulpit a raised platform where a person stands to give a worship service

guilty did something against the law; proven to have committed a crime

protest to speak out against something that seems unfair

hymn a song of praise to God

On Thursday evening, December 1, 1955, Mrs. Parks left work and started home. She was tired. Her shoulders ached from bending over the sewing machine all day. "Today, I'll ride the bus," she thought.

She got on and sat in the first seat for blacks, right behind the white section. After a few stops the seats were filled. A white man got on. He looked for an empty seat. Then he looked at the driver. The driver came over to Mrs. Parks.

"You have to get up," he said.

All of a sudden Mrs. Parks knew she was not going to give up her seat. It was not fair. She had paid her money just as the man had. This time she

This story is part of a biography about Rosa Parks. Notice how the writer begins by telling the real date when the story begins. Giving facts is important when telling a story that is true.

was not going to move.

"No," she said softly.

"You'd better get up, or I'll call the police," the driver said.

It was very quiet on the bus now. Everyone stopped talking and watched. Still, Mrs. Parks did not move.

"Are you going to get up?"

"No," she repeated.

The driver left the bus and returned with two policemen.

"You're under arrest," they told her.

Mrs. Parks walked off the bus. The policemen put her in their car and drove to the police station. One policeman stuck a camera in her face and took her

Being a hero is not always easy. People will not always like what you do. In this story, the writer often shows how other people react to Rosa Parks and to what she does. Why do you think the writer shows how other people feel about Mrs. Parks?

picture. Another took her fingerprints. Then she was locked in a cell.

Mrs. Parks felt very bad, sitting in that little room with iron bars. But she did not cry. She was a religious woman, and she thought of her faith in God. She said a silent prayer. Then she waited.

Someone who had seen Mrs. Parks arrested called Edgar Daniel Nixon of the NAACP. Mr. Nixon went right away to the police station and posted a hundred dollar **bond** for Mrs. Parks. This meant that she could leave, but that she promised to go to court on Monday for her trial.

Mrs. Parks left the police station. She had been locked up for two and a half hours. Mr. Nixon drove her home. At her apartment Mrs. Parks, her husband, Mr. Nixon, and Fred Gray, a lawyer, talked about what had happened. They thought they saw a way to solve the problem of the buses.

Mr. Gray would go into court with Mrs. Parks. He would prove that the bus company was not obeying the United States Constitution. The Constitution is an important paper that was written by the men who started the United States. It says that all the **citizens** of the United States must be treated fairly.

The next morning Mrs. Parks went to her job as usual. Her employer was surprised to see her. He had read about her arrest in the newspaper, and he thought she would be too upset to come in. Some of the white workers gave Mrs. Parks mean looks and would not speak to her. But she went on with her work.

That night Mrs. Parks met with a group of ministers and other black leaders of the city. Dr. Martin Luther King was one of the ministers. The black men and women of Montgomery were angry again. But this time they knew what to do.

"If the bus company won't treat us **courteously**," one leader said, "we won't spend our money to ride

The NAACP, or "N-double A-C-P", stands for The National Association for the Advancement of Colored People. This group was started in 1909 to win equal rights for blacks. Rosa Parks had worked for the local NAACP in her area before that famous day on the bus.

Because the Constitution says that everyone must be treated fairly, Mrs. Parks and her lawyer believed that the laws in Montgomery were not legal. Being forced to sit on the back of the bus because of your skin color is unfair treatment under the Constitution.

the buses. We'll walk!"

After the meeting some of the people printed little sheets of paper. These sheets of paper, called leaflets, said, "DON'T RIDE THE BUS TO WORK, TO TOWN, TO SCHOOL, OR ANYWHERE, MONDAY, DECEMBER 5." They also invited people to a church meeting on Monday night. The leaflets were left everywhere—in mail boxes, on porches, in drugstores.

On Sunday morning black ministers all over the city preached about Mrs. Parks in their churches. Dr. King preached from his **pulpit** at the Dexter Avenue Baptist Church.

The preachers said, "Brothers and sisters, if you don't like what happened to Rosa Parks and what has been happening to us all these years, do something about it. Walk!"

And the people said, "Amen. We'll walk."

On Monday morning, no one was riding the buses. There were many people on the street, but everyone was walking. They were cheering because the buses were empty.

Mrs. Parks got up early that morning. She went to court with her lawyer for her trial. The judge found her **guilty**. But she and her lawyer did not agree with him. Her lawyer said, "We'll get a higher court to decide. If we have to, we'll take the case to the highest court in the United States."

That night thousands of people went to the church meeting. There were so many people that most of them had to stand outside and listen through a loudspeaker.

First there was prayer. Then Rosa Parks was introduced. She stood up slowly. The audience rose to its feet and clapped and cheered. After Mrs. Parks sat down, several ministers gave their speeches. Finally Dr. Martin Luther King started to speak.

"We are tired," he said.

"Yes, Lord," the crowd answered.

How do other people feel about Mrs. Parks in this part of the story?

"We are tired of being kicked around," he said.

"Yes, Lord," they answered.

"We're not going to be kicked around anymore," Dr. King said. "We walked one day. Now we are going to have a real **protest**. We are going to keep walking until the bus company gives us fair treatment."

After Dr. King finished speaking, the Montgomery Improvement Association was formed to plan the protest. Dr. King was made president.

Then there was **hymn** singing and hand clapping. The people went home feeling good. All that walking was not going to be easy, but they knew they could do it.

The Montgomery Improvement Association and the churches bought as many cars and station wagons as they could afford. There were telephone numbers that people could call when they needed a ride. Women who worked at home answered the phones. Mrs. Parks was one of them. Her employer had told her that she was no longer needed. When someone called for a ride, Mrs. Parks would tell the drivers where to go. But there were not nearly enough cars.

Old people and young people walked. The children walked a long way to school. The men and women walked to work, to church, everywhere. In the morning it was like a parade. People were going to work, some riding on the backs of mules, some riding in wagons pulled by horses, but most of them walking. Sometimes they sang.

In the evening the parade went the other way, people going home. The newspapers called Montgomery "the walking city."

It was hard. Many people had to leave home long before daylight to get to work on time. They got home late at night. Their feet hurt. But they would not give up. The bus company kept saying it would not change. And black people kept on walking.

The enemies of the blacks tried to frighten them.

Why do you think Mrs. Parks is "no longer needed" by her employer? Do you think that it is fair that she is let go from her job?

They threw bottles at the walkers. Some homes were bombed.

One day Mrs. Parks's phone rang. She picked it up.

"Hello," she said.

"You're the cause of all this trouble," a voice said. "You should be killed."

Mrs. Parks hung up. The calls kept coming, day after day. Mrs. Parks was afraid, but she knew she could not stop.

After two months, more than a hundred leaders of the protest were arrested. Mrs. Parks was among them. A court had said that the protest was against the law. The leaders posted bond, and went right back to their work.

Here, the writer tells you how much time has passed and how many people are arrested. This information gives the reader more facts about this important event.

Reporters came to Montgomery from all over the United States and from other countries. They wrote stories in their newspapers about the arrests.

Mrs. Parks began to travel to other cities, making speeches. She told about the hardships of the people. Many of the people she spoke to helped. They gave her money to pay for bonds and to buy gas for the cars.

The black citizens of Montgomery walked all winter, all spring, all summer and fall in all kinds of weather. The bus company lost thousands of dollars.

In November, the Supreme Court, the highest court in the United States, said that the bus company had to change. It had not been obeying the Constitution.

That night the Ku Klux Klan paraded past the homes of the blacks. The people stood in their doorways and watched. They were no longer afraid. They had won.

Several weeks later, the bus company obeyed the Supreme Court and changed its rules. A year had passed since Mrs. Parks refused to give up her seat. Now blacks could sit in any seat. They would not have to get up for anyone.

Black people in other places read about Montgomery. They began to work for fair treatment of blacks in their own cities.

They said, "If Rosa Parks had the courage to do this, we can do it too." They called her the "Mother of the Civil Rights Movement."

One day a group of reporters went to Mrs. Parks's home. They took her to ride on the bus. She entered through the front door. For the first time she sat anywhere she chose. And she would stay there until the end of her ride.

No one could ever ask her to get up again.

The Ku Klux Klan (KKK) is a group that was formed after the Civil War by white Southerners who were angry about the end of slavery. They used violence to keep African Americans from voting. They also tried to stop African Americans from having equal rights.

Protest Without Fighting

Rosa Parks became famous for quietly but firmly keeping her seat on a public bus. Dr. Martin Luther King, Jr., helped African Americans by marching, making speeches, and asking people to boycott (not pay for or use) public buses. César Chávez helped farm workers in California get better treatment by marching, fasting (not eating), and boycotting grapes and lettuce.

These leaders learned how to get what they wanted without fighting from a man who lived far away in India. This man's name was Mahatma Gandhi. Gandhi helped all of India become free from British rule. He taught his people to stand up for what they believed in without hurting or killing anyone. Gandhi knew that his enemies would look bad to the rest of the world if they hurt people who would not fight. Gandhi and his people never gave up. He knew that his enemies would become tired of fighting him. It took many years, and many Indian people were arrested and hurt, but finally the British left India for good. The Indian people were able to win the freedom that they wanted.

Literature Practice

Answer these questions on a separate sheet of paper.

1. Why is Rosa Parks arrested and sent to jail?

2. What do the African Americans in Montgomery decide to do after Mrs. Parks is arrested?

3. How do African Americans get to work for the next year?

4. Is everyone in Montgomery happy with what is happening? How can you tell from the story how people feel?

5. How do people in the rest of the country find out about Mrs. Parks and what is happening in Montgomery?

Roberto Clemente: A Bittersweet Memoir
adapted from the article by Jerry Izenberg

Words to Know

LITERARY TERMS

quote the words that someone says, written with quotation marks (" ") around the statement

nonfiction a true story or article

SELECTION VOCABULARY

memoir a record of events in a person's life

prefer to choose one over another

recalled remembered

spectacular unusual, exciting

convinced made to feel sure

phony fake, false, not truthful or real

touched made to feel deeply

The record book will tell you that baseball player Roberto Clemente made 3,000 hits when he played in the major leagues. It will say that he came to bat 9,454 times and that he drove in 1,305 runs. It will say that during 18 years, he played 2,433 games.

But the record book won't tell you about Carolina, the town in Puerto Rico where Clemente was born. It won't tell you about María Isabella Casares. She was the woman Clemente called "teacher" until the day he died. Clemente said that Casares helped shape his life. The record book also won't tell you about Pedron Zarrilla, the man who made a young athlete into a major-league superstar.

The cold numbers in the record book won't begin to tell you who Clemente was. To understand what he

This is an article, or feature story, about a real person's life. Here, the writer is saying that a good article includes information about the subject's personal life. Cold facts are not enough to tell the reader about the whole person.

was all about, you have to begin where his life ended.

The place where Clemente's life ended is Puente Maldonado, Puerto Rico. Here the ocean pounds against the sharp rocks. It was here, on New Year's Eve 1972, that his plane went down in the angry water.

Clemente had been on his way to Managua, Nicaragua, where there had just been a terrible earthquake. He knew many people in Nicaragua because about a month earlier, he had taken a junior-league baseball team there. He had made many friends. And when Clemente made friends, he took those friendships seriously.

When the earthquake hit, Clemente did all he could to help. He went on Puerto Rican television. He asked the Puerto Rican people to give whatever they could to the Nicaraguans. He asked them to give

In telling the story, the writer changes the order of events in Clemente's life. The writer starts at the end of Clemente's life, because that one event best describes his entire life.

To help complete his description of Clemente, the author quotes people who knew him. Quoting someone means that you record *exactly* what the person says. Quotation marks (" ") around the words tell readers that this statement is a direct quote.

Here, the writer helps the reader feel the drama and emotion of the event. The writer does this by including both detailed facts and other people's reactions to what took place on the last day of Clemente's life.

Notice this quotation from someone close to Clemente who was in Puerto Rico at the time of Clemente's death.

The author asks a question to grab readers' attention. This tells the reader what to expect in the next part of the article.

supplies: medicine, food, shoes, clothes—everything would be used.

At 4:00 New Year's Eve day, Clemente was supposed to leave on a plane for Nicaragua. But the plane had engine trouble. All that afternoon, the plane had been worked on. But still it was not ready to fly.

Clemente's friend Rudy Hernandez came to the airport to give him money for the people of Nicaragua. "It's New Year's Eve, Roberto," Hernandez told him. "Let it wait."

But Clemente wanted to go. He said, "Who else will go? Someone has to do it."

The plane finally took off at 9 P.M., but minutes later the pilot sent a message to the airport at San Juan. He said, "We are coming back around."

Just that.

Nothing more.

And then there was a great silence.

Drawn together by their sadness, the people of San Juan went to the beach, to Puente Maldonado. A cold rain fell. It blended with their tears.

"I've lived on this island for more than twenty years," Hernandez said. "I have never seen a time or a sadness like that. The streets were empty, the radios silent. . . . All of us cried. All of us who knew him, and even those who didn't, wept that week."

Who was Roberto Clemente, really?

He was born in Carolina, Puerto Rico, in 1934.

María Isabella Casares, Clemente's favorite teacher, said that he was a very shy boy but that there was something very special about him.

One day, Clemente came to her and said, "Teacher, I have a problem."

He told her that Pedron Zarrilla, one of the biggest baseball names in Puerto Rico, had seen him play. And now Zarrilla wanted to sign him up for the

Santurce Crabbers team. Clemente didn't know what to do.

Casares told him, "This is your chance, Roberto. We are poor people in this town. This is your chance to do something. But if in your heart you **prefer** not to try, then, Roberto, that will be your problem—and your decision."

Clemente and his favorite teacher would always be close friends. Once, after he had become a famous baseball player, Clemente found out his teacher was ill. He went to her house, picked her up like a baby, and took her to the doctor. He visited her every day for 15 days and paid all her doctor bills.

When Clemente died, Casares said, "We must make sure that the children never forget how beautiful a man he was."

Another important person in Clemente's life was Pedron Zarrilla. He saw the young Clemente on a country softball team and signed him up for his Santurce team.

"He was a skinny kid," Zarilla **recalled**, "but even then he had those large, powerful hands. . . . I watched him, and I said to myself, 'This kid can throw and this kid can run, and this kid can hit. We will be patient with him.' "

Luis Olmo, a former outfielder with the Brooklyn Dodgers, remembered Clemente's first game with the Santurce team. He said, "I was managing the other team. . . . We had never seen him, so we didn't really know how to pitch to him. I decided to throw him a few bad balls and see if he'd bite.

"He hit the first pitch," Olmo exclaimed. "It was an outside fast ball, and he never should have been able to reach it. . . . He was the best bad-ball hitter I have ever seen.

"I played in the big leagues," Olmo said. "I know what I am saying. He was the greatest we ever had . . . maybe one of the greatest anyone ever had."

What does Clemente's relationship with his teacher tell you about him as a person?

Zarilla said that when Clemente was in the lineup, there was always a feeling of excitement in the ballpark. "You knew that if he was coming to bat, he would do something **spectacular**. You knew that if he was on first base, he was going to try to get to second base," Zarilla said.

Zarilla also knew that soon Clemente would be discovered by major-league scouts. "Sure I knew we were going to lose him," Zarilla said. "I knew it was just a matter of time. But I was grateful that we could have him if only for that little time."

Clemente first signed up with the Brooklyn Dodgers. Then he joined the Pittsburgh Pirates. In those days, the Pirates lost most of their games. Even Clemente couldn't make them winners right away.

The Pirates first winning year was 1960. They won the World Series against the New York Yankees. Clemente played a great Series. He batted over .300. But he didn't win the Most Valuable Player Award. He came in third.

Bob Friend, a player on the Pirates, said that Clemente felt as though he wasn't accepted. So Clemente started thinking, 'Well, I'm going to show them from now on so that they will never forget.'

Clemente went home to Puerto Rico and married Vera. He felt less alone. Now he could go on and prove what he had to prove.

Buck Canel, a sports writer for Spanish-language newspapers, recalled that Clemente often thought he wasn't accepted. "He would talk with me often about his feelings. You know, Clemente felt strongly about the fact that he was Puerto Rican and that he was a black man. In each of these things he had pride," Canel said.

"He wanted very much to prove to the world that he was a superstar," Canel added, "and that he could do things that in his heart he felt he had already proven."

"He batted over .300" means that Clemente hit a ball and got to a base three times out of every ten times he went to bat. This is a high average.

Even though Clemente was a great baseball player, some people called him names because he was black and because he was from Puerto Rico.

One season, Clemente was finally able to prove himself. In 1971, the Pirates made it to the World Series again. It had been 11 years since the last time they had played the Series. It was Clemente who led them there.

The Pirates were playing the Baltimore Orioles. Most people thought the Pirates would lose. In fact, they lost the first two games.

Most Valuable Player (MVP) is a title given to a baseball player who played the best games during the whole year. Each year, a new MVP is chosen by sportswriters from around the country.

In the third game, Clemente went to work. He led his team. In the five games that followed, he was a hero. He was the Most Valuable Player. He was everything he ever dreamed of being on a ball field.

Best of all, the whole country saw him do it on television. At last he had proven himself as a great ballplayer.

The next year, Clemente ended the season by making his 3,000th hit. At the time, only ten other men had ever done that in the history of baseball.

Willie Stargell, Clemente's closest friend on the Pirates, recalled that 3,000th hit. "He [Clemente] had thought of taking himself out of the lineup and resting for the playoffs. A couple of us **convinced** him that there had to be a time when a man had to do something for himself. So he [Clemente] went on and played and got it. I'm thankful that we convinced him, because, you know, as things turned out, that number three thousand was his last hit.

"When I think of Roberto now, I think of the kind of man he was," Stargell added. "There was nothing **phony** about him. . . . He was a man who chose his friends carefully. His was a friendship worth having.

"The way he died, you know, I mean on that plane carrying supplies to Nicaraguans who'd been dying in that earthquake. Well, I wasn't surprised he'd go out and do something like that. . . . I just never thought what happened could happen to him.

"But I know this," Stargell said. "He lived a full life. And if he knew at that moment what the Lord had decided, well, I really believe he would have said, 'I'm ready.'"

Roberto Clemente was 38 years old when he died. Few people **touched** the hearts of the Puerto Rican people the way he did. He touched a lot of other hearts, too. He touched hearts that beat inside people of all colors of skin.

He was one of the proudest of the Proud People.

For The Kids

Roberto Clemente was very proud to be Puerto Rican. He was also very proud to be of African descent. Some people treated him badly because of where he came from and because of the color of his skin. They did not give Clemente credit for being a really great baseball player. It was important to Clemente to change these people's minds. He wanted to be a good role model for young Puerto Ricans.

Clemente always wanted to build a place where all Puerto Rican boys and girls could play sports. After Clemente's tragic death, his wife Vera, his friends, and the government of Puerto Rico helped make his dream come true. In 1974, *Ciudad Deportiva*, or City of Sport, was built in Carolina, outside of San Juan. Built on 304 acres, the center is now a place where the children of Puerto Rico can learn to play sports of all kinds.

Literature Practice

Answer these questions on a separate sheet of paper.

1. How does the reader know this story is an article, or feature story?

2. Who is Roberto Clemente trying to help before he dies?

3. a.) What does Clemente want to prove to people in America?

   b.) Why is this difficult for Clemente?

4. What important record does Clemente set before he dies?

5. Why are so many people "touched" by Roberto Clemente?

Chapter Review

Summaries

- **Rosa Parks**—One evening in 1955, Mrs. Parks refuses to move when a white person wants her seat on a bus. She is arrested and sent to jail. As a result, the African Americans of Montgomery come together and boycott the bus company. They decide to walk to school and to work until the bus company changes its rules. Many people, including Dr. Martin Luther King, Jr., join the peaceful protest. Finally, after one long year of walking everywhere, the Supreme Court decides in Mrs. Parks's favor. The bus company must change its rules. Mrs. Parks takes a bus trip. For the first time, she chooses wherever she wants to sit.

- **Roberto Clemente: A Bittersweet Memoir**—Roberto Clemente was not just a famous baseball superstar. He was also a great person. The writer uses quotations to tell what Clemente was like as a husband, a friend, and a helper to people in need. A manager tells about Clemente's talent as a young man playing ball in Puerto Rico. Others describe his determination to be accepted by the big leagues. His teacher tells the world that his good deeds must not be forgotten. His friend tells how the people of Puerto Rico weep the day he dies. His plane is lost while carrying supplies to the people of Nicaragua. The *Ciudad Deportiva*, a park outside San Juan, is dedicated to his memory.

Chapter Quiz

Decide whether the statements below are true or false. Use a separate sheet of paper to explain your answers. Look back at the stories if you need to, and use details from them to support your answers.

1. When the story about Rosa Parks begins, it is the year 1964. She is riding a bus in Nashville, Tennessee.

2. Rosa Parks is arrested for refusing to give up her seat on the bus.

3. All of the people in Mrs. Parks's town are proud of what she did.

4. After Rosa is arrested, the bus company decides right away to change its rules because they are unfair.

5. Roberto Clemente was a famous football player.

6. When Clemente played baseball, many people thought he was exciting to watch.

7. In 1971, Clemente helped the Pittsburgh Pirates win the World Series.

8. Roberto Clemente died from fever when he was 59 years old.

Thinking and Writing

Answer the following questions on a separate sheet of paper. Write one or two paragraphs for each one.

1. Many people think of Rosa Parks as a hero. Describe Rosa Parks and what she did to make people think that she was a hero.

2. There are certain things a writer can do when writing nonfiction or a biography to make the reader feel the excitement or importance of the story. Choose one of the stories in this chapter. Explain what the writer does to make the reader feel the importance of the story.

3. Imagine that you are a fan of Roberto Clemente. Write a letter to Jerry Izenberg explaining why you think Clemente was a hero.

Unit Three Review

The following questions are about the selections you read in Chapters 5, 6, and 7. Write your answers on a separate sheet of paper.

A. The following statements are false. Rewrite each statement so that you can agree with it.

1. John Henry is famous for cutting down a lot of trees.
2. In "Thank You, M'am," Mrs. Jones is a thief.
3. Helen Keller does not learn to talk with her hands.
5. The Cheyenne learn how to fish and grow wheat from Sweet Medicine and Standing On The Ground.
6. In "The Midnight Ride of Paul Revere," Revere rides his horse to warn the British that the Patriots are coming.

B. Write one or two sentences to answer each of these questions about writing and storytelling. Look back at the selection if you need to.

1. What is the purpose of a ballad or narrative poem?
2. What is the difference between a tall tale and nonfiction?
3. Define personification. Then in one or two sentences, write your own example of personification.

C. Answer each question below in one or two paragraphs.

1. Make a list of all the qualities that you think a hero has. One quality might be great strength. Then choose one of the selections in this unit. Explain which qualities on your list the hero in the selection has.
2. If you could meet one of the heroes in this unit, who would it be? Explain your choice.
3. Write a short story or poem about someone you think is a hero.

Unit Four

NATURE

Chapter 8

A Visit to the Clerk of the Weather
an adapted story by Nathaniel Hawthorne
The First Tornado
by C. J. Taylor
River Man
by Teresa Pijoan de Van Etten

Chapter 9

Winter Animals
adapted from the essay by Henry David Thoreau
Shipwreck of the Whaleship Essex
adapted from the essay by Owen Chase
A Taste of Snow
an adapted essay by Jeanne Wakatsuki Houston

Chapter 10

Winter
by Nikki Giovanni
The Sky Is Low
by Emily Dickinson
Birdfoot's Grampa
by Joseph Bruchac
In Hardwood Groves
by Robert Frost
Sierra
by Diane Siebert
Big Yellow Taxi
by Joni Mitchell

Chapter 8

If Nature could talk, what do you think we would hear? We might hear the complaints of unhappy seasons. Perhaps we would hear wise words about life and living from a river. In this chapter, you will hear all these voices—and more—in stories about our natural world.

Chapter Learning Objectives

- Learn what a narrator does
- Learn to identify the first-person point of view
- Learn about myths
- Learn to identify similes
- Learn how a fable teaches a lesson

A Visit to the Clerk of the Weather
an adapted story by Nathaniel Hawthorne

Words to Know

LITERARY TERMS

narrator a person who tells a story

first-person point of view the story is told by the narrator, using the pronouns *I*, *me,* and *mine*

myths ancient stories that try to explain the mysteries of the world

SELECTION VOCABULARY

clerk an official in charge of records and accounts; an office worker

encircled made a circle around; surrounded

impulse a force that pushes forward or a sudden desire to act

pyramid a structure with a square base and four triangular sides that meet at the top

cavern a large cave

tolerably fairly good

neglected ignored; failed to care for

insulting disrespectful; hurting someone's feelings

assure make a person sure of something; comfort

forge a blacksmith's fire where metal is heated and shaped

"I don't know. I haven't spoken yet to the **clerk** of the weather," I said as a joke to my friend. He had asked me, "Do you think we shall have an early spring?"

We stood on the steps of the Mayfair Hotel. The night was not very dark, but falling snowflakes made it difficult to see. Still, I could plainly see a little old woman in a gray cloak. She was passing by at the moment and had caught my words. Her small black eyes looked at me through the mist as I spoke.

This tale borrows ideas from Greek and Roman myths. In ancient Greek myths, a god named Zeus controls the weather. The Romans have a similar god in their myths named Jupiter.

At the same moment, my friend shuddered, turned on his heel, and walked away. He went to warm up inside. The little old woman was by my side in an instant. When I tried to move away, her bony hand **encircled** my arm. It felt as if I were in the grasp of a skeleton.

"Let me go, madam, or by Heaven—"

"You have taken *his* name in vain often enough," she said in a hoarse whisper. "It is clear that you do not believe that he is real. Come with me. Now, don't hesitate, or I will weigh your manhood against the courage of an old woman."

"On, fool!" I exclaimed.

The old woman hurried away—and I followed. I was drawn by an **impulse** that I could not resist. We moved so rapidly that streets, houses, woods, and fences seemed to be running back as we progressed. At length, I was lifted from my feet and whirled

Who do you think *he* is?

Where do you think the old woman and the narrator are going? How are they traveling?

through the air. I traveled so fast that I nearly lost my breath.

The gray cloak of the old woman could be seen at some distance before me. The clouds split apart and rolled themselves on either side of her as she passed. They made a clear path for her and her follower. How far we traveled like this I cannot say. But suddenly we struck the land, and I stood upon the green grass. The sun flamed down on my head. And now, for the first time, I felt travel-worn and faint.

"I can assist you no farther," the old woman said. In a moment she had disappeared.

A little distance from where I stood was a pile of rocks. About a dozen tall, gray rocks, each several acres in height, had been thrown together in a circle. They formed a **pyramid,** with the points meeting at the top. I noticed a light smoke rising up through a small opening at the very top of this huge cone. I decided to enter this strange house. I no longer doubted that someone was living there.

I walked around the cone several times before I discovered an entrance. Several rocks had hidden it from my view. But the opening was large enough for a dozen horsemen to ride through it side-by-side. Slowly and carefully I entered the **cavern.** It was about five hundred yards all around.

Several objects drew my attention right away. Of course the living creatures were the first things I noticed. There were three huge beings in different parts of the room. And at the far side of the cavern sat a noble old man. He had long gray hair, and he was busily writing. He was the clerk of the weather.

Before I spoke to anyone, I glanced around the rocky cavern. In one corner, there was a pile of red-hot thunderbolts. Against the wall hung several second-hand rainbows. They were faded and covered with dust. Next, I saw several hundred cart loads of hailstones, two large sacks of wind, and a storm that

Do you think the first-person point of view helps make the adventure seem believable? Would a third-person point of view be as exciting? Find out by rereading a few sentences. Substitute *he* for *I* and *they* for *we.*

Here, the narrator is describing the great hall where the clerk of the weather lives.

was locked in iron chains.

Then I saw that the old man knew I was there. When he had half-risen from his seat, I hurried to present myself. As I got closer, I was struck by the size of his huge body and the fierce look in his eyes. He had stuck his pen behind his ear. This pen was the top of a tall tree. Some storm had rudely torn it from its trunk. And the old man had shaved the end down to the right size for dipping in his inkwell.

He took my hand into his big palm and squeezed it. His handshake was too strong for my comfort. But his friendliness helped ease the worry in my mind. I greeted him and asked how he was doing.

"I am **tolerably** well, thank you, for an old man of three-score centuries," he replied. "From where do you come?"

"I am from Boston, sir."

"I do not recall any planet of that name," he said.

"I beg your pardon—from Earth, I should have said."

He thought for a moment. "Yes, yes, I do remember a little mud-ball in this direction"—he pointed with his arm. "But, truly I had almost forgotten it. Hum! We have **neglected** you recently. It must be looked into. We owed Mr. Jack Frost a few favors. We had to give him permission to build some ice-palaces and snow forts. But he has gone too far. He must be stopped!"

"Really, sir, if you would pay more attention to us, not only would you have my thanks, but the whole world would thank you."

He looked serious for a moment. Then he shook his head and spoke. "But, sir, I have some complaints to make with you. I have been attacked and lied about by your fellows. You probably know that there are some people on your little planet who pretend to know what I am doing. They print information that says on such and such a day there shall be a snowstorm or thunder and lightning or a great heat

The clerk of the weather is "three-score centuries" old. A *score* is twenty. *Three-score* means three times twenty. A *century* is a hundred years. Multiply the three-score times one hundred to find out how old the clerk is.

In literature, Jack Frost is sometimes a cute elf and sometimes a nasty little man. How does Hawthorne describe Jack Frost?

THE FROST-KING.

wave. Some have even published **insulting** cartoons of me. And. . ."

Here we were interrupted by a loud, hissing noise. It startled me and caused me to turn around.

"You must be careful. You have burned your clothes, I fear," cried my host. He was speaking to a short, fat figure, who came walking slowly toward us. He was wrapped in sheets of ice and wearing a huge wig covered with snow.

"It is nothing, your Honor," answered the figure.

Who is this new character?

Who do you think this woman is?

Its hollow voice made my blood cold. "I only walked upon the cursed coil of chain lightning. Your servant has placed it near the door. This happens each time I visit you!"

I was too busy looking at this strange visitor to notice the entrance of another guest. She placed herself right between me and the clerk of the weather before I saw her. She was a lovely, young woman, dressed in a beautifully colored gown. On her head was a green hat and on her feet were green slippers.

The icy dwarf moved aside as she approached. He frowned at her from under his thick eyebrows. She glanced at him and pouted like a spoiled child. She then turned to me and spoke in the sweetest voice.

"You are the stranger from Earth, I guess!"

"At your service, fair lady," I said.

"I heard of your arrival and hurried to meet you," she said. "I wish to ask about my good friends, the people of your world. My name is Spring."

"My dear lady," I said. "Your face would gladden the hearts of us all. I can tell you that your presence has been wished and prayed for by all my fellow-sufferers."

"It is too upsetting!" she cried. She threw her green hat on the ground and stomped her feet. "I suppose I am blamed for my lateness by my children of the Earth. Heaven knows, I wish to leap over your valleys and hills and stay beside your running rivers as in days of yesterday. But that ugly, evil figure holds me in his power." Here, she pointed at Jack Frost, for that's who the strange, icy figure was.

"I took him to court last year," she said. "Before the case was decided, summer arrived. But **assure** your fellows that I will not neglect them in the future. I shall be among them early. Mr. Frost must take a journey to the north to get a polar bear for his wife. She has stayed among you Earth people for so long, she now follows some of your customs. She wants a substitute for a lap-dog." She then turned away and began to talk to the clerk of the weather.

I walked about the cavern to examine its contents. A giant fellow was sweating over the fire and cooking his master's breakfast. In a moment I saw him climb a sort of rope ladder. He picked a small white cloud out of the heavens and used it as milk for the coffee.

I wandered on until I came upon a heap of rocks. Behind it sat a dozen little black fellows sitting cross-legged. They were working with all their strength to weave a thunder gust. One part of this work seemed to puzzle them the most. They had to put in the thunderbolts, which they had to handle with long pincers. Another important part was sewing on the fringe, which was made of chain lightning.

While I stood looking at this, a huge fellow came stumbling towards me. He asked whether I had visited the **forge.** I told him that I had not. He said that it was not operating now because there were enough thunderbolts made for the present. But soon there might be an earthquake to fix.

Here, the narrator is watching lightning being created.

I noticed that his wrist was covered with a bandage. I asked him if he had been injured there. He said that he had gotten a small scratch there. Last year he had been ordered to fire several thunderbolts upon our Earth. He did it well, until he came to the last one. He hurled it toward our world, where unfortunately it landed on the head of a certain member of Congress. But the head was so hard that the bolt bounced back to the skies and scratched his wrist.

Nathaniel Hawthorne uses humor throughout this story. Here, he makes fun of a member of the U.S. Congress.

At this moment, someone grabbed me from behind. I turned my head and saw the little old woman in the gray cloak. I was quickly hurried from the great hall. Then I was sent with as much speed as before back to the world from which I had set out on this strange and wonderful adventure.

Zeus, Ruler of Sky and Weather

The sky rumbles. Mountains of dark clouds separate. A giant hand throws a fiery thunderbolt toward Earth. Zeus is angry!

Or maybe he is just amusing himself. Teasing the humans is one of Zeus's favorite pastimes. He enjoys watching them suffer through drought, wind storms, and flooding rains. Sometimes he even throws in a snowstorm.

Of course, this Greek god has his lighter moods. There are days when he dazzles humans with golden sunlight and scented breezes. A gentle shower to make the crops grow might please him, too. One never knows what the sky god will do!

What being or beings rule the sky in the stories of your culture?

Literature Practice

Answer these questions on a separate sheet of paper.

1. Why does the old woman take the narrator to visit the clerk of the weather?
2. a.) Why does the clerk of the weather complain about earthlings?
   b.) What have they done to make him angry?
3. Compare Hawthorne's descriptions of Jack Frost and Spring.
4. What do you think the narrator will do once he gets back on Earth?

The First Tornado
by C. J. Taylor

Words to Know

LITERARY TERM

simile a comparison of two things using *like* or *as*

SELECTION VOCABULARY

tornado a fierce, twisting wind

refresh make fresh again; renew

One summer day long ago the hot sun beat down on the people as never before. The heat came down like a blanket, leaving them with no air to breathe. The animals had all disappeared. Plants were dying in the dry earth. Even the snakes did not come out of their holes. The people felt they would soon dry up and die like the grass around them.

"Help us, please," they begged the Medicine Man. "Or we will become nothing but dried up bones."

"Go to the riverbed," the Medicine Man ordered, "and find some moist, red clay. Go immediately and bring it to me before it dries up."

The Medicine Man took the clay and, while the people watched, he shaped it into a horse with large white wings. He blew into its nostrils until the first sign of life appeared. Then he asked everyone to help him.

As they all blew together, the horse grew larger and larger. Its wings started to move and pull it upward. Soon the people could hold it down no longer. The horse flew up and around in a circle

Notice the simile in the second sentence. "The heat came down like a blanket." See if you can find one more simile in this story.

Medicine men are healers, storytellers, and wise elders.

Tipis, also spelled *tepees*, were what the Plains Indians lived in. Tipis were built and torn down by the women. Because Plains Indians, such as the Kiowa, were hunters, they needed to tear down their tipis quickly and move to where the buffalo were.

overhead, faster and faster. The wind from its wings blew everywhere, lifting tipis off the ground, breaking branches from the trees and swirling dust so that no one could see.

"What have you done?" the people cried out to the Medicine Man. "This wind is worse than the heat!"

The Medicine Man called to them over the noise of the wind storm. "It will be all right soon." Then he

shouted: "Horse! Go to your new home behind those dark clouds."

As the people watched, the horse disappeared behind the clouds, the skies calmed and the longed-for rains came, cooling them, filling the river again and returning life to the plants.

Now whenever terrible heat is followed by a **tornado,** the people know the horse has come down again. But they also know when it goes back behind the clouds, there will be rain to cool and **refresh** them.

Many cultures, such as the many Native American tribes, tell stories that explain how things came to be. They tell stories that explain why animals look the way they do. They also tell stories that explain the weather, such as this one which explains the creation of and reason for tornadoes.

The Kiowa

The name Kiowa means "a people who paint the two halves of the body or face different colors." Before whites invaded their territory, the Kiowa lived in the Plains, most specifically in what is now Southwestern Oklahoma and Texas. The Kiowa were hunters. Their main source of food came from buffalo. They hunted buffalo by driving the herds over cliffs or surrounding them and driving them into enclosed spaces. The Kiowa had strong taboos, or rules, against eating bears, birds, and fish.

After whites settled in Kiowa territory, the Texas Rangers rid the area of all Native Americans and forced the surviving Kiowa to live on reservations. The Texas Rangers were a specially chosen and trained group of law enforcers who had control over entire areas. Descendants of the Kiowa now live primarily in Oklahoma.

One of the most famous Native American writers—N. Scott Momaday—is part Kiowa. Momaday was born in Oklahoma, but he grew up in Arizona and New Mexico. Momaday often visited his grandparents in Oklahoma. He learned about his Kiowa ancestry from the stories his grandparents told him.

Literature Practice

Answer these questions on a separate sheet of paper.

1. When does this story take place?
2. What do the people ask the Medicine Man to do?
3. Why do you think it is necessary for everyone to help blow life into the horse?
4. Why do you think this tale has been important to the Kiowa people when there are tornadoes?

River Man

by Teresa Pijoan de Van Etten

Words to Know

LITERARY TERM

fable a short story that teaches a lesson

SELECTION VOCABULARY

channeled made into passageways

untapped not used

appliances household machines, such as dishwashers and refrigerators

mischievousness playfulness or naughtiness

pout frown; sulk

vaults safes where money or jewels are kept

glimpse a peek; a quick look

generosity willingness to give; unselfishness

balance steadiness; being stable

reflection an image given back, like from a mirror

The man in the river has always given each of us a little of himself—a bit of humor each time we drank some of his river water. But times change and with the times come new ideas and new devices. Men came here, men with modern ways, and told us not to drink the river water because it was unclean. They were right—people had thrown garbage in the river and the water was unclean.

The men brought in clean, shiny metal pipes. The earth was dug up and **channeled** to hold these metal pipes that contained the water. The river and ditches no longer carried it to the people. River water was

Animals, trees, or other natural things are often characters in fables. Who is the main character in this fable?

Why does modern technology bother the river man?

What qualities does the river man have?

Why do you think the river man is worried?

Why does the river man become mischievous?

forgotten. People even forgot to throw their garbage in the river. The water slowly became clean again.

The river was not used for washing, bathing, drinking, or cooking. The great humor of the river man was **untapped**. We were too busy using modern **appliances**, piped water, and water in bottles to think of river water.

The river man was left with his humor. He was saddened that the people who had once used river water would no longer have that little smile in the morning after drinking a cup of tea or coffee made with it. He worried about the children bathing in such pure, piped water—where would their **mischievousness** go? And the old ones—how would they keep their crooked smiles and sparkling eyes? How would they be now?

The river man waited. He waited for a long time. He listened to the big tractors and trucks that came by. Some of them tried to change his path, but he laughed at them and went the way he wished. While he waited, he worried. The river man knew that laughter and a good sense of humor keep the life alive in each of us.

The river man watched from his flowing river. He heard new babies cry—cry a *lot*. He heard small children complain and **pout** around their mothers and each other. The river man saw the old ones dry up in sadness. The river man didn't wait to see the old ones die. Oh, no. He made a plan.

The river man crept out of the river at night and went into people's houses. He went to the fancy new machines and pulled some wires; he went into the children's rooms and moved their toys around; he went to the old people's houses and took their false teeth.

The river man did mischief. He went to the house **vaults** of the rich ones, and he took their money and floated it in the river. The people became angry and irritable. We argued and fought.

One mother took her daughter out of school. She tried to teach her at home, but the little girl sat at the window and stared at the flowing river. The mother let her look, for she did not know what to do with the child.

One night, the river man came out of the river and took everyone's shadow. The children no longer had their shadows to play with. The lonely ones could no longer talk to their shadows. The old ones could no longer watch their shadows walk with them.

The little girl who lived with her mother stopped smiling, for her best friend was her shadow. She called for her shadow; she searched in the trees and the woods for her shadow. She didn't find it.

One afternoon she met a young man who was looking for his money. He was very rich, and he had seen his money mysteriously hurrying out the door toward the river early in the morning.

"Did you take my money?" the youth asked the little girl.

She laughed. "I would not take your money. I am searching for my shadow." They talked, and agreed to spend the night in a tree by the river to find out who was playing tricks. The mother gave her daughter some extra food for the young man.

The youth fell asleep, but not the little girl. She watched. She saw a man with long flowing silver hair come running from the town to the river. He ran right into the river and disappeared. She woke the young man, who just caught a **glimpse** of the old man's hair floating down into the river. The young man was greedy, and he wanted his money back. He dived into the river to get the old man. The girl dived in after him, for she feared what he would do to the old man.

Down they swam to an underwater house. They peered through the window. There were black shapes in the house, and the little girl recognized her shadow. She pushed open the door, and the young

Why do you think the river man takes away everyone's shadow?

The author uses an unusual point of view in this story. The narrator is a member of the river community and tells the story from the first-person "we." Do you think this point of view works for this story? Why or why not?

man followed her. The door slammed behind them. There stood the old man with the long flowing silver hair.

"What are you doing in my house?" the river man asked with a big grin.

"We are looking for things that we lost. Who are you?"

"I am the river man. I am the one who brings humor and joy into the lives of those that use my river water."

They listened to him. His wonderful, warm face glowed with a grand smile. They were happy to have found him and almost forgot all about their things. When at last the river man said he was tired, for he had had a busy night, they took what they needed. The young man only took a little of his money, and the girl took her shadow.

"If those who have things here will come to the river and use the river water, they will get their things back." The old man smiled and nodded off to sleep.

The next morning, the young man and the little girl went into town and told their story of the river man and his mischief and of the river water. The people were angry. How dared this river man make so much trouble for them! They went to the river, and those who tried to swim in it were amazed at how happy they felt. Those who washed their faces in the clean river water felt their lips stretch across their faces in almost-forgotten smiles. Slowly, small items came floating up from the river. The people—all of us—laughed and played in the water.

The river water brought joy, friendship, **generosity,** and good will back to us. The river man did not come up, but the flowing water rippled and slapped against the riverbank. We knew that he was pleased.

We use the river water every day now for different things, as we used to do, but now we use it and it brings **balance** to our lives. We respect the river and keep it clean.

In the **reflection** of the river water, we can see our own smiles. Look, and you can see yours, too.

Most fables end with a clearly stated lesson, or moral. What is the lesson of this fable?

Ol' Man River

The year is 1936. America is suffering through the Great Depression. Everywhere people are out of work and hungry. With the little money they have, people go to the movies to escape their troubles.

It is the opening night of the movie *Show Boat*. The audience is hushed as the famous African American singer Paul Robeson begins "Ol' Man River." It is a song about the Mississippi and the hard life of the African Americans who work on the river.

Robeson sings; the audience is spellbound. Many are openly weeping. Here are the unforgettable words:

> Ol' man river, dat ol' man river, He must know sumpin', but don't say nothin', He jus' keeps rollin', He keeps on rollin' along.

> Ah gits weary, an' sick of tryin', Ah'm tired of livin' an' skeered of dyin', But ol' man river, he jus' keeps rollin' along.

Why do you think the river is so important to many cultures?

Literature Practice

Answer these questions on a separate sheet of paper.

1. Why do the people stop using the river?
2. The author gives the river man the qualities of wisdom and patience. What other qualities does the river man have?
3. Why does the river man steal people's money, shadows, and belongings and do other mischievous things?
4. What is the moral of this story?

Chapter Review

Summaries

- **A Visit to the Clerk of the Weather**—The narrator jokes that he will ask the clerk of the weather if there will be an early spring. An old woman overhears the joke. She then takes the narrator to meet the clerk of the weather. There, the narrator meets the clerk, Jack Frost, and Spring. The clerk apologizes for neglecting Earth, but complains about the way humans joke about him. Spring promises to come to Earth soon.

- **The First Tornado**—This Kiowa tale tells how and why the first tornado was made. To end a drought, the Medicine Man makes a winged horse out of clay. He and the other people blow life into the horse. It then forms a tornado. When it flies into the clouds, the longed-for rains begin.

- **River Man**—A community pollutes and then forgets about its river. The man in the river gives the people joy. When he is forgotten, the people begin to lose the laughter that keeps them alive. To make people use the river again, the river man steals their valuables and shadows. The people go into the river to get their belongings back. The water makes them happy again. Now the community keeps the river clean, and they use it every day.

Chapter Quiz

Choose the letter of the correct answer. Rewrite the sentences on a separate sheet of paper.

1. In "A Visit to the Clerk of the Weather," why does the old woman get upset when the narrator jokes about the clerk of the weather?

   a. She thinks that the idea of a clerk who controls the weather is silly.

   b. She does not like jokes.

   c. She is angry that the narrator does not believe that the clerk of the weather is real.

   d. She is the being who controls winter.

2. The clerk of the weather complains about people on Earth because
   a. they lie about and insult him.
   c. they like him.
   b. they let Jack Frost stay too long.
   d. they only like Spring.

3. In "The First Tornado," why do the people ask for the Medicine Man's help?
   a. A tornado is coming.
   b. They want more heat.
   c. The hot sun is drying everything up.
   d. The wind is blowing.

4. What happens after the horse goes behind the clouds?
   a. The wind gets worse.
   b. The Medicine Man blows into the clay.
   c. It begins to rain.
   d. The sun gets hotter.

5. In "The River Man," what does the river water bring to the people?
   a. sickness
   b. seriousness
   c. garbage
   d. humor

Thinking and Writing

Answer the following questions on a separate sheet of paper. Write one or two paragraphs for each one.

1. "The River Man" is a fable, or a short story that teaches a lesson. What lesson do you think this story is trying to teach?

2. Why do you think "The First Tornado" helps people feel better about tornadoes?

3. The narrator in "A Visit to the Clerk of the Weather" meets Spring and Winter. Imagine that you visit the clerk of the weather. You meet a being that is called Fall. Describe what this being looks like and what you would talk to him about.

Chapter 9

As we walk the earth, we find that nature is both kind and not so kind. In the following nonfiction selections, you will share memories of both sides—from the beauty of a snowfall at Christmas to the terror of surviving a horrible shipwreck.

Chapter Learning Objectives

- Learn about nonfiction
- Learn to identify a topic sentence
- Learn what an autobiographical essay is
- Learn how an author uses a narrative hook
- Learn about comparison and contrast
- Learn how a writer uses description

Winter Animals

adapted from the essay by Henry David Thoreau

Words to Know

LITERARY TERMS

nonfiction literature that tells about things that are real

topic sentence the sentence that tells the main idea of a paragraph

SELECTION VOCABULARY

prowling sneaking, hiding out

skulk sneak away, slink

amid among, surrounded by

disputed argued, quarreled

flourishing growing well

densely thickly, close together

startled surprised

parings shavings, scraps

distinguished seen, identified, recognized

vigor power, strength, energy

At midnight, when there was a moon, I sometimes met hounds along my path. They would be **prowling** about the woods and would **skulk** out of my way. They acted as if they were afraid. They'd stand silently **amid** the bushes until I had passed.

Squirrels and mice **disputed** for my supply of nuts. There were dozens of pitch pines around my house, from one to four inches wide. They had been chewed up by mice the winter before. It had been a bitter, cold winter for them. The snow lay long and deep. They had to mix a large amount of pine bark with their other food.

This selection is nonfiction. Thoreau really did live in the woods. What he writes about truly happened.

These trees were alive and apparently **flourishing** at midsummer. Many of them had grown a foot. But after another winter they were without exception all dead. It is amazing that a single mouse should thus be allowed a whole pine tree for its dinner. But perhaps it is necessary in order to thin these trees. They have a habit of growing up **densely**.

The hares were very familiar. One stayed under my house all winter. She was separated from me only by the flooring. She **startled** me each morning. As soon as I began to wake up, she'd leave quickly. Thump, thump, thump—she'd strike her head against the floor timbers in her hurry.

Notice how Thoreau begins each paragraph with a topic sentence. The topic of the first paragraph is the hounds. In the topic sentence of the second paragraph, he names the mice he will tell about. What are the topics of the third and fourth paragraphs?

The hares used to come round my door each day at dusk. They'd nibble the potato **parings** I'd thrown out. These animals were similar to the color of the ground. They could hardly be **distinguished** from the ground when they were still. Sometimes in the twilight I would lose and then regain sight of one sitting still under my window. When I opened my door in the evening, off they'd go with a squeak and a bounce. Close by, they only excited my pity.

One evening, one sat by my door a few feet away. At first, it trembled with fear, but was unwilling to move. It was a poor wee thing, lean and bony. It had ragged ears, a sharp nose, a small tail, and slender paws. It looked as if Nature no longer contained the breed of stronger bloods. Its large eyes appeared young and unhealthy.

I took a step. And lo, away it jumped with an elastic spring over the snow-crust. It straightened its body and its limbs into graceful length. It soon put the forest between me and itself. It was wild and free, showing its **vigor** and the dignity of Nature. Not without reason was it slender. Such then was its nature.

Nonfiction usually ends with a closing statement. In that statement, the writer will make a point. What point about Nature does Thoreau make in the last few sentences?

The Smallest Winter Animals

It is the middle of the winter. You are taking a walk in the park. Although the day is a little warmer than it has been, there is still snow on the ground. Suddenly you notice some pepper sprinkled on the snow at the foot of a tree. How can that be? Then you notice that the pepper is moving. Looking closer, you see that the pepper is really a swarm of insects!

The insects that you see are called snow fleas. If you look at them with a magnifying glass, you'll notice that they have tails. Watch them tuck their tails under their bodies. They will use those tails as springs to hop about. That is why some people call them *springtails*.

Literature Practice

Answer these questions on a separate sheet of paper.

1. When does Thoreau meet hounds in the woods?

2. What winter animals does Thoreau mention in this selection?

3. Thoreau believes that Nature knows best. There is a reason for everything. What two examples does he give to support this idea?

4. Why do you think Thoreau is so interested in the animals?

Shipwreck of the Whaleship Essex
adapted from the essay by Owen Chase

Words to Know

LITERARY TERMS

autobiographical essay a composition about an event that happened in the writer's life

narrative hook the point in a story at which the author grabs the reader's attention

SELECTION VOCABULARY

destiny the future, fate

latitude the distance north and south from the Earth's equator

longitude the distance east and west from Greenwich, England

harpoon a spear used for whaling

knots a measurement of a ship's speed

helm a ship's steering wheel

thrashing whipping, tossing about

steward a person who takes care of the food and people on a ship

salvation rescue, deliverance from harm

casks kegs or barrels

A great deal of time has passed since it happened. Still, I cannot remember the scenes which I am about to describe without certain emotions. They are a mixture of horror and amazement at the incredible **destiny** that saved me and my companions from a horrible death.

On November 20th, we were cruising in **latitude** 0° 40′ south, **longitude** 119° 0′ west. Then a group of whales was discovered off in the distance. The weather

Notice how Owen Chase catches your interest in the first paragraph. In this narrative hook, he tells you that he was saved from a "horrible death." What other words hook you into reading on?

at this time was very fine and clear. At 8:00 A.M., the man at the lookout gave the usual cry of "there she blows."

Right away, we headed off in the direction where the whales were. Soon we had gotten within a half mile of the place where they'd been seen. All our boats were lowered down, manned, and we chased after them. The ship waited for us.

I had the **harpoon** in the second boat. The captain went in the first. We arrived at the spot where we thought the whales were. At first we could see nothing. We lay on our oars expecting the whales to come up somewhere near us.

Soon, one rose and spouted a short distance ahead of my boat. I sped toward it and struck it. The whale felt the harpoon in him. Then he threw himself, in agony, towards the boat. He gave a heavy blow with his tail. He struck the boat near the edge of the water and drove a hole in her.

I immediately grabbed a hatchet and cut the harpoon line. That separated the boat from the whale, which by this time was running off with great speed. I succeeded in getting clear of him, but we lost the harpoon and line. The water poured into the boat fast. I quickly stuffed three or four of our jackets in the hole. Then I ordered one man to keep bailing water and the other men to row immediately for the ship. We succeeded in keeping the boat afloat and shortly reached the ship.

The captain and the second mate were in the other two boats. They kept up the chase and soon struck another whale. At this time, I went forward, turned the ship around, and sailed in their direction. The boat, which had been damaged, was immediately lifted onto the ship. I examined the hole. I found that I could nail a piece of canvas over it and get her ready to join the chase.

I was in the act of nailing on the canvas when I noticed a very large sperm whale. As far as I could

What do you think the men are going after?

tell, it was about 85 feet in length. He broke water about 100 yards off our ship. He was lying quietly with his head pointed towards the ship.

He spouted two or three times and then disappeared. In less than two or three seconds, he came up again. He made directly for us at a speed of about three **knots**. The ship was then going at about the same speed. The whale's appearance and attitude at first gave us no worry. I stood watching his movements, as he came toward us with great speed. I ordered the boy at the **helm** to turn hard, intending to avoid him.

The words were hardly out of my mouth before he came down upon us with full speed. He struck the ship with his head. He slammed into us so hard that we nearly fell on our faces. The ship stopped suddenly, as if she'd struck a rock. It shook for a few seconds like a leaf.

We looked at each other in amazement. We did not even have the power to speak. Many minutes went by before we realized the awful accident that had taken place. During that time, the whale went under the ship and came up alongside her, facing the wind. He lay on top of the water for about a minute. He seemed stunned by the blow. Then suddenly he started off again.

After a few moments, we recovered from the confusion that had grabbed us. I saw that the whale had put a hole in the ship. I knew that it would be necessary to get the pumps going. They were set up and put in operation. However, they'd only been going for about a minute when I noticed something. The head of the ship was gradually settling down in the water.

I then ordered the signal for the other boats to sail off. Right after this, I again saw the whale. He was **thrashing** about on top of the water some 500 yards away. He was covered by the foam of the sea, which he had created by his moving about. I could clearly

A male sperm whale can grow to 50 feet in length. Its most outstanding feature is its huge, square head that takes up about one-third of its total body length. Sperm whales can dive more than 3,500 feet and stay under water for more than an hour! They prefer to eat giant squid, but they will also eat octopus and some fish. Although sperm whales generally stay in groups of 25 or 40, some males will wander from the group and will travel alone.

Sailors think of ships as being female. Most ships have female names and are referred to as *her*.

see him clamp his jaws together in rage and fury. He stayed a short time like this. Then he started off with great speed in the other direction.

By this time, the ship had sunk down quite a bit in the water. I gave her up as lost. However, I ordered the pumps to be kept constantly going. I turned to the two boats that were still with the ship. I intended to get them ready for use, if there were no other choice left. While I was paying attention to that, I heard the cry of a man. "Here he is—he's making for us again."

I turned around. I saw him about 500 yards directly ahead of us. He was coming down with twice his usual speed. And he seemed to be ten times angrier.

The surf flew in all directions about him. His path toward us was marked by white foam about five yards wide, which he made by thrashing his tail. His head was about half out of water. And in that way he came up and again struck the ship.

I yelled up to the helmsman, "hard up." But the ship had barely moved before we took the second shock. He completely smashed in her bow. Then he passed under the ship again and went off in the other direction. We saw no more of him.

Our situation at this point is difficult to describe. Misfortune found us at a moment when we did not dream of any accident. We had looked forward to earning money from our work. Now we were faced with disaster.

We were more than a thousand miles from the nearest land. And there was nothing more than a light, open boat to provide safety for myself and my companions.

I ordered the men to stop pumping and everyone to provide for himself. I grabbed a hatchet and cut away the ropes on the spare boat. I cried out to those near me to take her as she came down. They did so and carried her as far as mid-ship.

At the same time, the **steward** had gone down into the cabin twice. He had saved some equipment, and the captain's trunk and mine. All of this was quickly thrown into the boat along with two compasses I had saved. The steward tried to go back down again. But by this time the water had rushed in, and he returned without success.

By this time, the ship had filled with water. She was going down. We shoved our boat as quickly as possible into the water. All hands jumped in her at the same time, and we pushed off clear of the ship. We were barely two boat's lengths distant from her when she fell over and sunk.

Shock and despair now took hold of us. We thought with horror about the sudden tragedy that had overtaken us. None of us spoke a word for several minutes. Everyone seemed to be under a spell of confusion.

From the time we were first attacked by the whale until the ship sunk, not more than ten minutes had passed. My companions had not saved a single thing

Predict what you think will happen next.

The author says that "shock and despair now took hold" of the sailors when the ship sank. What do you think is going through their minds as they watch it go down?

What do the sailors take off the sinking ship? Why do you think it is important for the men to save those things?

except what they had on their backs. But I was quite satisfied, if one could be satisfied by such a gloomy situation. We had been lucky enough to save our compasses and other tools.

The first shock of what happened was over. Then I happily thought of these tools as the likely source of our **salvation**. Without them, all would have been dark and hopeless. What a picture of distress and suffering I began to imagine!

The crew of the ship, 20 men, were saved. But all that was left to carry us across the stormy waters, thousands of miles, were three open light boats. The idea of getting any food or water from the ship was now very doubtful. How many long and watchful nights would we have? How many long days of near starvation would we have to suffer through? When could we expect some relief from our troubles?

We lay in our boat about two ship's lengths from the wreck. We were silent and calm, thinking about

our lost ship. Soon, we saw the other boats rowing up to us. They had shortly before discovered that some accident had happened to us. But they did not know the nature of the accident.

The ship's sudden and mysterious disappearance was first discovered by the boat steerer in the captain's boat. With horror on his face, he shouted, "Where is the ship?" A general cry of shock and horror came from the lips of every man. They immediately made their way toward us.

The captain's boat was the first to reach us. He stopped a short distance away. But he had no power to say a single word. He was overpowered with the sight before him. He sat down in his boat, pale and speechless. I hardly recognized his face. Finally, he was able to ask me a question.

"Mr. Chase, what is the matter?"

"We have been struck by a whale," I answered. I then briefly told him the story.

He thought for a few moments. Then he said we must cut away the ships' masts. This would allow the ship to rise up a bit. Then we could get something out of her to eat. Our thoughts were now set on saving from the wreck whatever we might want. So, for this purpose, we rowed up and got on to her.

We cut away the masts as fast as we could. The ship came up about two-thirds out of the water. We now began to cut a hole through the planks right above two large **casks** of bread. From them, we were able to get about 600 pounds of bread.

Other parts of the deck were then torn up. We took as much freshwater as we dared to carry in the boats. Each one was supplied with about 65 gallons. We also got from one of the lockers a gun, some gunpowder, and about two pounds of boat nails. In the afternoon, a wind came up to blow a strong breeze. By then we had taken everything we could think of. So, we began to prepare for our safety during the night.

A boat's line was tied to the ship. One of the other boats was tied to the other end of it about 300 feet away. Another boat was then attached to the first one about 50 feet to one side. Then the third boat was attached to the second about the same distance away.

Night came on just as we had finished our work. And such a night as it was to us! We were worried and distracted. None of us was able to sleep.

After several hours of sorrow, I began to think about the accident. I thought about by what destiny this sudden and deadly attack had been made upon us. It had been made by an animal never before known to attack in such a planned, violent way.

Every fact made me believe that the attack did not happen by chance. The whale made two attacks upon the ship. Both attacks were designed to do us the most harm. His actions were horrible and filled with fury. He came directly from the group of whales where we had struck three of his companions. It was as if he wanted revenge for their suffering.

Why do you think the narrator says the whale attacks them because it wants revenge?

However, one point may be made by observers. The whale's usual way of fighting is either with repeated strokes of its tail or by snapping its jaws together. A case similar to this one has never before been heard of among the oldest and most experienced whalers.

To this I have an answer. The build and strength of the whale's head is well-designed for this kind of attack. The whale's head is as hard and tough as iron. A harpoon would not make the slightest dent there. The eyes and the ears are far from this front part of the head. So, they are not in any way put in danger when the attack is made.

An autobiography tells about the author's whole life, or most of it. How is an autobiographical essay, like this one, different from an autobiography?

All the events taken together, which happened before my eyes, lead me to feel correct in my opinion. It is certainly in all ways, up to now, an unheard of event. Perhaps it is the most extraordinary event in the history of fishing.

Stranger Than Fiction

Here is a sea story that is just as unbelievable as "Shipwreck of the Whaleship Essex." But like that bizarre whale tale, it is a true story!

About a hundred years ago, a fishing boat was returning home to Gloucester, on the coast of Massachusetts. When it was 300 miles from land, the crew saw the impossible. Swimming in the water, all alone, was a giant black dog! The captain immediately stopped the boat and ordered his crew to bring the strange beast on board.

As it turned out, the dog was a Newfoundland. This strong, intelligent breed is often used to rescue drowning swimmers. Its large web-like feet and powerful build make it a strong swimmer. But could it swim 300 miles?

The town of Gloucester adopted the friendly Newfoundland, and it lived out its life in comfort.

Yet, the dog's mystery was never solved. Had it jumped overboard from a ship? Had it survived a shipwreck? Was it dragged out to sea by a storm?

We will never know.

Literature Practice

Answer these questions on a separate sheet of paper.

1. What kind of whale attacks the ship?
2. Why does the author think the whale attacks the ship?
3. This story almost sounds unbelievable. What is the author's explanation of how the whale sank the ship?
4. How do you feel about the whale in this story?
5. Why is this story called an autobiographical essay?

A Taste of Snow

an adapted essay by Jeanne Wakatsuki Houston

Words to Know

LITERARY TERMS

comparison and contrast writing that tells how things are alike and how they are different

description writing that uses details and the senses to give the reader a feeling of "being there"

SELECTION VOCABULARY

barracks a plain building used as temporary housing

muffled made less loud or less clear; deadened the sound

pier a landing or walkway extending out into a body of water

appreciate value, cherish

cranes large birds with very long legs and necks and long, straight bills

---

I first saw snow one Christmas. I was nine years old, living in the high desert of Owens Valley in California. It was during World War II. It was the first winter my family and I spent at Manzanar. When the first flakes of snow fell down, they looked like bits of coconut. They danced on the wind. I ran out between the **barracks**. I danced in circles. I opened my mouth to catch the icy flakes. The snow was like cotton candy—very light—and gone with one lick of the tongue.

I was surprised by how sharp and cold the air was. The beautiful snow had a price. It made my feet

During World War II, Japan and the United States were enemies. In 1942, the U.S. government sent about 120,000 Japanese Americans to internment camps, such as Manzanar, and treated them as spies. The camps were like military bases.

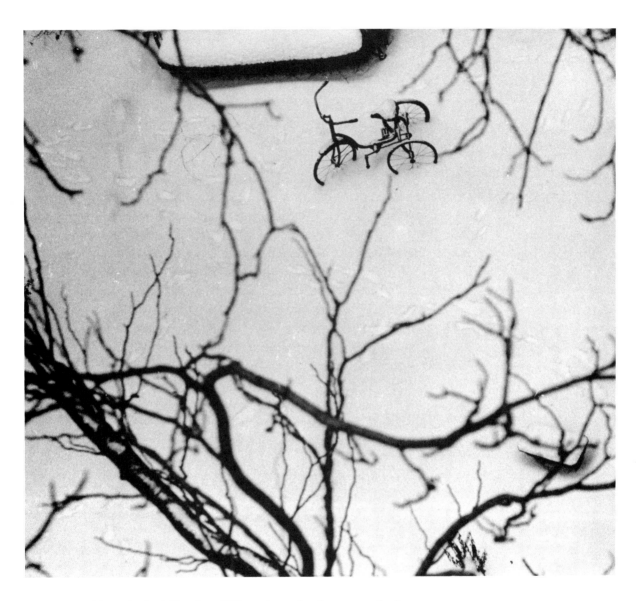

and hands feel like ice. When it melted on my clothes, my clothes became cold and wet. Still, the snow was so beautiful, I soon forgot how cold and wet it made me.

Other people came out of the barracks. They saw that their world was changed by the snow. Some people carried bright Japanese umbrellas and wore high wooden shoes called *getas*. The *getas* kept their

The author uses description to make us *see* the crystal flakes, *feel* the cold and wet, and *taste* the powdery ice. What sound does she describe in the third paragraph?

feet from getting wet. Because of the snow, there was no "kata-kata" sound of wooden shoes scraping across the sand and gravel. The snow **muffled** sounds. It also made the thin roofs of the barracks look thicker. The barracks and the land around it looked softer.

The snow was strangely peaceful to me—so quiet and calm. It brought tears to my eyes.

There is a reason I remember this first snow so well. Before my family was sent to Manzanar, we lived in Ocean Park. Our house was on Dudley Avenue. It was one block away from the beach. Ocean Park **Pier** was my playground. All the kids who lived in our neighborhood played on the wide cement sidewalk next to the beach. That sidewalk went all the way from Ocean Park to Venice. Here, we played ball and skated on rollerskates.

Notice how the author describes the similarities and differences between Manzanar and Ocean Park. She uses comparison and contrast to tell the reader about her experiences.

My memories of Ocean Park are warm ones. I remember hot days on the beach and making sand castles. I played *Tarzan* and *Jungle Girl*. I jumped off the stands where the lifeguards sat and hurt my ankles. The Fourth of July was a warm evening with crowds of people waiting by the pier for the fireworks to fill the sky. Easter had as many colors as the eggs our service club hid in the sand for us to find. Christmas was just another time of high spirits and fun that my family had before the war.

Christmas morning at Ocean Park seemed always clear and sunny. We walked along that wide sidewalk. I wore a new dress with orange flowers and shoes with high tops. I pushed a doll carriage that Santa had left under the big tree in our living room. I showed off my gifts and myself with pride. So did all the other children in my neighborhood. My oldest brother Bill was in his twenties then. He walked with me. He helped me feed popcorn to the pigeons that were around our feet. Then he rushed me off in his old blue car to see his girlfriend Molly. Molly played the violin while Bill sang, and I fell asleep.

It is like a story inside a story, or a memory inside a memory. I cannot think of another Christmas except these two. These two Christmas days are like *yin* and *yang*—each part is necessary to **appreciate** the other. I don't remember Christmas trees in Manzanar. But we found pieces of wood in the creeks. Those creeks came down from the Sierra Nevada Mountains across the high desert. We made our tree with this wood. In my mind they are together: the big green tree with lights in Ocean Park and the brown branch we found near Manzanar that we decorated with paper **cranes**.

Even today, when I travel in the high country, the beautiful snow can make me cry. And I remember my first taste of snow.

—1983

Yin and *yang* are opposites. They are night and day, female and male, cold and hot. They are the world's necessary opposites.

In 1983, a U.S. government commission stated that the internment camps were not necessary for national security. The commission's report has been taken by many people to be an apology for the treatment of Japanese Americans.

Literature Practice

Answer these questions on a separate sheet of paper.

1. List the similarities and differences between Christmas at Manzanar and Christmas at Ocean Park.

2. Why does the author say the two Christmases are *yin* and *yang?*

3. The author does not say that one Christmas was good and one was bad, even though she spent one in an internment camp. Why do you think she does not judge the two Christmases?

4. The author specifically notes the date of her writing. How do you think the happenings of that year, 1983, may have affected her writing?

Chapter Review

Summaries

- **Winter Animals**—Thoreau writes about his observations of several animals. Through examples of animal behavior, he hints that everything in nature has a purpose. The wild mice kill huge pine trees. But the forest is actually improved by the thinning of the trees. The hares are lean in winter. Perhaps, Thoreau says, that is why they can run so fast from danger.

- **Shipwreck of the Whaleship Essex**—Chase tells of his terrifying adventure at sea. Chase is on a voyage to hunt whales. Then, a thousand miles from land, his ship is attacked by a large sperm whale and is sunk. Chase believes that the whale attacked to revenge the harpooning of its companions.

- **A Taste of Snow**—Houston compares two Christmases. First, she describes a Christmas at an internment camp in Manzanar, California. It is there that she sees, feels, and tastes snow for the first time. The author then contrasts the snowy Christmas with the memory of a previous childhood Christmas in sunny Ocean Park, California. The two events are *yin* and *yang*, necessary opposites, she concludes. Each memory is needed to understand the other.

Chapter Quiz

Choose the letter of the correct answer. Rewrite the sentences on a separate sheet of paper.

1. In "Winter Animals," Thoreau feels sorry because the hares are so thin but then he realizes
   a. Nature must have made a mistake.
   b. he can feed them potato parings.
   c. the hares are sick.
   d. they are thin for a reason.

2. Why does Owen Chase think that the whale attacks the ship in "Shipwreck of the Whaleship Essex"?
   a. It is frightened of the ship.
   b. It is warning them to stay away.
   c. It thinks the ship is a shark.
   d. It wants revenge.

3. Why does Chase say he was saved from a horrible death right when the story begins?
   a. He wants to give away the ending.
   b. He writes in the third person.
   c. He is using a narrative hook.
   d. The story is too confusing.

4. Where was her family living when Jeanne Wakatsuki Houston first saw snow?
   a. an internment camp in Manzanar
   b. their house on Dudley Avenue
   c. near the beach
   d. Ocean Park Pier

5. Why are the two Christmases linked in Houston's mind?
   a. Both times she saw snow.
   b. One happened a year before the other.
   c. One is necessary to appreciate the other.
   d. Both happened in the same place.

Thinking and Writing

Write answers to the following questions on a separate sheet of paper.

1. Owen Chase said that the experience he described in "Shipwreck of the Whaleship Essex" still made him feel a mix of emotions. List the emotions you think he felt. Then write a sentence explaining how Chase felt about this experience.

2. Choose one piece of art that you especially liked in this chapter. Tell whether you think it is a good illustration for the story.

3. If you wanted to write about an event in your life that relates to nature, what event would you choose? Explain.

Chapter 10

The mystery and beauty of nature has inspired people through the ages. All around us, the wonders of nature's glory continue to amaze us. Think about how nature has inspired the poets in this chapter.

Chapter Learning Objectives

- Learn to identify alliteration
- Learn how poets use assonance
- Learn how writers personify nature
- Learn about tone in writing
- Learn about theme
- Learn how rhyme adds to a poem
- Learn what a couplet is
- Learn how to recognize a ballad
- Learn what a refrain does
- Learn to identify stanzas

Winter
by Nikki Giovanni

Words to Know

LITERARY TERMS

alliteration the repeating of consonant sounds

assonance the repeating of vowel sounds

SELECTION VOCABULARY

burrow dig a hole in the ground

store keep; collect

Frogs **burrow** the mud
snails bury themselves
and I air my quilts
preparing for the cold
5 Dogs grow more hair
mothers make oatmeal
and little boys and girls
take Father John's Medicine

Bears **store** fat
10 chipmunks gather nuts
and I collect books
for the coming winter

Look at how alliteration ties parts of this poem together. The words *burrow* and *bury* both start with the same consonant sound.

Vowel sounds, too, are used to tie this poem together. Listen to the assonance of the long *o* in *cold, grow,* and *oatmeal.*

A Long Winter's Nap

Do bears really hibernate? No they don't. Are you surprised? Most people think bears sleep through the winter. But the truth is that they simply become less active. Like the chipmunk, raccoon, and skunk, they will come out of their dens on nice days to look for food.

The animals that do hibernate are reptiles, amphibians, and insects. Only a few mammals will sleep through the winter. One that really does is the groundhog. During its six-month hibernation, the groundhog's body temperature can drop 60 degrees! Its heart will beat only four times per minute rather that its normal 160 beats per minute. What's more, it only needs to breathe once a minute. Now that's a real winter's nap!

Once the groundhog wakes up and comes out of his den, if he sees his shadow, there will be an early spring—or so the story goes.

Literature Practice

1. a.) What do you think Father John's Medicine is?
   b.) Why do you think children take it to prepare for winter?

2. In what words is alliteration used in the last two lines of the poem?

3. The poet uses assonance in the words *air* and *preparing*. What word in line 5 has the same vowel sound?

4. What do you do to prepare for winter?

The Sky Is Low

by Emily Dickinson

Words to Know

LITERARY TERM

personification objects, animals, or ideas are given human qualities

SELECTION VOCABULARY

rut a track made in the ground by wheels

debates thinks about; tries to decide

diadem a crown

The Sky is low—the Clouds are mean.
A Traveling Flake of Snow
Across a Barn or through a **Rut**
Debates if it will go—

5 A Narrow Wind complains all Day
How some one treated him.
Nature, like Us is sometimes caught
Without her **Diadem**.

Notice the use of capital letters and dashes. Dickinson's use of capitalizing all nouns is her trademark.

Nature is supposed to be noble and like a queen.

Literature Practice

1. When the poet says "the Clouds are mean," she is using personification. She has given the clouds a human personality. Find three other examples of personification in the poem.

2. Tell in a few sentences what is happening in the poem.

3. Why do you think the poet describes the clouds as "mean"?

4. The poet describes clouds, snow, and wind in this poem. What part of nature would you add to this poem? Write a third stanza, or section, to this poem in which you describe a different part of nature.

5. Emily Dickinson did not write titles for her poems. Publishers usually use the first line or part of the first line as the title. What title would you give this poem?

Birdfoot's Grampa
by Joseph Bruchac

Words to Know

LITERARY TERM

tone the feeling the writer shows toward the subject of the poem or story

SELECTION VOCABULARY

accept admit, give in to

leathery like leather

The old man
must have stopped our car
two dozen times to climb out
and gather into his hands
5   the small toads blinded
by our lights and leaping,
live drops of rain.

The rain was falling,
a mist about his white hair
10   and I kept saying
you can't save them all,
accept it, get back in
we've got places to go.

But, **leathery** hands full
15   of wet brown life,
knee deep in the summer
roadside grass,
he just smiled and said
they have places to go to
20   *too.*

The poem is told from the point of view of Birdfoot.

The first two stanzas of this poem have a different tone from the last. In the first two, the narrator seems impatient with the old man. How does the narrator's attitude change in the last stanza?

Frog or Toad?

Can you tell the difference between a frog and a toad? Most people can't. As a rule of thumb, toads have a rougher skin and live on land. Frogs have smooth skin and prefer water. Perhaps because frogs do so much swimming, they have developed smaller eyes than toads, too. Toads are also chubbier and slower than their more streamlined cousins.

Who would win a jumping contest? Not the toad!

Literature Practice

Answer these questions on a separate sheet of paper.

1. a.) Who is the narrator in this poem?
   b.) Who is the old man?
2. Why does the old man stop the car?
3. What is the "wet brown life" mentioned in the last stanza?
4. What does the old man's actions tell us about his attitude toward nature?
5. How does Grampa feel about nature?
6. What is the tone of this poem?

In Hardwood Groves

by Robert Frost

Words to Know

LITERARY TERM

theme the main idea of a story, novel, play, or poem

SELECTION VOCABULARY

groves clumps of trees; forest

texture surface; the way a certain
surface feels

faded dull; no longer bright

mount rise; go up

shade color

decayed rotten; plants which are
slowly broken down

pierced made a hole; stabbed; broke
through

The same leaves over and over again!
They fall from giving shade above
To make one **texture** of **faded** brown
And fit the earth like a leather glove.

5 Before the leaves can **mount** again
To fill the trees with another **shade,**
They must go down past things coming up.
They must go down into the dark **decayed.**

They *must* be **pierced** by flowers and put
10 Beneath the feet of dancing flowers.
However it is in some other world
I know that this is the way in ours.

A hardwood grove could include trees, such as oak, maple, and birch.

Theme was very important to Robert Frost. He believed a poem should have a main idea and that every line should relate to that idea.

Literature Practice

Answer these questions on a separate sheet of paper.

1. In this poem, Frost repeats words and phrases. He even uses the same word in two different ways. Find two examples of repeated words.

2. Explain why you think Frost uses repetition.

3. Where do the leaves have to go before they can become part of the tree again?

4. Why do you think Frost italicized the word *must* in "They *must* be pierced by flowers . . ."?

5. How does this poem make you feel? Explain.

6. What is the theme of this poem?

Make Your Own Compost

Do you live in the city? Chances are there is a community garden near you. Or maybe you have a vegetable patch in your backyard. No matter where you garden, you can use a compost pile.

Decaying plants and leaves that are added to garden soil are called compost. Composting is important because it keeps the soil healthy and fertile. Nature makes its own compost, of course. The leaves that drop from the trees and the plants that die in the fall become compost. But when we garden, we need to give nature a helping hand. Here's how.

Find an old barrel or 50-gallon drum. Punch holes in the bottom and sides. Now imitate nature. Put a layer of twigs on the bottom for circulation. Autumn leaves and grass clippings can be added next. Toss in some earthworms, too. Also throw in kitchen scraps, such as fruit and vegetable peels, egg shells, and coffee grounds. Just don't add meat or fat. Let the snow or rain keep the compost moist.

By spring your barrel will be filled with a rich, soft compost that you can add to your community garden or backyard vegetable patch.

Sierra

by Diane Siebert

Words to Know

LITERARY TERMS

rhyme the repetition of sounds in the words of a poem

couplet two lines of poetry—one right after the other—that rhyme

SELECTION VOCABULARY

sentinel a guard

glaciers huge layers of ice

ravines valleys

clefted split; divided

gnarled knotty; twisted

quest a search

lairs animals' homes; dens

I am the mountain,
　Tall and grand.
And like a **sentinel** I stand.
Surrounding me, my sisters rise
5　With watchful peaks that pierce the skies;
From north to south we form a chain
Dividing desert, field, and plain.
　　I am the mountain.
　　Come and know
10　Of how, ten million years ago,
Great forces, moving plates of earth,
Brought, to an ancient land, rebirth;
Of how this planet's faulted crust
Was shifted, lifted, tilted, thrust
15　Toward the sky in waves of change
To form a newborn mountain range.

The narrator of this poem is a mountain in the Sierra Nevada mountain range. Who are the narrator's sisters?

I am the mountain,
Young, yet old.
I've stood, and watching time unfold,
20 Have known the age of ice and snow
And felt the **glaciers** come and go.
They moved with every melt and freeze;
They shattered boulders, leveled trees,
And carved, upon my granite rocks,
25 The terraced walls of slabs and blocks
That trace each path, each downward course,
Where through the years, with crushing force,
The glaciers sculpted deep **ravines**
And polished rocks to glossy sheens.
30 At last this era, long and cold,
Began to lose its frigid hold
When, matched against a warming sun,
Its final glacier, ton by ton,

Retreated, melting, making way
35   For what I have become today:
A place of strength and lofty height;
Of shadows shot with shafts of light;
Where meadows nestle in between
The arms of forests, cool and green;
40   Where, out of **clefted** granite walls,

Spill silver, snow-fed waterfalls.
Here stand the pines, so straight and tall,
Whose needles, dry and dying, fall
Upon my sides to slowly form
45 A natural blanket, soft and warm;
Their graceful, swaying branches sing
In gentle breezes, whispering
To junipers, all **gnarled** and low,
That here, in stubborn splendor, grow.
50 And on my western slope I hold
My great sequoias, tall and old;
They've watched three thousand years go by,
And, in the endless **quest** for sky,
This grove of giants slowly grew
55 With songs of green on silent blue.
          I am the mountain.
          In each breath
I fell the pull of life and death
As untamed birds and beasts obey
60 The laws of predator and prey.
On me, the hunted ones reside,
Sustained by foods my plants provide:
I keep the pikas, small and shy,
That spread their gathered grass to dry.
65 I shelter rodents. In my trees
Live pinecone-loving chickarees,
While tunnels, crevices, and holes
Hold marmots, ground squirrels, chipmunks, voles.
I cradle herds of graceful deer
70 That drink from waters cold and clear;
I know each buck with antlers spread
Above his proud, uplifted head.
I know each doe, each spotted fawn,
In sunshine see, in shadows, gone.
75 I know these creatures, every one.
They, to survive, must hide or run;
As food for those that stalk and chase,
Within life's chain, they have a place.

Notice how *sky* rhymes with *by,* and *blue* rhymes with *grew.* This poem is made up of couplets, or pairs of rhymed lines. Groups of couplets are separated by the line *I am the mountain.*

Then, too, the predators are mine,
80 Each woven into earth's design.
I feel them as they wake and rise;
I see the hunger in their eyes.
These are the coyotes, swift and lean;
The bobcats, shadowy, unseen;
85 The martens in their tree-branch trails;
The masked raccoons with long, ringed tails;
The mountain lions and big black bears
That live within my rocky **lairs;**
The owls that prowl the skies at night;
90 The hawks and eagles, free in flight.
I know them all. I understand.
They keep the balance on the land.
They take the old, the sick, the weak;
And as they move, their actions speak
95 In tones untouched by right or wrong:
          We hunt to live.
          We, too, belong.
          I am the mountain.
          From the sea

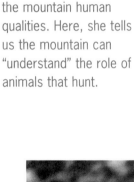

Diane Siebert uses personification to give the mountain human qualities. Here, she tells us the mountain can "understand" the role of animals that hunt.

100 Come constant winds to conquer me—
Pacific winds that touch my face
And bring the storms whose clouds embrace
My rugged shoulders, strong and wide;
And in their path, I cannot hide.
105 And though I have the strength of youth,
I sense each change and know the truth:
By wind and weather, day by day,
I will, in time, be worn away;
For mountains live, and mountains die.
110 As ages pass, so, too, will I.
But while my cloak of life exists,
I'll cherish winds and storms and mists,
For in them, precious gifts are found
As currents carry scent and sound;
115 As every gust and playful breeze
Helps sow the seeds of parent trees;
As silver drops and soft white flakes
Fill laughing streams and alpine lakes;
As lightning fires, hot and bright,
120 Thin undergrowth, allowing light
To reach the fresh, cleared soil below
So roots can spread and trees can grow.
      I am the mountain,
      Tall and grand,
125   And like a sentinel I stand.
Yet I, in nature's wonders draped,
Now see this mantle being shaped
By something new—a force so real
That every part of me can feel
130 Its actions changing nature's plan.
Its numbers grow. Its name is MAN.
And what my course of life will be
Depends on how man cares for me.
      I am the mountain,
135   Tall and grand.
      And like a sentinel I stand.

Climb the Highest Mountain

Which mountain is Diane Siebert writing about in this poem? The poet never says. Perhaps it is Mount Whitney. Not only is this the tallest mountain in the Sierra Nevada range, it is also the highest in the continental United States!

Giant Mount Whitney stands 14,495 feet above sea level. It is truly "tall and grand" and "like a sentinel" it stands.

Literature Practice

Answer these questions on a separate sheet of paper.

1. How many times does the line "I am the mountain" appear in the poem? Why do you think the line is repeated?

2. What animals make the mountain their home?

3. What is the new force that the mountain mentions at the end of the poem?

4. What does the course of the mountain's life now depend on?

5. What can humans do to take care of the mountain?

Big Yellow Taxi
by Joni Mitchell

Words to Know

LITERARY TERMS

ballad a story told or sung in rhyme

refrain lines repeated in a poem or song

SELECTION VOCABULARY

paved put a road surface on   **boutique** a small, fashionable shop

paradise a heaven on earth

They **paved paradise**
And put up a parking lot
With a pink hotel, a **boutique**
And a swinging hot spot
5 Don't it always seem to go
That you don't know what you've got
Till it's gone
They paved paradise
And put up a parking lot.

10 They took all the trees
And put them in a tree museum
And they charged all the people
A dollar and a half just to see 'em
Don't it always seem to go
15 That you don't know what you've got
Till it's gone
They paved paradise
And put up a parking lot.

"Big Yellow Taxi" is written in true ballad form. The second and fourth lines rhyme in three of the stanzas. Which stanza breaks with that form?

Each stanza ends with the refrain. How many lines make up this refrain? What are they?

Hey farmer farmer
20 Put away that DDT now
Give me spots on my apples
But leave me the birds and the bees
Please!
Don't it always seem to go
25 That you don't know what you've got
Till it's gone
They paved paradise
And put up a parking lot.

Late last night
30 I heard the screen door slam
And a big yellow taxi
Took away my old man
Don't it always seem to go
That you don't know what you've got
35 Till it's gone
They paved paradise
And put up a parking lot.

Literature Practice

Answer these questions on a separate sheet of paper.

1. What do you think the paradise in this ballad looked like before they put up a parking lot, pink hotel, boutique, and hot spot?

2. What does the poet say she didn't appreciate, or like, until it was gone?

3. What is the lesson, or theme, of this poem?

4. Think about other things we don't appreciate until they're gone. Then add another stanza to this ballad. Remember to make your second and fourth line rhyme. The last five lines should include the refrain.

Chapter Review

Summaries

- **Winter**—This poem tells how animals, people, and the poet herself prepare for winter.

- **The Sky Is Low**—This poem uses personification to describe a change in the weather. Low, dark clouds and a whining wind are threatening an approaching snowstorm.

- **Birdfoot's Grampa**—The young narrator of the poem is at first impatient with his grandfather. The old man insists on stopping the car to rescue toads from the wet roads. By the end of the poem, the narrator and the reader have a better understanding of the old man and his respect for life.

- **In Hardwood Groves**—In this poem, Robert Frost describes the way trees recycle their leaves. Frost tells how the fallen leaves become soil and nourish the trees so they can grow more leaves.

- **Sierra**—This poem is told from the point of view of a mountain. The mountain tells the history of the Sierra Nevada range from its birth millions of years ago. The mountain also tells of the plants and animals of the Sierra and the roles they play in the mountain's life. At the end of the poem, the mountain says that its future depends on the care it receives from people.

- **Big Yellow Taxi**—Joni Mitchell reminds us all that we cannot get back what we destroy. She tells how we do not appreciate nature and human relationships until they are gone.

Chapter Quiz

Choose the letter of the correct answer. Rewrite the sentences on a separate sheet of paper.

1. The theme of "Winter" is that
   a. everyone prepares for winter.
   b. winter is almost over.
   c. animals and humans do different things.
   d. no one is prepared for the cold.

2. In "The Sky Is Low," Emily Dickinson describes nature as
   a. boring.
   b. unpleasant.
   c. beautiful.
   d. funny.

3. In "Birdfoot's Grampa," why does the old man move the toads?
   a. He wants to save their lives.
   b. They might hurt the car.
   c. He hates toads.
   d. It is raining.

4. Robert Frost, in his poem "In Hardwood Groves," explains
   a. how things die.
   b. how nature recycles over and over.
   c. how leaves fill the trees.
   d. how flowers grow.

5. In "Sierra," the new force that is changing nature's plan is
   a. animals.
   b. earthquakes.
   c. humans.
   d. the mountain.

6. In "Big Yellow Taxi," nature is destroyed because
   a. people don't appreciate what they have until it is gone.
   b. the old man leaves in the big yellow taxi.
   c. everyone thinks a parking lot is a paradise.
   d. the tree museum needs to be built.

Thinking and Writing

Write answers to the following questions on a separate sheet of paper.

1. In "The Sky Is Low," Emily Dickinson personifies, or gives human qualities to, the weather on a winter day. Think about what human qualities you might give to summer. Then write two or three sentences that personify summer.

2. In "Birdfoot's Grampa," the narrator thinks that saving the toads is not important. The grandfather thinks it is important. Write a short paragraph explaining which person you agree with and why.

Unit Four Review

A. The following questions are about some of the selections you read in this unit. Write one or two sentence answers on a separate sheet of paper.

1. Why does Owen Chase believe the whale attacked in "Shipwreck of the Whaleship Essex"?
2. In "A Taste of Snow," why does Jeanne Wakatsuki Houston say the two Christmases are yin and yang?
3. How does the story "The First Tornado" explain tornadoes?
4. What is the lesson that "River Man" teaches?
5. Why do you think the old man in "Birdfoot's Grampa" saves the toads?
6. Why does Thoreau stop feeling sorry that Nature makes the hares thin?
7. Describe how nature recycles itself in Robert Frost's "In Hardwood Groves."
8. What is the strange experience that the narrator has in "A Visit to the Clerk of the Weather"?

B. Choose two of the essay questions below. Answer them on a separate sheet of paper. Write one or two paragraphs for each one.

1. Some of the selections in this unit teach people to respect nature. Choose one. Explain how your choice teaches this lesson. Use specific examples from the selection.

2. Many of these poems and stories use personification. What example of personification did you enjoy most? Explain.

3. Poems and stories about nature can have different themes. The theme of "Winter" is how people and animals prepare for winter. The theme of "Shipwreck of the Whaleship Essex" is that nature can be dangerous. Think of a theme that relates to nature. Then write a poem or an outline of a short story about nature. Make sure what you write reflects your theme.

CONFLICT

Chapter 11

Narrative of the Life of Frederick Douglass
  adapted from the autobiography by Frederick Douglass
Little Things Are Big
  an adapted essay by Jesus Colon
Chief Seattle's Oration
  adapted from the speech by Chief Seattle

Chapter 12

Ribbons
  an adapted story by Laurence Yep
Amigo Brothers
  an adapted story by Piri Thomas

Chapter 13

Ballad of Birmingham
  by Dudley Randall
Taught Me Purple
  by Evelyn Tooley Hunt
Simple-song
  by Marge Piercy
War Is Kind
  by Stephen Crane

Chapter 11

In the nonfiction selections you are about to read, three lives are shaped and challenged by social injustices. Yet, for each person, the challenge leads to a stronger understanding of who they really are.

Chapter Learning Objectives

- Learn about conflict
- Learn how to compare two things using an analogy
- Learn how genre names a type of literary work
- Learn what a paradox is
- Learn how figurative language makes writing memorable

Narrative of the Life of Frederick Douglass
adapted from the autobiography by Frederick Douglass

Words to Know

LITERARY TERMS

conflict a fight or a battle between two or more characters

analogy a comparison between two different things

genre a type of literary work, such as a novel, short story, poem, drama, biography, or autobiography

SELECTION VOCABULARY

reputation what people generally think about a person; fame

discipline punishment, correction

brute beast, animal

plantation a large piece of property on which crops are grown

moorings weights to hold down ships

fast held tight, fastened

hopper grain bin

curry groom, brush

assurance confidence

determination firmness of purpose or mind

My master and myself had quite a number of differences. He found me unfit for his purpose. . . . One of my greatest faults was to let his horse run away. It would go down to his father-in-law's farm, which was about five miles from St. Michael's. I would then have to go after it.

I had a reason for this kind of carelessness, or carefulness. The reason was that I could always get something to eat when I went there. Master William Hamilton, my master's father-in-law, always gave his

Frederick Douglass was born a slave. This story is from Douglass's autobiography. It describes one event that happened while Douglass was a slave. An autobiography is one type of genre in which the author writes about his or her own life.

slaves enough to eat. I never left there hungry, no matter how fast I had to return.

Master Thomas finally said that he couldn't take it any longer. I had lived with him for nine months. During that time he had given me a number of whippings, all to no good purpose. He was set to hurt or, as he said, to break my spirit. For this purpose, he loaned me for one year to a man named Edward Covey.

Mr. Covey was a poor man, a farm-renter. He rented the place upon which he lived and al' the field hands who worked on the farm. Mr. Covey had gotten a very high **reputation** for breaking young slaves. This reputation was of great value to him. It let him get his farm tilled at much less cost than he could have had it done without such a reputation. Some slave holders thought it wasn't much of a loss to allow Mr. Covey to train their slaves for one year. He could hire young help easily because of his reputation.

Mr. Covey was a professor of religion. He was a member and a class-leader in the Methodist church. All of this added weight to his reputation as a "slave-breaker." I was aware of all these facts. I had been told about them by a young man who'd lived there. Still, I made the change gladly. This way I was sure of getting enough to eat. This was not an easy task for a hungry man.

I went to live with Mr. Covey on January 1, 1833. For the first time in my life, I was now a field hand. . . . My first six months with Mr. Covey were the worst time of my life as a slave. We were worked in all kinds of weather. It was never too hot or too cold. It could never rain, blow, hail, or snow too hard for us to work in the field.

I was somewhat hard to manage when I first went there. But a few months of this **discipline** tamed me. Mr. Covey succeeded in breaking me. I was broken in body, soul, and spirit. My ability to bounce back from things was crushed. My mind became weak. My desire

On January 1, 1863, President Abraham Lincoln issued the Emancipation Proclamation, a law that freed slaves.

to read disappeared. The dark night of slavery closed in upon me. See a man turned into a **brute**.

Sunday was my only time to relax. I spent this day in a sort of beast-like state, between sleep and wake, under some large tree. At times I would rise up. A flash of energy and freedom would race through my soul. That feeling flickered for a moment and then vanished. I sank down again, mourning over my terrible condition. I sometimes thought of taking my life and that of Covey. But I was prevented by a combination of hope and fear. Now my sufferings on that **plantation** seem like a dream rather than a reality.

Our house stood within several yards of Chesapeake Bay. I have often, in the stillness of a summer's Sunday, stood all alone upon the banks of that noble bay. I've looked upon the waters with a sad heart and a tearful eye. I have traced the countless number of sails moving off to the mighty ocean. The sight of these sails always affected me powerfully. My thoughts would force me to speak. With no audience but God, I would pour out my soul's complaint. In my rude way, I would speak to the great number of moving ships.

"You are loosed from your **moorings** and are free. I am **fast** in my chains and am a slave! You move happily before the gentle breeze. And I sadly before the bloody whip! You are freedom's angels that fly around the world. I am bound in bands of iron! O, that I were free! O, that I were on one of your bold decks and under your protecting wing!

"Alas! Between me and you the muddy waters roll. Go on, go on. O, that I could also go! Could I but swim! If I could fly! O, why was I born a man of whom to make a brute! O, God, save me! God, deliver me! Let me be free! Is there any God? Why am I a slave?

"I will run away. I will not stand it. Only think of it—100 miles straight north, and I am free! Try it? Yes! I will take to the water. And when I get to the

Southern plantation owners bought slaves to work on their property and to grow crops in their fields. Many slaves were used on cotton plantations.

Here Douglass is comparing his life to a ship on an ocean. The ship is free and is like an angel that flies around the world. What does Douglass say his life is like?

head of the bay, I will turn my canoe loose. Then I will walk straight through Delaware and into Pennsylvania. When I get there, I shall not be required to have a pass. I can travel without being bothered.

"Let the first opportunity offer, and I am off. Meanwhile, I will try to be strong. I am not the only slave in the world. Why should I worry? I can take as much as any of them. It may be that my misery in slavery will only increase my happiness when I get free. There is a better day coming."

This I used to think. And this I used to say to myself. I was driven almost to madness at one moment. Then at the next, I accepted my terrible condition.

I have already said how terrible my condition was during my first six months with Mr. Covey. Then events caused a change in the way he treated me. You have seen how a man was made a slave. You shall see how a slave was made a man.

It was one of the hottest days of the month of August 1833. Bill Smith, William Hughes, a slave named Eli, and myself were busy fanning wheat. The work was simple. It required strength rather than brains. Yet to someone not used to such work, it was very hard. At about three o'clock that day, I broke down. I was gripped with a violent headache. I felt very dizzy. I was shaking in every part of my body.

Knowing what was coming, I gathered my nerves. I thought it wouldn't help to stop working. I stood for as long as I could stagger to the **hopper** with grain. When I couldn't stand it any longer, I fell. I felt as if I was being held down by a great weight. Of course, the fan stopped. Every one had his own work to do. No one could do someone else's work and have his own go on, too.

Mr. Covey was at the house, about 100 yards from where we were fanning. He heard the fan stop. He left

What is the conflict in this story? Predict what you think happens to change the way Mr. Covey treats Douglass.

Fanning wheat is a process of separating the parts of the wheat that can be made into flour from the parts that are unuseable.

right away and came to the spot where we were. He quickly asked what was the matter. Bill said that I was sick. There was no one to bring the wheat to the fan.

By this time, I had crawled away under the side of the fence that surrounded the yard. I was hoping to find relief by getting out of the sun. Mr. Covey asked where I was. One of the field hands told him. He came over to me and looked at me awhile. Then he asked me what was the matter. I told him as well as I could. I had barely enough strength to speak.

He then gave me a savage kick in the side. He told me to get up. I tried to do so but fell back down. He gave me another kick and again told me to rise. I again tried and this time succeeded in getting to my feet. I stooped to get to the tub with which I was feeding the fan. As I did, I again staggered and fell.

I lay down in this position. Then Mr. Covey took up the hickory stick that Hughes had been using to strike off the wheat. Mr. Covey used it to give me a heavy blow upon the head. It made a large wound, and the blood ran freely. Then he told me again to get up.

I made no effort to do so. I had made up my mind to let him do his worst. In a short time after receiving this blow, my head felt better. Mr. Covey had now left me to my fate. . . .

I spent the next day mostly in the woods. I had two choices. I could go home and be whipped to death. Or I could stay in the woods and be starved to death. That night I met up with Sandy Jenkins, a slave I knew. He had a free wife who lived about four miles from Mr. Covey's farm. Because it was Saturday, he was on his way to see her.

I told Sandy what happened. He very kindly invited me to go home with him. I did, and we talked this whole matter over. I got his advice as to what course was best for me to take. He told me, seriously, that I must go back to Covey. However, he said that before I went, I must go with him to another part of the woods.

Douglass runs away at this time.

There we would find a certain *root*, which he wanted
me to carry *always on my right side*. If I did, he said it
would make it impossible for Mr. Covey, or any other
white man, to whip me. Sandy said he had carried it for
years. Since he'd done so, he'd never been hit.

At first, I turned down the idea. I thought that the
simple carrying of this *root* would not do what he said
it would do. I did not want to take it. But Sandy told me
it was necessary. He said it could do no harm, even if it
did no good.

To please him, I finally took the *root*. Then
according to his direction, I carried it upon my right
side. It was Sunday morning. I started for home right
away. When I entered the yard gate, Mr. Covey came
out. He was on his way to a meeting. He spoke to me

very kindly. He told me to drive the pigs from a lot nearby. Then he walked toward the church.

Now this conduct of Mr. Covey really made me stop and think. Perhaps there was something in the *root* that Sandy had given me. I half believed the *root* was something more than I at first had taken it to be.

All went well until Monday morning. On this morning, the power of the *root* was fully tested. It was long before daylight. I was called to go and rub, **curry**, and feed the horses. I obeyed and was glad to obey.

While I was throwing down some blades from the loft, Mr. Covey entered the stable. He had a long rope with him. I was half out of the loft. Mr. Covey caught hold of my legs and began tying me up. I gave a sudden spring. As I did so, I was brought sprawling to the stable floor.

Mr. Covey now seemed to think he had me. He thought he could do what he pleased. But at this moment, I made up my mind to fight. I grabbed Covey hard by the throat. As I did so, I rose. He held on to me, and I to him.

My holding back was so unexpected, that Covey seemed startled. He shook like a leaf. This gave me **assurance**, and I held him. . . . He asked me if I planned on continuing to hold back. I told him I did, no matter what. I told him he had used me and beat me for six months. I was determined not to be used that way any longer.

With that, he tried to drag me to a stick that was lying just outside the stable door. He meant to knock me down. Just as he was leaning over to get the stick, I grabbed him by the collar. I brought him suddenly to the ground.

By this time Bill came. Covey called upon him for help. Bill wanted to know what he could do. Covey said, "Take hold of him!" Bill said his master had hired him out to work and not to help whip me. So he left Covey and myself to fight our own battle.

We were at it for nearly two hours. Covey finally let me go. He was rapidly puffing and blowing. He said that if I had not resisted, he wouldn't have whipped me half as much. The truth was that he had not whipped me at all. I thought he had gotten entirely the worst end of the fight. He had drawn no blood from me, but I had from him.

I spent six months more with Mr. Covey. In that time, he never laid a finger upon me in anger. He'd sometimes say he didn't want to get hold of me again. "No, you need not," I thought. "For you will come off worse than before."

Douglass makes an analogy between becoming free and being reborn. What is similar about these two things?

This battle with Mr. Covey was the turning-point in my career as a slave. It gave me a new **determination** to be free. I felt as I never felt before. It was a glorious rebirth, from the tomb of slavery, to the heaven of freedom.

I now promised myself something. For however long I remained a slave in form, the day had passed forever when I could be a slave in fact. I also let a fact be known about me. Whichever white man expected to succeed in whipping, must also succeed in killing me.

Douglass escaped to freedom in 1838. He then spent his life speaking against slavery.

From this time, I was never again what might be called fairly whipped. I remained a slave for four years longer. And I had several fights. But I was never whipped.

Literature Practice

Answer these questions on a separate sheet of paper.

1. What kind of man is Frederick Douglass?
2. What kind of man is Mr. Covey?
3. What is the conflict in this story?
4. Who do you think won the conflict? Why?
5. Douglass uses an analogy to compare freedom to rising from the dead. Write an analogy of your own that compares freedom to something else.

Little Things Are Big
an adapted essay by Jesus Colon

Words to Know

LITERARY TERM

paradox a statement that at first seems impossible but that may actually be or feel true

SELECTION VOCABULARY

subway a train that runs underground

platform where one waits for a train

courtesy good manners, kindness

prejudiced intolerant, closed-minded, racist

explode blow up, go off

racism the belief that some people are superior to others, bigotry

It was very late. It was the night before Memorial Day. She came into the **subway** at the 34th Street Pennsylvania Station. I am still trying to remember how she was able to get on the train. She had so much to deal with. She was holding a baby on her right arm. She had a travel bag in her left hand. There were two children, a boy and a girl about three and five years old, walking behind her. She was a nice looking white lady in her early twenties.

At Nevins Street, in Brooklyn, we saw her getting ready to get off at the next station. The next station was Atlantic Avenue. I had to get off at that station, too. I knew it was going to be hard for her to get off with a baby, two small children, and a medium-sized travel bag.

And here I was, ready to get off, too. I had nothing

The title of this selection is a paradox. Big and little are opposites. How can little things be big?

This story is set in New York City's subway system.

Subway trains are trains
that are underneath the
ground. Many people
think that subways are
very unsafe. They do not
expect other people to
be helpful on subways.

to carry. I did not even have a book. I almost always
carry a book. Without a book, I feel like I don't have all
my clothes on. But that night I had nothing.

The train came in to the Atlantic station. Some
white man got up from his seat and helped her out. He
put the children on the long, empty platform. There
were only two adults on the **platform** some time after
midnight on the night before Memorial Day.

I could see the long, steep steps going down to the
street. Should I offer to help her, as the white man had
done? Should I take the girl and the boy by their hands
and lead them down the long steps?

Puerto Ricans are known for their **courtesy**. And

here I was—a Puerto Rican—with people who needed help. It was past midnight. A white lady, a baby, and two white children needed help getting down the stairs.

But how could I go up to this woman? I am an African American man and a Puerto Rican. This white lady might be **prejudiced** against African Americans. How would she feel about an African American coming up to her in an empty subway station late at night?

What would she say? How would she react? Perhaps she was coming to the city from a small town with her children and a travel bag. Would she say: Yes, of course, you can help me. Or would she think I was just trying to get too friendly with her? Or would she think something worse than that? What would I do if she screamed when I walked up to her?

The author's questions help readers follow his thoughts as he tries to make a decision.

Could I be wrong about her? Every day, so many bad things are written in the papers about African Americans and Puerto Ricans. For a long, long minute, I could not decide what to do. Inside me were the manners that every Puerto Rican passes on from father to son. These manners were struggling inside me. If I went to her, the situation could **explode**. The prejudices people learn could suddenly burst out. These are the prejudices that keep people apart.

The conflict in this story is called internal conflict. The narrator is fighting with his own fears and feelings as he decides whether to help the woman.

It was a long minute. Then I walked by her as though I had seen nothing. I acted as though I did not care that she needed help. I was like a rude animal walking on two legs. I moved away from her on the long platform. I was almost running. I left the children and the travel bag and her with the baby on her arm. I reached the steps and ran down them two at a time. When I came out on the street, the cold air slapped my face.

This is what **racism** and prejudice can do to people and to a nation! This is what happens when

Why do you think the author addresses the woman directly here?

these false walls keep us apart from each other.

Dear lady, if you were not prejudiced, I failed you. I know there is one chance in a million that you will read what I have written here. I will take that chance, anyway. If you were not prejudiced, I failed you, lady. I failed your children. I failed myself.

I buried my courtesy early on the morning of Memorial Day. But I am making a promise to myself. If something like this ever happens to me again, I am going to offer to help.

Then I will have my courtesy with me again.

Literature Practice

Answer these questions on a separate sheet of paper.

1. Why does the narrator want to help the woman?
2. What is the conflict in this essay?
3. Why does the narrator decide not to help the woman?
4. Who does the narrator say he has failed?
5. Why do you think the author titled this story with the paradox "Little Things Are Big"?

Chief Seattle's Oration

adapted from the speech by Chief Seattle

Words to Know

LITERARY TERM

figurative language words that describe something by making comparisons

SELECTION VOCABULARY

oration a speech

centuries periods of a hundred years time

ancestors people in your family who came before you, such as your parents and grandparents

harbors places where ships can land

abandoned left alone, deserted

sacred holy; coming from God

regret to feel sorry for something that happened

visions things that are seen, especially in a dream or while praying

descendants people in your family who come after you, such as your children and grandchildren

invisible cannot be seen

Chief Seattle was a Native American leader in the Pacific Northwest. In 1854, he made a famous speech. During this time, the U.S. government took land from the Native Americans. Then Native Americans were forced onto small pieces of land called reservations. The governor of the Northwest offered to buy the land from Chief Seattle's people. In his speech, Chief Seattle accepted this offer. He really did not have a choice. Chief Seattle's speech describes many of the differences between the way Native Americans and whites think about the world.

—— ⊗⊗⊗ ——

Chief Seattle's speech is filled with figurative language. It begins with a personification of the sky. He says the sky "has wept loving tears" upon his people.

"But my words are like the stars that never change," is a simile, which is another kind of figurative language. Look for other examples of figurative language as you continue reading.

. . . The sky above us has wept loving tears upon my people for **centuries**. Although the sky seems changeless, it changes. Today the sky is clear. Tomorrow it may be covered with clouds. But my words are like the stars that never change. Whatever I say, the Great White Chief at Washington can be as sure of as he is that the sun will rise each day.

The Great White Chief at Washington says he wants to be our friend. This is kind of him. We know he does not need our friendship in return. His people are many. They are like the grass that covers huge

prairies. My people are few. We are like a few trees in a plain swept by storms.

The Great White Chief tells us that he wants to buy our lands. But he will allow us to keep enough land to live comfortably. This offer seems fair, even generous. He no longer has to respect our rights. And since there are so few of us left, we no longer need as much land.

There was a time when our people covered the land like the waves of the sea cover its sandy floor. But that time has long since passed. Now the greatness of our tribes is just a memory. I will not talk about how our end came too early. I will not blame my paleface brothers for causing it to happen sooner. We may also have been somewhat to blame.

Young people can be foolish. When our young men feel they are wronged, they get angry. They paint their faces black to show that their hearts are black. They can be cruel. Our old men and old women cannot stop them. It has always been this way.

It was this way when the White Men first pushed our **ancestors** west. But we hope that war between the Red Men and the White Men will never break out again. We would have everything to lose and nothing to gain. Young men think taking revenge is good, even if they die. But old men who stay at home in times of war know better. And mothers who have sons to lose know better as well.

Our good father at Washington tells us that if we do what he wants, he will protect us. His warriors will be our wall of strength. His ships of war will fill our **harbors**. Then our old enemies—the Hydas and Tsimpsians—will not frighten our women, children, and old men. Then he really will be our father, and we will be his children.

But can that ever be? Your God is not our God! Your God loves your people and hates mine. He puts his strong arms lovingly around the paleface. He

Chief Seattle refers to the President of the United States as the "Great White Chief at Washington." Elsewhere, he calls the President "our good father at Washington."

Chief Seattle also uses figurative language to describe white settlers and Native Americans. Phrases, such as "paleface brothers" and "Red Men," were once used to refer to the two groups. These phrases are not commonly used today.

The Great Spirit is the one spirit from which all other spirits came. Many Native Americans believe that everything has a spirit, including the sky, the earth, wind, trees, rocks, animals, and so on.

Seattle uses imagery from nature to tell of his people's troubles. Here, he uses imagery from the Pacific Ocean, which borders his lands. His people, he says, will disappear like a tide that goes out and never returns. Look for other references to nature as you continue reading.

leads you by the hand as a father leads his baby son. But he has **abandoned** his red children—if we are really his.

Our God, the Great Spirit, seems also to have abandoned us. Your God makes your people stronger every day. Soon you will fill all of the land. Our people are disappearing. We are like a tide that goes out and will never return. The White Man's God cannot love our people or he would protect us. We are like orphans who can look nowhere for help.

How can we be brothers with the White Men? How can your God become our God? Can he make our lives better? Can he make our people great once again? If the Red Men and the White Men have the same God, he must like the White Men better. He came to his paleface children. We never saw him. He gave you laws. But he had no word for his red children who once filled this huge land like stars fill the sky. No, White Men and Red Men are two separate races. We have separate pasts and separate futures. There is little in common between White Men and Red Men.

To us, the ashes of our ancestors are **sacred**. Their graves are holy. You leave the graves of your ancestors and seem to have no **regret**. Your religion was written upon tables of stone. It was written by the iron finger of your God so that you could not forget. The Red Man could never understand nor remember it. Our religion is the tradition of our ancestors. It is the dreams of our old men, given to them at night by the Great Spirit. Our religion is the **visions** of our leaders—it is written in the hearts of our people.

Your dead stop loving you and the land of their birth as soon as they die. They are soon forgotten and never return. Our dead never forget the beautiful world that gave them being. They still love its green valleys, its whispering rivers, and its great mountains. They love the people who are still living.

Our dead often return from the Happy Hunting Ground to visit, guide, and comfort us.

Day and night cannot live together. The Red Man flees when the White Man comes, like the morning mist flees before the sun.

However, your offer seems fair. I think my people will accept it. They will live on the reservation you offer them. Then White Men and Indians will live apart in peace.

It does not matter where we spend the rest of our days. We do not have many days left. The Indians' night promises to be dark. Not a single star of hope is in the sky. Sad-voiced winds moan in the distance. Death seems to be on the Red Man's trail. Wherever we go, we will hear the footsteps of Death behind us.

The Happy Hunting Ground is similar to heaven. It is the place where the dead live in peace.

And we will prepare to meet our end. We are like the wounded deer who hears the footsteps of the hunter.

A few more moons. A few more winters. Then not one of the **descendants** of the great people who lived in this land will remain. No one will be here to cry over the graves of our people who were once more powerful than yours. But why should I cry about my people's death? Tribe follows tribe, and nation follows nation. It is like the waves of the sea. It is the order of nature. Regret is useless. Your people's time of death may be far in the future. But it will surely come. Even the White Man cannot escape death. We may be your brothers after all. We will see.

We will think about your offer. When we decide, we will let you know. But if we accept it, it is only on one condition. We must be allowed to visit the tombs of our ancestors, friends, and children. Every part of this soil is sacred to my people. Every hill, valley, and plain has been made holy by some sad or happy event in the past.

Even the rocks are full of memories of events in the lives of my people. Even the dust upon which you now stand loves our footsteps more than yours. This is because it is rich with the blood of our ancestors. Our bare feet feel its loving touch. Our people who have died—braves, kind mothers, happy maidens, and even little children—love this earth. At night, we greet these returning spirits.

Then some day the last Red Man will die. And the memory of my tribe will become a myth among the White Men. Then these shores will be full of the **invisible** dead of my tribe. When your children's children think they are alone, they will not be alone. At night, when your city streets are silent, you will think there is no one there. But the streets will be full of our people that once lived and still love this beautiful land. The White Man will never be alone. Be kind to my people, because the dead are not powerless. Dead, did I say? There is no death, only a change of worlds.

Do you think most white settlers understood the Native Americans' feelings about nature and the land? Explain.

Chief Seattle's people and other Native American groups believe that when a person dies, he or she is alive in a different reality, or world.

Chief Seattle

Chief Seattle, or Seathl, became a chief at a very young age when his father died. He was a great orator, or speaker. Seattle, Washington, the largest city to be named for a Native American, was named in honor of this man who showed great friendship for white people.

In 1851, the first permanent white settlement was established in Chief Seattle's part of Puget Sound. Seattle welcomed newcomers to his country. At Seattle's suggestion, the white settlers set up a trading post in what is now the heart of the city of Seattle, Washington. In 1852, the settlement's name, Alki Point, was changed to Seattle.

In 1854, when Seattle was about 66 years old, Native Americans were beginning to be removed from the area and relocated onto reservations. Later that same year, many tribes developed a plan to drive the settlers out of their country. Chief Seattle's speech was made to Governor Stevens as a last attempt to save his land.

In 1855, all the tribes of the Puget Sound were moved onto a reservation. Seattle lived the rest of his life on the reservation. He died in 1866.

Literature Practice

Answer these questions on a separate sheet of paper.

1. Does Chief Seattle think the President's offer is fair? Explain.
2. How has the President promised to protect Chief Seattle's people?
3. According to Chief Seattle, what are some of the differences between white people and Native Americans?
4. Find three examples of figurative language in Chief Seattle's speech.

Chapter Review

Summaries

- **Narrative of the Life of Frederick Douglass**—Frederick Douglass describes being a slave. He is sent to Mr. Covey to be "broken." Douglass was beaten even when he was very sick. He runs away but must come back. Then he decides to fight back when Mr. Covey tries to beat him again. Douglass wins the fight. He is never beaten again.

- **Little Things Are Big**—Colon describes what happens on a subway train one night. He sees a white woman struggling with a travel bag, an infant, and two small children. Colon wants to help her. But he thinks she might be afraid of him because he is African American and Puerto Rican. He then decides not to help her. Later, he is sorry that he did not help her.

- **Chief Seattle's Oration**—Chief Seattle was a Native American leader in the Pacific Northwest in 1854. This speech tells how Chief Seattle's people have no choice but to sell their land to the United States government. Chief Seattle tells how his people and the white settlers are different. He asks only that respect be given to his people and to the spirits of his people's ancestors.

Chapter Quiz

Choose the letter of the correct answer. Rewrite the sentences on a separate sheet of paper.

1. In "Narrative of the Life of Frederick Douglass," why is Douglass sent to Mr. Covey?

   a Master Thomas wants Douglass "broken."

   b. Mr. Covey pays more money than usual for Douglass.

   c. Master William Hamilton does not give Douglass enough to eat.

   d. Master Thomas is very happy with Douglass.

2. Why does Mr. Covey stop whipping Douglass?

    a. Douglass gives up.   c. Mr. Covey has a root.

    b. Douglass fights back.   d. Douglass runs away.

3. In "Little Things Are Big," Jesus Colon tries to decide whether to

    a. help a white woman.   c. get off on Atlantic Avenue.

    b. admit he is Puerto Rican.   d. talk to someone on the subway.

4. Colon is afraid that the woman might be prejudiced against African Americans and Puerto Ricans, but he wants to

    a. explode.   c. struggle with the man.

    b. show courtesy.   d. act like he does not care.

5. In "Chief Seattle's Oration," Chief Seattle compares his people to

    a. a tide that goes out and   c. stars that never change.
       will never return.   d. the sky.

    b. the Great White Chief.

Thinking and Writing

Answer the following questions on a separate sheet of paper. Write one or two paragraphs for each one.

1. Why is the battle with Mr. Covey a turning-point in Frederick Douglass's time as a slave? Explain in your own words.

2. What does Chief Seattle say is one important difference between his people and white people?

3. Imagine that you are the woman from "Little Things Are Big." You have read Jesus Colon's essay, and you want to write back to him. Write him a short letter explaining how you felt that night. Tell him how you feel about his promise to himself.

Chapter 12

Sometimes we find it difficult to communicate with those closest to us. The stories in this chapter teach the joy—and the difficulty—of reaching out to one another.

Chapter Learning Objectives

- Learn about colloquial language
- Learn about conflict, including internal and external conflict
- Learn about dialogue
- Learn about the omniscient point of view

Ribbons

an adapted story by Laurence Yep

Words to Know

LITERARY TERMS

turning point the event in a story that leads to a solution of the problem

drawing conclusions combining your own experience with story details to figure out what is happening

foreshadowing hints that tell the reader what might happen in a story

SELECTION VOCABULARY

ballet a kind of dance, made up of special jumps and turns, that requires great skill

drool to let liquid run out of the mouth, as a baby does

stumped walked in a stiff way with heavy feet

belongings luggage; things that belong to someone

exotic unfamiliar; as if from another country

fluttered moved like wings flapping rapidly

alien strange; coming from another country

calloused hardened thick skin

assumed thought something was true

tainted ruined; damaged

spine the part of a book where the pages are bound together

The sunlight swept over the broad grassy square, across the street, and onto our living-room rug. In that bright, warm rectangle of light, I practiced my **ballet**. Ian, my little brother, giggled and ran around me while I did my exercises.

A car stopped outside, and Ian rushed to the window. "She's here! She's here!" he shouted

As you read, try to guess what the problem, or conflict, in this story will be.

Ballet is important to the narrator. Because the grandmother came, the narrator had to stop ballet lessons. How do you think this will make her feel about the grandmother?

excitedly. "Paw-paw's here!" *Paw-paw* is Chinese for grandmother—for "mother's mother."

I squeezed in beside Ian so I could look out the window, too. Dad's head was just disappearing as he leaned into the trunk of the car. A pile of luggage and cardboard boxes wrapped in rope sat by the curb. "Is that all Grandmother's?" I said. I didn't see how it would fit into my old bedroom.

Mom laughed behind me. "We're lucky she had to leave her furniture behind in Hong Kong." Mom had been trying to get her mother to come to San Francisco for years. Grandmother had finally agreed, but only because the British were going to return the city to the Chinese Communists in 1997. Because Grandmother's airfare and legal expenses had been so high, there wasn't enough money for Madame Oblomov's ballet school. I'd had to stop my daily ballet lessons.

The rear car door opened, and a pair of carved

black canes poked out like six-shooters. "Wait, Paw-paw," Dad said, and slammed the trunk shut. He looked sweaty and tired.

Grandmother, however, was already using her canes to get to her feet. "I'm not helpless," she insisted to Dad.

Ian was relieved. "She speaks English," he said.

"She worked for a British family for years," Mom explained.

Turning, Ian ran towards the stairs. "I've got the door," he cried. Mom and I caught up with him at the front door and made him wait on the porch. "You don't want to knock her over," I said. For weeks, Mom had been preparing us for just this moment. Ian was supposed to wait, but in his excitement he began bowing to Grandmother as she struggled up the outside staircase.

Grandmother was a small woman in a padded silk jacket and black pants. Her hair was pulled back behind her head. On her small feet she wore a pair of cotton slippers shaped like boots, with furred tops that hid her ankles.

"What's wrong with her feet?" I whispered to Mom.

"They've always been that way. And don't mention it," she said. "She's ashamed of them."

I was instantly curious. "But what happened to them?"

"Wise grandchildren wouldn't ask," Mom warned.

Mom bowed formally as Grandmother reached the porch. "I'm so glad you're here," she said.

Grandmother gazed past us to the stairway leading up to our second-floor apartment. "Why do you have to have so many steps?" she said.

Mom sounded just like a child. "I'm sorry, Mother," she said.

Dad tried to change the subject. "That's Stacy, and this little monster is Ian."

Here, the author makes the reader curious about the grandmother's feet, too.

In China, people bow to show respect.

"*Joe sun, Paw-paw,*" I said. "Good morning, Grandmother." It was afternoon, but that was the only Chinese I knew, and I had been practicing it.

Mother had taught us a proper Chinese greeting for the last two months. I thought Grandmother also deserved an American-style bear hug. However, when I tried to put my arms around her and kiss her, she stiffened in surprise. "Nice children don't **drool** on people," she snapped at me.

To Ian, anything worth doing was worth repeating, so he bowed again. "*Joe sun, Paw-paw.*"

Grandmother brightened in an instant. "He has your eyes," she said to Mom.

Mom bent and lifted Ian into her arms. "Let me show you our apartment. You'll be in Stacy's room."

Grandmother didn't even thank me. Instead, she **stumped** up the stairs after Mom, trying to get a smile from Ian, who was staring at her from over Mom's shoulder.

Grandmother's climb was long, slow, and difficult. *Thump, thump, thump.* Her canes struck the boards as she slowly climbed the steps. It sounded like the slow, steady beat of a heart.

Mom had told us her mother's story often enough. When Mom's father died, Grandmother had strapped my mother to her back and walked across China to Hong Kong to escape the Communists who had taken over her country. I had always thought her journey was heroic, but it seemed even braver when I realized how wobbly she was on her feet.

I was going to follow Grandmother, but Dad waved me down to the sidewalk. "I need you to watch your grandmother's things until I finish bringing them up," he said. He took a suitcase in either hand and set off, catching up with Grandmother at the foot of the first staircase.

While I waited for him to come back, I looked at Grandmother's pile of **belongings**. The boxes, laced with tight cords, were covered with words in Chinese and English. I could almost smell their **exotic** scent, and in my imagination I pictured sunlit waters lapping at beautiful docks. Hong Kong was probably as exotic to me as America was to Grandmother. Almost without thinking, I began to dance.

Dad came back out, his face red from climbing the stairs. "I wish I had half your energy," he said. Crouching, he used the cords to lift a box in each hand.

I pirouetted, and the world spun round and round. Madame Oblomov said that I should still practice every day. I had waited for this day, not only for Grandmother's sake but for my own. "Now that Grandmother's here, can I begin my ballet lessons again?" I asked.

Dad turned toward the house. "We'll see, honey."

Disappointment made me protest. "But you said I had to give up the lessons so we could bring her from Hong Kong," I said.

"Well, she's here."

Dad hesitated and then set the boxes down. "Try to understand, honey. We've got to set your grandmother up in her own apartment. That's going to take even more money. Don't you want your room back?"

Poor Dad. He looked tired and worried. I should have shut up, but I loved ballet almost as much as I loved him. "Madame put me in the fifth division already. If I'm gone much longer, she might make me start over again with the beginners."

"It'll be soon. I promise." He looked guilty as he picked up the boxes and struggled toward the stairs.

Dad had taken away the one hope that had kept me going during my time away from Madame. Suddenly I felt lost, and the following weeks only made me more confused. Mom started laying down all sorts of new rules. First, we couldn't run around or make noise because Grandmother had to rest. Then we couldn't watch our favorite TV shows because Grandmother couldn't understand them. Instead, we had to watch Westerns on one of the cable stations because it was easier for her to figure out who was the good guy and who was the bad one.

Worst of all, Ian got all of her attention—and her candy and anything else she could bribe him with. It finally got to me on a warm Sunday afternoon a month after she had arrived. I'd just returned home from a long walk in the park with some friends. I was looking forward to something cool and sweet, when I found her giving Ian an ice cream bar I'd bought for myself. "But that was *my* ice cream bar," I complained as he gulped it down.

"Big sisters need to share with little brothers," Grandmother said, and she patted him on the head to encourage him to go on eating.

When I complained to Mom about how Grandmother was spoiling Ian, she only sighed. "He's a boy, Stacy. Back in China, boys are everything."

It wasn't until I saw Grandmother and Ian together the next day that I thought I really understood why she treated him so much better. She was sitting on a kitchen chair with her head bent over next to his. She had taught Ian enough Chinese so that they could hold short, simple conversations. With their faces so close, I could see how much alike they were.

Ian and I both have the same brown eyes, but his hair is black, while mine is brown, like Dad's. In fact, everything about Ian looks more Chinese. Except for the shape of my eyes, I look as white as Dad. And yet, people sometimes stare at me as if I were a freak. I've always told myself that it's because they never learned manners, but it was really hard to have my own grandmother make me feel that way.

Even so, I kept telling myself: Grandmother is a hero. She saved my mother. She'll like me just as much

Here, the mother refers to traditional Chinese culture. Boys were often thought to be more important than girls.

as she likes Ian once she gets to know me. And, I thought in a flash, the best way to know a person is to know what she loves. For me, that was the ballet.

Ever since Grandmother had arrived, I'd been practicing my ballet alone in the room I now shared with Ian. Now I got out the special box that held my satin toe shoes. I had been so proud when Madame said I was ready to use them. As I lifted them out, the satin ribbons **fluttered** down around my wrists. I slipped one of the shoes onto my foot, but when I tried to tie the ribbons around my ankles, the ribbons came off in my hands.

I could have asked Mom to help me reattach them, but then I remembered that at one time Grandmother had supported her family by being a seamstress.

Grandmother was sitting in the big chair in the living room. She stared uneasily out the window as if she were gazing not upon the broad, green lawn of the square, but upon an **alien** desert.

A seamstress sews clothing.

"Paw-paw," I said, "can you help me?"

Grandmother gave a start when she turned around and saw the ribbons dangling from my hand. Then she looked down at my bare feet, which were **calloused** from three years of daily lessons. When she looked back at the satin ribbons, it was with a hate and disgust that I had never seen before. "Give those to me." She held out her hand.

I clutched the ribbons tightly against my stomach. "Why?"

"They'll ruin your feet." She lunged toward me and tried to snatch them away.

Angry and confused, I took a few steps back and showed her the shoe. "No, they're for dancing!"

All Grandmother could see, though, was the ribbons. She managed to struggle to her feet without the canes and almost fell forward on her face. Somehow, she caught her balance. Arms reaching out, she stumbled after me. "Lies!" she said.

"It's the truth!" I backed away so fast that I bumped into Mom as she came running from the kitchen.

Mom immediately **assumed** it was my fault. "Stop yelling at your grandmother!" she said.

By this point, I was in tears. "She's taken everything else. Now she wants my toe-shoe ribbons."

Grandmother panted as she leaned on Mom. "How could you do that to your own daughter?"

"It's not like you think," Mom tried to explain.

However, Grandmother was too upset to listen. "Take them away!"

Mom helped Grandmother back to her easy chair. "You don't understand," Mom said.

All Grandmother did was stare at the ribbons as she sat back down in the chair. "Take them away. Burn them. Bury them."

Mom sighed. "Yes, Mother."

As Mom came over to me, I stared at her in amazement. "Aren't you going to stand up for me?"

But she acted as if she wanted to break any ties between us. "Can't you see how worked up Paw-paw is?" she whispered. "She won't listen to reason. Give her some time. Let her cool off." She worked the ribbons away from my fingers. Then she also took the shoe.

For the rest of the day, Grandmother just turned away every time Mom and I tried to raise the subject. It was as if she didn't want to even think about satin ribbons.

That evening, after the dozenth attempt, I finally said to Mom, "She's so weird. What's so bad about satin ribbons?"

"She connects them with something awful that happened to her," Mom said.

That puzzled me even more. "What was that?"

She shook her head. "I'm sorry. She made me promise never to talk about it to anyone."

The next morning, I decided that if Grandmother was going to be mean to me, then I would be mean to her. I began to ignore her. When she entered a room I was in, I would turn around and leave.

For the rest of the day, things got more and more tense. Then I happened to go into the bathroom early that evening. The door wasn't locked, so I thought it was empty, but Grandmother was sitting fully clothed on the edge of the bathtub. Her slacks were rolled up to her knees and she had her feet soaking in a pan of water.

"Don't you know how to knock?" she snapped, and dropped a towel over her feet.

However, she wasn't quick enough, because I saw her bare feet for the first time. Her feet were like taffy that someone had stretched out and twisted. Each foot bent downward in a way that feet were not meant to, and her toes stuck out at odd angles, more like lumps than toes. I didn't think she had all ten of them, either.

This is the turning point of the story. Stacy is shocked by the sight of Paw-paw's feet. Can you draw a conclusion about why the ribbons may have upset Paw-paw so much?

"What happened to your feet?" I whispered in shock.

Looking ashamed, Grandmother flapped a hand in the air for me to go. "None of your business. Now get out."

She must have said something to Mom, though, because that night Mom came in and sat on my bed. Ian was outside playing with Grandmother. "Your grandmother's very upset, Stacy," Mom said.

"I didn't mean to look," I said. "It was horrible." Even when I closed my eyes, I could see her twisted feet.

I opened my eyes when I felt Mom's hand on my shoulder. "She was so ashamed of them that she didn't even like me to see them," she said.

"What happened to them?" I wondered.

Mom's forehead frowned as if she wasn't sure how to explain things. "There was a time back in China when people thought women's feet had to be shaped a certain way to look beautiful. When a girl was about five, her mother would gradually bend her toes under the sole of her foot."

"Ugh!" Just thinking about it made my own feet ache. "Her own mother did that to her?"

Mom smiled sadly. "Her mother and father thought it would make their little girl pretty so she could marry a rich man. They were still doing it in some of the back areas of China long after it was outlawed in the rest of the country."

I shook my head. "There's nothing lovely about those feet."

"I know. But they were usually wrapped in silk ribbons." Mom brushed some of the hair from my eyes. "Because they were a symbol of the old days, Paw-paw undid the ribbons as soon as we were free in Hong Kong—even though they kept back the pain."

I was even more puzzled now. "How did the ribbons do that?"

Mom began to brush my hair with quick, light strokes. "The ribbons kept the blood from flowing freely and bringing more feeling to her feet. Once the ribbons were gone, her feet ached. They probably still do."

I rubbed my own foot in sympathy. "But she doesn't complain."

"That's how tough she is," Mom said.

Finally the truth dawned on me. "And she thought my toe-shoe ribbons were like her old ones."

Mom lowered the brush and nodded. "And she didn't want you to go through the same pain she had."

I guess Grandmother loved me in her own way. When she came into the bedroom with Ian later that evening, I didn't leave. However, she tried to ignore me—as if I had become **tainted** by her secret.

When Ian demanded a story, I sighed. "All right. But only one."

Naturally, Ian chose the fattest story he could, which was my old collection of fairy tales by Hans Christian Andersen. Years of reading had cracked the **spine** so that the book fell open in his hands to the story that had been my favorite when I was small. It was the original story of "The Little Mermaid"—not the cartoon. The picture in the tale showed the mermaid posed like a ballerina in the middle of the throne room.

"This one," Ian said, and pointed to the picture of the Little Mermaid.

When Grandmother and Ian sat down on my bed, I began to read. However, when I got to the part where the Little Mermaid could walk on land, I stopped.

Ian was impatient. "Come on, read," he ordered, patting the page.

"After that," I went on, "each step hurt her as if she were walking on a knife." I couldn't help looking

Stacy finds out why Paw-paw thinks her ribbons are bad. How will Stacy show Paw-paw that her ribbons are different? Think about this as you complete the story.

"The Little Mermaid" is about a mermaid who falls in love with a prince. She gives up her tail to have legs. But walking on her new legs is very painful. When Paw-paw listens to the story, she thinks about her own feet. She sees herself in the same position as the mermaid.

up at Grandmother.

This time she was the one to pat the page. "Go on. Tell me more about the mermaid."

So I went on reading to the very end, where the Little Mermaid changes into sea foam. "That's a dumb ending," Ian said. "Who wants to be pollution?"

"Sea foam isn't pollution. It's just bubbles," I explained. "The important thing was that she wanted to walk even though it hurt."

"I would rather have gone on swimming," Ian insisted.

"But maybe she wanted to see new places and people by going on the land," Grandmother said softly. "If she had kept her tail, the land people would have thought she was odd. They might even have made fun of her."

When she glanced at her own feet, I thought she might be talking about herself—so I seized my chance. "My satin ribbons aren't like your old silk ones. I use them to tie my toe shoes on when I dance." Setting the book down, I got out my other shoe. "Look."

Grandmother fingered the ribbons and then pointed at my bare feet. "But you already have calluses there."

I began to dance before grandmother could stop me. After a minute, I struck a pose on half-toe. "See? I can move fine."

She took my hand and patted it clumsily. I think it was the first time she had showed me any sign of love. "When I saw those ribbons, I didn't want you feeling pain like I do."

I covered her hands with mine. "I just wanted to show you what I love best—dancing."

"And I love my children," she said. I could hear the pain in her voice. "And my grandchildren. I don't want anything bad to happen to you."

Suddenly I felt as if there were an invisible ribbon binding us, tougher than silk and satin, stronger even than steel; and it joined her to Mom and Mom to me.

I wanted to hug her so badly that I just did. Though she was stiff at first, she gradually softened in my arms.

"Let me have my ribbons and my shoes," I said in a low voice. "Let me dance."

"Yes, yes," she whispered fiercely.

I felt something on my cheek and realized she was crying, and then I began crying, too.

"So much to learn," she said, and began hugging me back. "So much to learn."

Literature Practice

1. Why does Stacy have to stop her ballet lessons?
2. What happened to Paw-paw's feet?
3. How does Stacy show Paw-paw that her toe-shoe ribbons are different?
4. Name two events that foreshadow the problem between Stacy and Paw-paw.

Amigo Brothers

an adapted story by Piri Thomas

Words to Know

LITERARY TERMS

colloquial language the everyday language people use when talking to friends

conflict a struggle or fight that a character undergoes

internal conflict conflict within a person; the character struggles to make a difficult decision

external conflict a character's struggle against something outside himself or herself, such as society, nature, or another person

dialogue the conversation between characters

omniscient point of view the author tells the thoughts and feelings of all the characters; the omniscient narrator uses the third person, *he, she*, and *they*, and stays outside the story

SELECTION VOCABULARY

lightweight a weight class for boxers from 127 to 135 pounds

bouts fights or matches

slugger hitter

division in boxing, a group or class of boxers

draw a tie; the fighters have equal points at the end of the match

sparring boxing

amigo a friend; an amigo brother is a best friend

champion the winner of a match or series of matches

challenger in boxing, the one who ights the champion

referee the person who judges the match

Antonio Cruz and Felix Varga were both seventeen years old. They were such close friends that they felt like brothers. They had known each other since they were children. They had grown up on the lower east side of Manhattan in the same apartment building.

Antonio was thin and had light skin. Felix was short and had a heavier, dark body. Antonio's hair was always falling over his eyes. Felix wore his dark hair in an Afro.

Both boys had a dream. Each wanted to be the **lightweight** champion of the world. Every chance they had, the boys worked out.

Before the sun came up, they would go running along East River Drive. They wore sweat shirts, short towels around their necks, and handkerchiefs around their foreheads.

While some kids were into negative stuff on the street, Antonio and Felix were positive. They slept, ate, rapped, and dreamed positive. The boys had a bigger collection of *Fight* magazines than anyone. They had a scrapbook of torn tickets from every boxing match they had ever been to. They could answer any question about a fighter.

Both boys had fought many **bouts** for their community. They had won medals—gold, silver, and bronze. Each boy had his own fighting style, too. Antonio's thin body and long arms and legs made him the better boxer. Felix's short body, with its heavy muscles, made him the better **slugger**. When the boys practiced with each other, it had always been a tough fight.

Now a big day was coming. The boys would fight each other in the **division** finals for the Boy's Club. The fight was August seventh, two weeks away.

The boys still ran together along East River Drive. But even when they were joking with each other, they could feel a wall going up between them.

One morning, they met as usual for their workout. They fooled around with a few punches in the air, slapped skin, and then ran along the edge of the dirty East River.

After they had run a mile or so, Felix said, "Let's

stop a while, bro. I think we both got something to say to each other."

Antonio nodded. They couldn't act as though nothing unusual was going on. Not when two buddies were going to be competing with each other in a few short days.

Antonio said, "It's about our fight, right?"

"Yeah, right," Felix said.

"Ever since I found out it was going to be you against me, I've been thinking about it," Antonio said. "I've been awake at night. I've been pulling punches on you, trying not to hurt you."

"Same here," Felix said. "I mean, we are both

Antonio's external conflict is with Felix. What is their conflict?

good fighters, and we both want to win. But only one of us can win. There ain't gonna be no **draw** in this fight."

Antonio nodded. "Yeah. We both know that in the ring, the best man wins. Friend or no friend. Brother or no brother."

"Let's promise something right here," Felix said. "When we get into the ring, it's gonna be like we never met. We gotta be like two strangers who want the same thing—and only one can have it. See what I mean?"

Antonio smiled. *"Si,* (Yes) I know. No pulling punches. We go all the way."

"Yeah, that's right," Felix said, "and listen, don't you think it's a good idea if we don't see each other until the day of the fight? I'm going to stay with my Aunt Lucy in the Bronx. I can use Gleason's gym for working out. My manager says he's got some **sparring** partners who fight like you."

Antonio said, "Watch yourself, Felix. I hear there's some pretty heavy dudes up in the Bronx. "Be careful, okay?"

"Okay," Felix said. "You watch yourself, too."

The **amigo** brothers were not ashamed to hug each other tightly.

The days before the fight passed much too slowly. The boys kept out of each other's way.

The night before the big fight, Antonio went up to the roof of his building. He tried not to think of Felix. He thought he had prepared his mind pretty well for the fight. But he wouldn't really know until he got in the ring. He wanted to knock out Antonio quickly, so his friend would not get hurt.

Up in the South Bronx, Felix went to a movie. He wanted to stop thinking about hitting Antonio's face with his fists. The movie was *The Champion* with Kirk Douglas.

In the movie, the champion was getting beat up. His face was being pounded into raw, wet hamburger. His eyes were cut and bleeding. One eye was swollen.

Notice how Piri Thomas uses dialogue to tell what is happening in the story. Here, he is using dialogue to explain the external conflict between the boys. Some of the words the author uses in the dialogue are colloquial. "There ain't gonna be no draw in this fight" is an example of colloquial language.

As Felix watches the movie, he begins to imagine that he and Antonio are in the movie. He sees himself as the champion. He sees Antonio as the fighter who is challenging Felix's championship title.

The other eye was almost swollen shut. He was saved only by the sound of the bell.

Felix became the **champion**, and Antonio became the **challenger**.

The champion was bent over. His nose was broken and bloody. The challenger thought he had the champ beat. He hit the champ with a left. The champ came back with a right that exploded into the challenger's brains.

Instead of the face on the movie screen, Felix saw Antonio's face. Felix saw himself in the ring. He blasted Antonio against the ropes. The challenger fell slowly to the ground. He was a broken, bloody mess.

Felix had found how to get himself ready for the fight. It was Felix the Champion vs. Antonio the Challenger.

Antonio was still out on the roof, worrying about the upcoming fight. He wondered what the fight would do to his friendship with Felix. He started having doubts. He cut out the negative thinking real quickly by doing some fancy fighting steps. He filled the night air with fast punches. Felix would not be his *amigo* brother tomorrow. He would just be another fighter to beat. Like Felix, Antonio hoped to win by knocking his friend out in the first round.

All over the neighborhood, people were interested in the fight. There were posters for the fight on the walls of stores. Lots of people bet on the fight. They bet everything from a can of soda to real money on the fighter they thought would win.

The fight was in Tompkins Square Park. That morning, the park was as busy as a beehive. Workers set up the ring, the seats, and the guest speakers' stand. The fights began shortly after noon. But people started coming into the park much earlier.

Community leaders got up to speak. Great boxers who had fought years ago also spoke.

At last it was time for the main event. Felix stepped into one corner as Antonio stepped into the opposite corner. The crowd roared. Antonio and Felix bowed to each other and raised their arms in the air.

The **referee** told the fighters, "No low hits. No punching on the back of the head. Let's have a clean fight."

BONG! BONG! ROUND ONE. Felix wasted no time. He came quickly up to Antonio with a left punch. Antonio slipped away from the punch. He hit Felix with one-two-three left punches. This series of punches snapped Felix's head back. Felix felt a shock go through his body. He knew now that Antonio was going to fight his hardest, friend or no friend.

Bong! It was the end of the round. Felix walked back to his corner. His ear was still ringing from Antonio's punches.

In this paragraph, you can almost imagine two people arguing inside Antonio's head. One voice is saying "You must win! Forget about Felix being your best friend." The other voice is saying, "How can you hurt Felix? Will he still be your *amigo* brother if you beat him?" This is Antonio's internal conflict.

Antonio danced back to his corner. Burns from Felix's gloves had made angry red marks on his ribs.

Bong! *Bong*! Round two. Felix rushed out of his corner like a bull. He gave Antonio a hard right punch to his head.

Antonio hit back with quick lefts and rights, giving Felix some painful blows.

Felix rushed at Antonio. He made a move with his right fist, then hit Antonio with his left. But Antonio ducked the blow and hit Felix on the chin. Lights exploded in Felix's head.

The crowd went wild as Felix's legs wobbled. He fought off Antonio's punches. Then he came back with a strong right punch that taught Antonio a lesson.

Antonio came back with a left hook. He got Felix in the eye. The pain was a haze in front of Felix's face. He swung out. He couldn't really see Antonio. But the roar of the crowd told him he had knocked Antonio down. Antonio got up, ducked, and threw a right punch that dropped Felix on his back.

Felix got up as fast as he could. His head was in a fog. The bell rang. It was the end of the round.

In the other corner, Antonio was doing what all fighters do when they are hurt. They sit and smile at everyone.

Bong! Round three—the last round. Up to now, the boys had fought an even fight. But everyone knew there would be no draw. This round was it.

This time it was Antonio who came out fast from his corner. Antonio's fists came fast and hard. Felix was pounded against the ropes.

The crowd loved it. So far the two boys had fought with *mucho corazón* (a lot of heart).

Both boys punched away. Felix's left eye was tightly closed. Blood poured from Antonio's nose. They fought toe-to-toe.

The crowd was quiet now. The sound of the boys'

This story is told from the omniscient point of view. The author tells the thoughts and feelings of both Felix and Antonio by using the pronoun *he*.

punches could be heard around the park. The referee could not believe how hard they were fighting each other.

Bong! *Bong*! *Bong*! The bell rang but Felix and Antonio didn't even hear it. They kept on punching. They were out of control.

Finally, the referee pulled Felix and Antonio apart. Cold water was poured over the boys.

The boys looked around. Then they ran toward each other. The crowd cried out. It looked like the boys were going to try to kill each other! But the fear of the crowd changed to cheers. The two *amigos* met and hugged.

No matter who won, they knew they would always be champions with each other.

The announcer got up to speak. He said, "Ladies and Gentlemen. The winner is . . ."

He turned to point to the winner. But suddenly he saw that he was alone in the ring. The two champions had already walked away, arm in arm.

Why do you think Antonio and Felix keep fighting even after the bell rings? What does the author mean when he says, "They were out of control"?

Literature Practice

Answer these questions on a separate sheet of paper.

1. Look at the first line of dialogue in "Amigo Brothers." Felix calls Antonio "bro." Find other examples of colloquial language in the dialogue.
2. Why do you think the colloquial language makes the dialogue in this story more interesting?
3. What is the conflict between Antonio and Felix?
4. What is their internal conflict?
5. From what point of view is this story being told? How do you know?
6. Why don't the boys stay to find out who won the fight?

Chapter Review

Summaries

- **Ribbons**—Paw-paw, Stacy's Grandmother, comes from Hong Kong to live with the family. It costs a lot of money to move Paw-paw to the United States. The parents can no longer afford to pay for Stacy's ballet lessons. When Paw-paw arrives, she acts cold toward Stacy. But she is warm and friendly to Stacy's brother. Stacy feels bad. She decides to show Paw-paw her dancing. But Paw-paw gets upset when she sees Stacy's dancing shoes and ribbons. Paw-paw tells the mother to take away Stacy's ribbons. Then Stacy finds out Paw-paw's secret. Paw-paw's feet were bound with ribbons when she was a baby. Paw-paw thinks that Stacy's ribbons will hurt Stacy's feet. Then Stacy explains that her ribbons are different. Now Stacy and Paw-paw understand each other.

- **Amigo Brothers**—This story is about the competition between two best friends, Felix and Antonio. They are both serious boxers. Both dream of becoming the lightweight champion of the world. In the division finals for the Boy's Club, however, they must fight each other. Felix and Antonio agree that they will not hold back. They both worry that they won't want to hurt each other. They also worry that the fight will hurt their friendship. The boys prepare for the fight physically and mentally. The fight is intense. After the fight, the boys hug each other. Then they leave together, without finding out who won.

Chapter Quiz

Choose the letter of the correct answer. Rewrite the sentences on a separate sheet of paper.

1. The conflict in "Amigo Brothers" results because
   a. Felix doesn't want to be friends anymore.
   b. Antonio wins the boxing match.
   c. two friends have to fight each other.
   d. some kids are into negative stuff.

2. Why do Felix and Antonio leave without finding out who is the winner?
   a. They knew they would always be champions with each other.
   b. The crowd was cheering too loudly for them to hear anything.
   c. The referee did not see that he was alone in the ring.
   d. They were out of control.

3. In "Ribbons," Stacy's parents cannot afford to continue her ballet lessons because they must pay for
   a. Chinese classes for Ian.
   b. new ballet shoes and ribbons.
   c. Paw-paw's airfare and expenses.
   d. airplane tickets to Hong Kong.

4. How does Stacy show Paw-paw that the ballet shoes and ribbons do not hurt her feet?
   a. She dances around the room.
   b. She shows Paw-paw her calluses.
   c. She sees Paw-paw's feet.
   d. She yells at Paw-paw.

Thinking and Writing

Write the answers to the following questions on a separate sheet of paper.

1. Imagine that you are a newspaper reporter in "Amigo Brothers." Write a short article describing the fight between Antonio and Felix. Make the story exciting. Include the fact that the boys are friends.

2. Imagine that you are Paw-paw in "Ribbons." Describe how you might tell your version of the story.

3. Both of these stories are about conflict between people who are close. Which story could you relate to the most? Why?

Chapter 13

In this chapter, you will read poetry about events that changed people's lives forever. The conflicts that each poem describes are difficult. But out of these conflicts, came strength and courage.

Chapter Learning Objectives

- Learn how setting can make a story come alive
- Learn what a quatrain is
- Learn the difference between a word's connotation and denotation
- Learn about rhyme schemes
- Learn what lyric poetry tells us
- Learn what a metaphor is
- Learn about verbal irony
- Learn how a poet uses apostrophe

Ballad of Birmingham
by Dudley Randall

Words to Know

LITERARY TERMS

irony the difference between what seems to be real and what is real

setting the time and place of a story

quatrain a four-line stanza

SELECTION VOCABULARY

fierce violent, cruel

choir a singing group

explosion blast from a bomb bursting

clawed to have dug with nails

"Mother, dear, may I go downtown
instead of out to play,
and march the streets of Birmingham
in a freedom march today?"

5 "No, baby, no, you may not go,
for the dogs are **fierce** and wild,
and clubs and hoses, guns and jails
ain't good for a little child."

"But, mother, I won't go alone.
10 Other children will go with me,
and march the streets of Birmingham
to make our country free."

The story told in this poem is based on fact. On September 15, 1963, in Birmingham, Alabama, four African American girls died when a bomb was thrown into their church.

The poet uses dialogue to explain what is happening in the story. The dialogue also shows one conflict in the poem—the conflict between a mother and her child.

What *seems* to be a dangerous situation to the mother? What is the *real* danger? What literary term names this difference between what seems real and what is real?

"No, baby, no, you may not go,
    for I fear those guns will fire.
15 But you may go to church instead,
    and sing in the children's **choir**."

She has combed and brushed her nightdark hair,
    and bathed rose petal sweet,
    and drawn white gloves on her small brown hands,
20 and white shoes on her feet.

The mother smiled to know her child
was in the sacred place,
but that smile was the last smile
to come upon her face.

25 For when she heard the **explosion**,
her eyes grew wet and wild.
She raced through the streets of Birmingham
calling for her child.

She **clawed** through bits of glass and brick,
30 then lifted out a shoe.
"O, here's the shoe my baby wore,
but, baby, where are you?"

Like most ballads,
Dudley Randall's is made
up of a series of
quatrains. How many
are in his ballad?

Literature Practice

Answer these questions on a separate sheet of paper.

1. What words and images tell us that the child in this poem is a girl?
2. In 1963, newspapers around the world reported thebombing of the Alabama church. How would a news reporter's telling of this story differ from "Ballad of Birmingham"?
3. There were many terrible happenings during the fight for civil rights in the 1960s. Why do you think the poet chose the bombing of a Birmingham church to write about?
4. Name two of the conflicts in the poem.

Taught Me Purple
by Evelyn Tooley Hunt

Words to Know

LITERARY TERMS

connotation an idea or feeling suggested by a word

denotation the plain meaning of a word

rhyme scheme the pattern of rhyme in a poem

SELECTION VOCABULARY

tenement apartment building

orbit area stayed in

molding the trim on a wall or ceiling

lack need

My mother taught me purple
Although she never wore it.
Wash-gray was her circle,
The **tenement** her **orbit**.

5 My mother taught me golden
And held me up to see it,
Above the broken **molding**,
Beyond the filthy street.

My mother reached for beauty
10 And for its **lack** she died,
Who knew so much of duty
She could not teach me pride.

The color *purple* suggests royalty. Long ago, the color purple was worn only by kings and queens. This connotation gives meaning to the poem. The mother tries to teach her child to be queenly. She wants her child to see beauty even in the dirty, poor city where they live.

Notice the rhyme scheme in each stanza. The last word of every other line rhymes.

Literature Practice

Answer these questions on a separate sheet of paper.

1. Where do the mother and child live? Use words from the poem to support your answer.

2. What connotation of the word *golden* in line 5 comes to mind?

3. a.) Why does the speaker of the poem say that her mother could not teach her pride?
   b.) Why might learning pride be important to the speaker of the poem?

4. Why do you think the mother wanted her child to see beauty?

5. The rhyme scheme in the following nursery rhyme is a a b c c b. The first rhyme is labeled *a*, the second is *b*, and the third is *c*. What is the rhyme scheme of "Taught Me Purple"? Hint: The rhymes will go up to the letter *e*.

Doctor Foster	a
Went to Gloucester	a
In a shower of rain.	b
He stepped in a puddle	c
Right up to his middle,	c
And never went there again.	b

6. What do you think is the conflict in this poem?

Simple-song
by Marge Piercy

Words to Know

LITERARY TERMS

lyric poem a poem that is like a song; it expresses strong feelings about something

metaphor a comparison that does not use the words *like* or *as*

SELECTION VOCABULARY

communicate talk; express thoughts and feelings

weary tiresome

clumsy awkward

outlive last longer than someone or something else

When we are going toward someone we say
you are just like me
your thoughts are my brothers and sisters
word matches word
5 how easy to be together.

When we are leaving someone we say
how strange you are
we cannot **communicate**
we can never agree
10 how hard, hard and **weary** to be together.

"Simple-song" is free verse. It has no rhyme scheme or rhythm pattern. Yet, it holds together well. Here's how:
1. Each stanza has repeated words.
2. The first and last lines of the first two stanzas are similar.
3. Each stanza is a complete idea.

Look back at the definition of the literary term *lyric poem*. How does "Simple-song" fit that definition?

We are not different nor alike
but each strange in his leather bodies
sealed in skin and reaching out **clumsy** hands
and loving is an act
15 that cannot **outlive**
the open hand
the open eye
the door in the chest standing open.

Literature Practice

Answer these questions on a separate sheet of paper.

1. The metaphor in the first stanza compares a loved one's thoughts to "brothers and sisters." Make up a metaphor that compares those same thoughts when the relationship is ending.

2. The last line of the first stanza sounds light and happy: "how easy to be together." Compare its sound to the line: "how hard, hard and weary to be together." How is that line different? What makes it sound so different?

3. Reread the last stanza. Explain in your own words what the poet is saying. What is the conflict she sees in human relationships? Refer to lines in the poem in your explanation.

War Is Kind

by Stephen Crane

Words to Know

LITERARY TERMS

verbal irony what is meant may be the opposite of what is said

apostrophe in this figure of speech, the poet talks to, or addresses, a person or thing that is not present

SELECTION VOCABULARY

affrighted frightened

steed war horse

hoarse grating, harsh

regiment group of soldiers

corpses bodies of dead people

trenches ditches, gullies

virtue goodness, uprightness, excellence

slaughter killing, slaying

shroud cloth used to cover the dead

The poet says war is kind, but he tells how war is terrible. The poet says we should not cry for the thousands of men who die. We must tell soldiers that killing and dying are good. But the poet tells how young women lose their lovers in war, babies lose their fathers, and mothers lose their sons. Men die terrible deaths in war. War is not kind, but cruel.

—∞∞∞—

Do not weep, maiden, for war is kind.
Because your lover threw wild hands toward the sky
And the **affrighted** **steed** ran on alone,
Do not weep.
5 War is kind.

There are three apostrophes in "War Is Kind." In the first line, Crane addresses a young woman whose boyfriend is killed in battle. "Do not weep, maiden . . ." he tells her. What are the other two apostrophes in the poem? Whom do they address?

Hoarse, booming drums of the **regiment**,
Little souls who thirst for fight,
These men were born to drill and die.
The unexplained glory flies above them,
10 Great is the battle-god, great, and his kingdom—
A field where a thousand **corpses** lie.

Do not weep, babe, for war is kind.
Because your father tumbled in the yellow **trenches**,
Raged at his breast, gulped and died,
15 Do not weep.
War is kind.

Swift blazing flag of the regiment,
Eagle with crest of red and gold,
These men were born to drill and die.
20 Point for them the **virtue** of **slaughter**,
Make plain to them the excellence of killing
And a field where a thousand corpses lie.

Mother whose heart hung humble as a button
On the bright splendid **shroud** of your son,
25 Do not weep.
War is kind.

Is war kind? Of course not! This poem is filled with this kind of *verbal irony*. In verbal irony, what is meant may be the opposite of what is said.

America's War with Itself

It was the spring of 1861. The newspaper headlines said, "War!" The Civil War had started. America's men threw their hats in the air and cheered.

From Maine to Florida, young men raced to join their side's army. Everyone thought the war would be over in a month. No one wanted to be left out of the excitement!

Few living Americans had seen war. Only a few people who fought in the American Revolution were still alive. Only they could remember how horrible war can be. Who would have listened to them, anyway?

Four long years later, over 600,000 Americans had died in the war. All over the country were fields "where a thousand corpses lie." Death was all around. Cities were destroyed, orphanages were filled, starvation was everywhere. America had seen war. It no longer seemed exciting.

Literature Practice

Answer these questions on a separate sheet of paper.

1. List two examples of Crane's verbal irony.
2. a.) What lines from the first stanza does Crane repeat in the poem?
   b.) Why do you think he repeats these lines?
3. Who do you think Crane blames for war?
4. Who suffers during war?
5. Write a final stanza for "War Is Kind." Follow the pattern set by Crane in the six-line stanzas.

Chapter Review

Summaries

- **Ballad of Birmingham**—A girl asks her mother if she can go on a civil rights march. Her mother says no. The mother tells her that it is not safe to march. Instead, the mother sends her daughter to church. But it is not safe there, either. The church is bombed, and the child is killed.

- **Taught Me Purple**—This poem is about a mother and child who live in a poor, dirty city. Even though there is ugliness all around them, the mother teaches her daughter about beauty.

- **Simple-song**—This poem contrasts the beginning of a relationship with the end. The poet tells of the different ways someone else is seen at the beginning and at the end of a relationship. People try to reach out toward others. For love to last, people have to be open with each other.

- **War Is Kind**—Stephen Crane uses verbal irony to describe the horrors of war. Using apostrophes, Crane addresses a young woman, a child, and a mother who have lost loved ones in war. Crane shows that war is *not* kind.

Chapter Quiz

Choose the letter of the correct answer. Rewrite the sentences on a separate sheet of paper.

1. In "Ballad of Birmingham," how does the mother try to protect her child?
   a. She tells her child not to play outside.
   b. The mother does not allow her to march.
   c. The mother lets her child march in the streets of Birmingham.
   d. She tells her child to play outside, instead of marching.

2. What happens to the child in the church?
   a. She is killed by a bomb.
   b. She calls for her mother.
   c. She goes to the march anyway.
   d. She plays in a safe place.

3. The mother's conflict in "Taught Me Purple" is that she
   a. does not like the color purple.
   b. can see many colors.
   c. lacks beauty in her life.
   d. does not know her duty.

4. In "Simple-song," what do people say when they are leaving each other?
   a. how easy it is to be together
   b. you are just like me
   c. how hard and weary it is to be together
   d. your thoughts are my brothers and sisters

5. In "War Is Kind," Stephen Crane shows the reader that war is really
   a. great.
   b. happy.
   c. kind.
   d. cruel.

Thinking and Writing

Write answers to the following questions on a separate sheet of paper.

1. What conflict in U.S. society was "Ballad of Birmingham" written about? Explain.

2. Reread the last stanza of "Simple-song." Do you agree that people must be open or love does not last? Why or why not?

3. To which poem in this chapter did you feel a strong reaction? Explain why. Use examples from the poem in your explanation.

Unit Five Review

A. The following questions are about the selections you read in this unit. Write one or two sentence answers on a separate sheet of paper.

1. How does the little girl die in "Ballad of Birmingham"?
2. In "Amigo Brothers," why do Felix and Antonio believe that they are champions to each other?
3. What two groups of people are in conflict in "Chief Seattle's Oration"?
4. What is the message of "War Is Kind"?
5. What happens after Frederick Douglass fights Mr. Covey in the "Narrative of the Life of Frederick Douglass"?
6. How do racism and prejudice affect Jesus Colon's decision in"Little Things Are Big"?
7. In "Simple-song," what does Marge Piercy say loving cannot outlive?
8. Where do the mother and child live in "Taught Me Purple"?
9. Why does Paw-paw think Stacy's shoes and ribbons should be taken away in "Ribbons"?

B. Choose two of the essay questions below. Answer them on a separate sheet of paper. Write one or two paragraphs for each one.

1. In "Taught Me Purple," the poet uses the colors purple and gold to contrast with the gray ugliness of the city. If you were writing a poem about your own life, what colors would you use to describe it? Explain the connotation, or feelings, these colors have for you.

2. List each selection in this unit. Then tell whether it is about an internal conflict, an external conflict, or both. Which kind of conflict do you relate to the most? Explain.

3. Of all the genres covered in this unit, which is your favorite? Give an example of the genre by naming a selection. Then explain why you prefer that genre over the others.

FAMILY

Chapter 14

from Childtimes
   by Eloise Greenfield and Lessie Jones Little
The Medicine Bag
   an adapted story by Virginia Driving Hawk Sneve
Abuela
   an adapted story by Rosa Elena Yzquierdo

Chapter 15

I Ask My Mother to Sing
   by Li-Young Lee
My Father's Song
   by Simon J. Ortiz
Mother to Son
   by Langston Hughes
Lineage
   by Margaret Walker
Abuela
   by Denise Alcalá
Grandma Ling
   by Amy Ling
Aunt Sue's Stories
   by Langston Hughes
Bailando
   by Pat Mora
To My Dear and Loving Husband
   by Anne Bradstreet

Unit Review

Chapter 14

A family has many kinds of people in it. Some members are wiser, and they help us along. Other members are younger, and they learn from our experiences, as well as have their own. Our families are always a part of us. Sometimes, we try to forget that. Other times, that is wonderful to remember.

Chapter Learning Objectives

- Learn to identify an autobiography
- Learn about the first-person point of view in storytelling
- Learn to understand characters' motivations
- Learn to understand the conflict in a story
- Learn to draw conclusions about the reading

from Childtimes
by Eloise Greenfield and Lessie Jones Little

Words to Know

LITERARY TERMS

autobiography   a true story about a person, told by that person

first-person point of view   in an autobiography, the writer telling the story with the pronoun *I*

SELECTION VOCABULARY

lopsided uneven

pout make a face to show you are unhappy

joint a section of a finger

mantel a shelf over a fireplace

commence start; begin

challenging daring someone to a contest

stroke a sudden attack of illness

descendants family that comes after someone

procession people moving forward one after another

Mama Sewing

I don't know why Mama ever sewed for me. She sewed for other people, made beautiful dresses and suits and blouses, and got paid for doing it. But I don't know why she sewed for me. I was so mean.

It was all right in the days when she had to make my dresses a little longer in the front than in the back to make up for the way I stood, with my legs pushed back and my stomach stuck out. I was little then, and I trusted Mama. But when I got older, I worried.

This passage is written from the first-person point of view. That means that the person telling the story, or the narrator, is part of the story. What do you know so far about the narrator?

Mama would turn the dress on the wrong side and slide it over my head, being careful not to let the pins stick me. She'd kneel on the floor with her pin cushion, fitting the dress on me, and I'd look down at that dress, at that **lopsided**, raw-edged, half-basted, half-pinned *thing*—and know that it was never going to look like anything. So I'd **pout** while Mama frowned and sighed and kept on pinning.

Sometimes she would sew all night, and in the morning I'd have a perfectly beautiful dress, just right for the school program or the party. I'd put it on, and I'd be so ashamed of the way I had acted. I'd be too ashamed to say I was sorry.

But Mama knew.

Pa

"Leave the children alone," he used to tell mamas and daddies. "They ain't doing nothing."

Pa was a sharecropper. He worked in the fields, farming the land for the white man who owned it, and got paid in a share of the crops he raised. Along with that, he had almost always had some kind of little business going, even when Daddy was a boy—a meat market, an icehouse, a cleaner's, a grocery store.

Long before I was born, Pa had been a member of the Marcus Garvey group that used to meet in Parmele on Sunday afternoons. It was one of thousands of branches of the United Negro Improvement Association headed by Marcus Garvey. They met to talk about the beauty and strength of blackness, and to plan the return of black people to Africa.

I didn't think my grandfather was afraid of anything except the frogs that came out of the mud-filled ditches at night and flopped across the yard, and he knew plenty of names to call them. The thumb on his right hand looked like a little baldheaded man. The top **joint** had been cut off in a farm accident, and he had put it in

The author tells what a sharecropper is. What new information does knowing that Pa is a sharecropper give you about who the narrator is?

Marcus Garvey was a well-known African American leader. Based only on what you have read here, what do you know about Garvey's beliefs and those of Pa?

a jar of preserving liquid that stayed on the front-room **mantel**. I never got tired of looking at it.

Children hung around Pa, nieces and nephews and neighbors, listening to his stories, giggling at his jokes. Some nights there would be just us—Wilbur, Gerald, and me, with our grandfather—sitting on the porch where the only light was that of the stars and the nearest house was a long way down the road. He'd tell scary stories, and get really tickled when we got scared. He swore his ghost stories were true.

"One night," he'd say, "me and my brother John was coming 'cross that field over yonder." He'd make his arm tremble and point toward the woods across the highway. "And we **commence** to hearing this

What more do you know about the narrator now? Who else is part of the family? What details give you that information?

strange sound. Ummmmm-*umph!* Ummmmm-*umph!* And we looked up and saw this . . . this *haint!*"

He'd twist his face and narrow his eyes in horror as he stared out into the darkness, and I could just feel all those haints hovering behind us, daring us to turn around and run for the door.

Sometimes Pa would stop right in the middle of a story.

"Then what happened, Pa?" one of us would ask.

"Oh, I left after that," he'd say, and he'd laugh. Then we'd laugh, small nervous laughs, wanting to believe that it had all been just a joke.

Every year when it was time for us to leave, a sudden change would come over Pa. One minute he'd be **challenging** Daddy to a foot race that never took place, and the next minute he was weak and sick, trying to get us to stay. He didn't think he would live to see us the following summer, he'd say. At breakfast he'd begin the blessing with, "Lord, I sure do thank You for allowing me to see my family one last time before You call me home," and he'd pray a long, sad prayer that brought tears to our eyes.

But finally, when nothing worked, Pa would give up and help Daddy load the car with suitcases and with sacks of fresh corn and peanuts. There'd be hugs and kisses and more tears, and then we'd drive away, leaving him and Granny standing on the side of the road, waving, waving, waving, getting smaller and smaller, until they blended into one and disappeared.

Pa never liked to leave home. Granny came to visit us a few times over the years, but Pa always made an excuse. He couldn't get away right then, he had too much work to do, or something. One year, though, he had to come. He'd had a **stroke**, and Mama and Daddy brought him to Washington to take care of him. The stroke had damaged his body and his mind, so that he didn't understand much of what was going on around him, but he knew he wasn't where he

From what you have read and from your own experience, what relation is Pa to the narrator? Use details from the story to support your answer.

wanted to be. Mama would take him for a walk and he'd ask people on the street, "Which way is Parmele?"

My grandfather never got back to Parmele. He lived in Washington for eighteen months, and then, in 1951, at the age of seventy-eight, he died.

Martha Ann Barnes Ridley

I called my great-grandmother Mama Ridley, because that's what Mama called her. Actually, though, I don't think I ever really called her anything, except in my mind. I guess I must have talked to her sometimes, but I don't remember those times. I just remember that she was the small lady who lived in a bed, upstairs in Grandma's house.

Mama Ridley had fallen and broken her hip, and she never got out of bed again. She couldn't turn herself over, Grandpa had to do it, and she was in pain much of the time. But Mama told me that Mama Ridley loved her great-grandchildren. Whenever we got dressed up to go out, she'd say, "Let the children come in here before you go, so I can see what they got on." But nothing of her voice comes back to me. I can only see her lying there.

I was eight years old when Mama Ridley died. I wish so much that I had known her better. Hearing Mama and Grandma talk about her makes me know how much I missed.

Family

Family. All this running through my mind. . .

Saturday Sunday mornings Daddy making pancakes big as the plate Daddy making fat hamburgers leftover stuffed with rice green peas enough for everybody. Hot nights leave our hot one room sleep till midnight pillows blankets grass bed

Is Grandma the same grandmother who was married to Pa and lived in Parmele? How do you know?

beside the river. Lincoln Park evenings Mama other mothers bench-talk children playing.

Give Mama her lesson take my piano lesson teach Mama. Downtown Wilbur Gerald Eloise wait in the car have fun get mad have fun get mad. Go for a ride park car New York Avenue hill dark watch trains wave passengers sitting in lighted window squares sliding by. Gerald tell us the movie tell us show us be the gangster be the good guy be the funny guy tell us show us. Look out the window wait wait snow

This part of the story is run together without much punctuation. Why might a writer change his or her way of writing like this?

stopping Daddy going to make snow ice cream ready to eat without freezing.

Vedie little sister turning somersaults we laugh. Vera baby sister fat baby laughing we laugh. Play games I'm thinking of a word I'm thinking of a word that starts with *S* guess give a clue it's blue. Radio hear-see squeaking door ghosts scary music. Parade take turns on Daddy's shoulder watch the floats watch the firemen march watch the horns watch the sound of the bass drum.

Easter Monday picnic zoo dyed eggs lionhouse popcorn polar bear picnic. Merry-go-round Mama laughing. Sparrow's Beach sun water-splashing sandy legs Mama laughing. Mama laughing. . . .

All this running through my mind now, running through my mind now.

Family.

Well—our stories are told. Grandma's, Mama's, and mine. It's been good, stopping for a while to catch up to the past. It has filled me with both a great sadness and a great joy. Sadness to look back at suffering, joy to feel the unbreakable threads of strength.

Now, it's time for us to look forward again, to see where it is that we're going. Maybe years from now, our **descendants** will want to stop and tell the story of their time and their place in this **procession** of children.

A childtime is a mighty thing.

Why might the author believe that "childtime is a mighty thing"?

Literature Practice

Answer these questions on a separate sheet of paper.

1. From what point of view is the story written?

2. Why does the author pout when her mother sews her clothes?

3. Which one or more of the following words accurately describes Pa? Explain your answer.

   funny   old   brave   proud   scary   sick

4. What does the author remember most about Mama Ridley?

5. Why might the author have written the last part of "Family" without very much punctuation?

The Medicine Bag

an adapted story by Virginia Driving Hawk Sneve

Words to Know

LITERARY TERM

character's motivation the reason a character does what he or she does in a story

conflict the problem that needs to be solved in a story

SELECTION VOCABULARY

impressed made someone think highly of something

exaggerated made something seem better than it really is

authentic genuine; real

stately appearing important and worthy of respect

muttered said softly

trembling shaking; shivering

reluctantly not wanting to do something; unwillingly

descendants family that comes after someone

patiently calmly putting up with something

seldom not often; rarely

protection defense against harm or danger

My kid sister Cheryl and I liked to brag about our grandpa, Joe Iron Shell. He was a Sioux Indian. Our friends had always lived in the city. They only knew about Indians from movies and TV. They were **impressed** by our stories. Maybe we **exaggerated** and made Grandpa and the reservation seem wonderful. But when we came back to Iowa after visiting Grandpa, we always had some exciting story to *tell*.

The narrator is the person or character telling the story. In the first two paragraphs, the narrator tells how proud he is of his grandfather. What details help you to understand how the narrator feels about his grandfather?

We always had some **authentic** Sioux article to show our friends. One year Cheryl had new moccasins that Grandpa had made. On another visit Grandpa gave me a drum. It was small, flat, and round and was made from cow skin. On the drum was a painting of a warrior riding a horse. Grandpa taught me a real Sioux chant to sing while I beat the drum with a stick. The stick was covered with leather and had a feather on the end. Man, my friends thought that was great.

We never showed our friends a picture of Grandpa. Not that we were ashamed of him. But we knew the great stories we told didn't go with the real thing. Our friends would have laughed if they'd seen a picture of Grandpa. He wasn't tall and **stately** like Indians on TV. His hair wasn't in braids. It hung in gray strings on his neck. And he was old. He was our great-grandfather. He lived all by himself on the Rosebud Reservation in South Dakota. He didn't live in a teepee, but in a shack made out of logs and tar-paper. So when Grandpa came to visit us, I was so ashamed and embarrassed I wanted to die.

In the second sentence of this paragraph, the author says, "Not that we were ashamed of him." At the end of the paragraph, the narrator says he *is* ashamed. How might someone be both proud and ashamed of somebody?

There are a lot of yapping poodles and other fancy little dogs in our neighborhood. Most of the time you'll hear them barking one at a time from their yard. But that day it sounded as if a whole pack of them was barking together in one spot.

I got up and walked to the curb to see what all the fuss was about. About a block away, someone was walking down the middle of the street. Around this person a crowd of little kids were yelling and dogs were yapping and growling.

Predict who this person will be. What do you think will be the conflict, or problem, in the story?

I watched the group as it slowly came closer. At the center of all the kids and dogs was a man wearing a tall black hat. He'd slow down now and then to look at something in his hand. Then he'd look at the houses on both sides of the street. All of a sudden I

knew who the man was. I felt hot and cold at the same time. I whispered, "Oh, no! It's Grandpa!"

I stood on the curb. I wanted to run and hide, but I couldn't move. Then I got mad when I saw how the yapping dogs were growling and nipping at the old man's baggy pants leg. He poked at them in a tired way with his cane. "Stupid dogs," I said. I ran to help Grandpa.

I kicked and yelled at the dogs to drive them away. They put their tails between their legs and ran in all directions. The kids ran to the curb where they watched me and the old man.

"Grandpa," I said. My voice cracked and made me feel dumb. I bent to pick up his beat-up suitcase, which was tied shut with a rope. But he put the suitcase right down in the street and shook my hand.

"*Hau. Tazoka,* Grandchild," he said in Sioux.

The whole neighborhood was watching. All I could

Was your prediction correct? What details in the story tell you what the conflict in the story will be?

do was stand there and shake the old man's hand. I saw how his gray hair hung down from his big black hat. The hat had a tired-looking feather in it. His suit was wrinkled. It hung like a sack on his body. As he shook my hand, his coat fell open. He was wearing a bright red shiny shirt. His tie was a string tie with beads on it. His clothes wouldn't look strange on the reservation, but they sure did here. I wanted to sink right into the street.

"Hi," I **muttered** with my head down. When I felt his bony hand **trembling,** I tried to pull my hand away. I looked at his face and saw how tired he was. I felt like crying. I couldn't think of anything to say. I picked up Grandpa's suitcase and took his arm. I led him up the driveway to our house.

Mom was standing on the steps. I don't know how long she'd been watching us. Her hand was over her mouth. She looked as if she couldn't believe what she saw. Then she ran to us.

She went to hug Grandpa, then stopped herself. I remembered that the Sioux didn't do things like that. It would have embarrassed Grandpa.

"*Hau,* Marie," Grandpa said as he took Mom's hand. She smiled and took his other arm.

We helped him up the steps. Just then the door opened with a bang. Cheryl came running out of the house. She was all smiles. It was clear that she was glad to see Grandpa. I was ashamed of how I felt.

Cheryl gave a happy yell. She said, "Grandpa! You came to see us!"

Grandpa smiled. Mom and I let go of him as he held out his arms to my ten-year-old sister. She was still young enough to be hugged.

"*Wicincala,* little girl," he said, and then he fell over. He had passed out. Mom and I carried him into her sewing room. We had a spare bed in there.

We put Grandpa on the bed. Mom stood there, patting his shoulder. She didn't seem to know what to do.

I said, "Shouldn't we call the doctor, Mom?"

Cheryl, the narrator's sister, is not ashamed of her grandfather. The narrator is. Why do you think the two characters think so differently about their grandfather?

Here you learn the narrator's name for the first time. Add this detail to what you already know about him.

This bag might be important to the story. Predict what you think the importance of the bag might be.

"Yes," she said with a sigh. "You get Grandpa into bed, Martin."

I **reluctantly** moved to the bed. Grandpa wouldn't have wanted Mom to take his clothes off. But I didn't want to, either. He was so skinny that his coat slipped off easily. When I untied his tie and opened his shirt collar, I felt a small leather bag. It hung from a leather string around his neck. His old cowboy boots were tight. It seemed to hurt him a little as I jerked them off.

I put the boots on the floor and saw why they fit so tightly. Each one was stuffed with money. I looked at the money and started to ask about it, but Grandpa's eyes were closed again.

Mom came back with some water. She said, "The doctor thinks Grandpa is worn out from the heat." She wiped Grandpa's face with a washcloth. Then she gave a big sigh. "*Oh, hinh,* Martin," she said. "How do you think he got here?"

We found out after the doctor left. Grandpa was sitting up in bed. He was angry because Mom was trying to feed him soup.

Dad had come home from work just as the doctor was leaving. "Grandpa," he said, "tonight you let Marie feed you." He gently pushed Grandpa back against the pillows. Dad went on, "You're not really sick. The doctor said you just got too tired and hot after your long trip."

Grandpa took it easy then. Between sips of soup, he told us about his trip. After our visit to see him, he thought that he would like to see where his only living **descendants** lived and what our home was like. Also, he felt lonely after we left.

I knew everyone felt as badly as I did, and Mom felt the worst. Mom was the only family Grandpa had left. Even after Mom married Dad, who's a white man and teaches college in our city, and even after Cheryl and I were born, Mom made sure that every summer we spent a week with Grandpa.

How does the storyteller feel about his grandfather now? How have his feelings changed? Predict whether you think Martin's conflict is over. Why or why not?

I never thought that Grandpa would feel lonely after our visits. And none of us noticed how old and weak he had become. But Grandpa knew how old he was getting, and so he came to us. He had ridden buses for two and a half days. When he came to the city, he was tired and stiff from sitting so long. He had set out, walking, to find us.

Grandpa had stopped to rest on the steps of some building downtown. A policeman found him. Grandpa said that the cop was a good man. The cop had taken Grandpa to the bus stop. He'd waited with Grandpa until the bus came and then told the bus driver to let Grandpa out at Bell View Drive. After Grandpa got off the bus, he started walking again. But when he walked on the sidewalk, he couldn't see the house numbers on the other side of the street. So he walked in the middle of the street. That's when all the little kids and dogs followed him.

I knew everybody felt as badly as I did. Yet, I was proud of Grandpa. After all, he was eighty-six years old, and he had never been away from the reservation. But he was brave enough to take a long trip alone.

Grandpa asked Mom, "You found the money in my boots?"

Mom said, "Martin did. Grandpa, you shouldn't have carried so much money. What if someone had stolen it from you?"

Grandpa laughed. He said, "I would have known if anyone tried to take the boots off my feet. I've saved the money for a long time. It's a hundred dollars—for my funeral. But you take it now. Use it to buy food while I'm here. I don't want my visit to be hard for you."

Dad said, "You don't need to do that, Grandpa. It's good to have you here with us. I'm only sorry we didn't think of bringing you home with us this summer. You wouldn't have had to make such a long, hard trip."

Now you learn more about the medicine bag around Grandpa's neck. Why will Grandpa give the medicine bag to Martin instead of Martin's father?

A medicine bag holds objects that protect the person wearing it.

What is Martin's conflict, or problem, now? How do you think he will work the problem out?

This made Grandpa happy. He said, "Thank you. But do not feel bad that you didn't bring me with you. I would not have come then. It was not time." The way he said it, no one could argue with him. To Grandpa and the Sioux, a thing would be done when it was the right time to do it. That's the way it was.

Grandpa went on, looking at me. He said, "Also, I have come because soon it will be time to give Martin the medicine bag."

We all knew what that meant—Grandpa thought he was going to die. When a man in the family died, the medicine bag, along with its story, was passed on to the oldest male child.

Grandpa kept looking at me. He said, "Even though the boy has a white man's name, the medicine bag will be his."

I didn't know what to say. I had the same hot and cold feeling that I had when I first saw Grandpa in the street. The medicine bag was the dirty leather bag I had found around his neck. I thought, "I could never wear such a thing." I almost said it out loud. I thought of having my friends see it in gym class or at the swimming pool. I thought of the smart things they would say. But I knew I would have to take the medicine bag. I swallowed hard and took a step toward the bed.

But Grandpa was tired. He said, "Not now, Martin. It is not the time. Now I will sleep."

So that's how Grandpa came to be with us for two months. My friends kept asking to come to see him. I kept making up reasons why they couldn't. I told myself that I didn't want them laughing at Grandpa. But it really wasn't Grandpa I was afraid they'd laugh at.

Cheryl was happy to bring her friends to see Grandpa. Every day after school, she'd bring home a group of kids. There would be a group of giggling girls or little boys with their eyes wide with wonder.

Grandpa would sit on the patio, and they'd crowd around him.

Grandpa would smile in his gentle way. He would **patiently** answer all their questions. He'd tell them stories of brave warriors, ghosts, and animals. The kids listened without a sound. Those little guys thought Grandpa was great.

Finally, my friends came over. This was because nothing I said had stopped them. Hank, who was supposed to be my best friend, said: "We're going to see the great Indian of Bell View Drive. My brother has seen him three times, so he ought to be well enough to see us."

When we got to my house, Grandpa was sitting on the patio. He had on his red shirt. But today he also wore a leather vest decorated with beads. Instead of his cowboy boots, he wore moccasins with beads. Of

Grandpa got dressed up. Why do you think he does this?

course, he had his old black hat on—he was **seldom** without it. But his hat had been brushed. The white feather in it looked bright and proud. His silver hair lay over his shirt collar.

I stared at him. So did my friends. I heard one of my friends say in a low voice, "Wow!"

Grandpa looked up. When his eyes met mine, they looked as if they were laughing. He nodded to me, and my face got all hot. Grandpa had known all along I was afraid he would embarrass me in front of my friends.

"*Hau, hoksilas*, boys," he said and held out his hand.

My friends shook his hand one by one as I told Grandpa their names. They were so polite that I almost laughed. They said, "How, there, Grandpa," and even, "How-do-you-do, Sir?"

I said, "You guys want some lemonade or something?" No one said anything. They were listening to Grandpa. He was telling them how he'd killed the deer his vest was made from.

Grandpa did most of the talking while my friends were there. I was so proud of him. I couldn't believe how quiet and polite my friends were. Mom had to tell them to leave when it was time for supper. As they left, they shook Grandpa's hand. They said to me, "Martin, he's really great!"

"Yeah, man! Don't blame you for keeping him to yourself."

"Can we come back?"

But after they left, Mom said, "No more visitors for a while, Martin. Grandpa won't say so, but his strength hasn't come back. He likes having people visit, but it makes him tired."

That evening, before he went to sleep, Grandpa called me to his room. He said, "Tomorrow, when you come home, it will be time to give you the medicine bag."

I felt a hard squeeze where my heart is supposed to be. I was scared, but I said, "OK, Grandpa."

All night I had strange dreams about thunder and lightning on a high hill. From far away, I heard the slow beat of a drum. When I woke up in the morning, I felt as if I hadn't slept at all. School seemed like it would never end. When it finally did end, I ran home.

Grandpa was in his room, sitting on the bed. The shades were down, and the place was dark and cool. I sat on the floor in front of Grandpa, but he didn't even look at me. It seemed like a long time before he spoke.

At last, Grandpa said, "I sent your mother and sister away. What you will hear today is only for a man's ears. What you will be given is only for a man's hands." Then he was silent. I felt a cold wave down my back.

Why does Grandpa tell Martin that what he will hear is "only for a man's ears"?

When a Sioux boy turns twelve, it is time for him to seek the spirit that will guide and protect him for the rest of his life. He will find this spirit on a vision quest. The boy goes somewhere to be alone. For three or four days and nights, he does not eat or drink anything. As he grows weaker, he begins to dream. After the four days are over, he tells the holy man, or medicine man, about his dreams. The medicine man explains the dreams and tells the boy what his spirit guide is. Boys are often renamed after their first vision quest. The name is based on their vision and becomes their adult name.

According to the Sioux, Wakantanka is the greatest spirit and creator of the world.

Grandpa began, "Soon after my father became a man, he made a vision quest to find a spirit guide for his life. You don't know how it was back then. That is when the great Sioux of the Teton mountains were made to stay on a reservation. The Sioux had a great need for *Wakantanka*, the Great Spirit, to guide them. But too many of the young men were full of hate. They had no hope. They thought it was no good to look for a vision. Why should they, when the best part of their life was gone—when there was nothing for them but the reservation, which they hated? But my father kept to the old ways.

"My father got ready for his quest with a sweat bath, to make himself clean inside and out. Then he went alone to a high hill, without food, to pray. After three days he was given his sacred dream. In the dream he looked a long time, and then he found the white man's iron.

"My father did not understand this vision of finding iron. This belonged to the white people and at that time they were the enemy.

"He came down from the hill to wash himself in the stream below. There, he found a place where a camp had been. At the place where a fire had been built, there was a broken iron kettle. The broken kettle was like a shell. This was a sign that meant his dream was true.

"My father took a piece of the iron for his medicine bag. He had made the bag from elk skin years before, to use for his vision quest.

"My father went back to his village. He told his dream to the wise old men of the tribe. They gave him the name *Iron Shell*. But they, too, did not understand my father's dream. My father, now Iron Shell, kept the piece of iron with him at all times. He believed that it gave him **protection** from the evil things that went on in those sad days.

"Then a terrible thing happened to Iron Shell.

Soldiers took him and several other young men away from their homes. The young men were sent far away to a white man's school. Iron Shell was angry and lonely. He missed his parents and the young girl he had just married.

"At first, Iron Shell would not try to learn. He would not let the teacher try to change him. One day it was his turn to work in the school's blacksmith shop. As he walked into the shop, he knew his medicine had brought him there. Now he would learn and work with the white man's iron.

A blacksmith is a person who makes metal objects, such as horseshoes.

"Iron Shell became a blacksmith. That was his work when he came back to the reservation. All his life he kept the medicine bag with him, and never let it go. When he was old, and I was a man, he gave it to me. This was because no one made the vision quest anymore."

Grandpa stopped talking. Then he covered his face with his hands. I stared at him. I couldn't believe what I saw. Grandpa's shoulders were shaking with quiet sobs. I looked away until he began to speak again.

He said, "I kept the bag until my son, your mother's father, was a man and had to leave us. He had to fight in the war across the ocean. I gave him the bag. I felt it would keep him safe when he was fighting. But he did not take it with him. He was afraid that he would lose it. He died in a far-off place."

If Grandpa's son is Martin's mother's father, who is he to Martin? What relation is Grandpa to Martin?

Again Grandpa was still. I felt his sadness around me.

Grandpa cleared his throat. He said, "My son had only a daughter—your mother. It is not right for her to know these things."

He opened his shirt, pulled out the leather bag, and lifted it over his head. He held the bag in his hand. He turned it over and over as if he wanted to remember forever how it looked.

Grandpa opened the bag and took out two things that were inside. He said, "In the bag is the broken

Sage is an herb that is believed to have the power to purify, or clease, oneself.

piece of the iron kettle, a small rock from the hill of the vision quest, and a piece of the sacred sage." He held the bag upside down and dust—what was left of the sage—fell out.

Grandpa said, "After the bag is yours, you must put a piece of sage inside. Never open the bag again until you pass it on to your son." Grandpa put back the small stone and the piece of iron. Then he tied the bag.

Somehow I knew it was time to stand up. Grandpa slowly got up from the bed. He stood in front of me and held the bag before my face. I closed my eyes. I waited for him to put the bag over my head.

Grandpa said, "No, you do not need to wear it." He put the soft leather bag in my hand. He closed my other hand over it. He said, "It would not be right to wear it. In this time and place no one will understand. Put it away in a safe place until you are on the reservation again. Wear it then, when you put in a new piece of the sacred sage."

How do Grandpa's words to Martin show that he understands the conflict Martin feels? How does he help Martin solve that conflict?

Grandpa turned and sat again on the bed. He leaned his head against the pillow in a tired way. He said, "Go. I will sleep now."

I said, "Thank you, Grandpa," in a soft voice. I left with the bag in my hands.

That night Mom and Dad took Grandpa to the hospital. Two weeks later, I stood alone on the land of the reservation. I put the sacred sage in my medicine bag.

The Sioux Nation

The Sioux are not a single tribe of American Indians. They are a nation of tribes. The Dakota were the Mother tribe. Over time, the Dakota split into three tribes. These three tribes are the Dakota, Lakota (or Teton), and Yankton (or Nakota). Each tribe is also broken into smaller groups called bands. Originally, the Sioux lived on the American plains. This area is now Iowa, Minnesota, and North and South Dakota.

But, in the 1800s, the United States expanded. Settlers from the east coast moved through Sioux land in the 1840s and 1850s. There were many conflicts. Then, in 1874, gold was discovered on Sioux land. Settlers rushed into the area. Shortly after the gold rush, the U.S. government forced the Sioux onto reservations.

Conditions on reservations were terrible. There were too many people for too little land. People often did not have enough to eat. Many got sick and died. Even on the reservations, the conflicts were not over. In 1890, U.S. soldiers attacked the Sioux at Wounded Knee, South Dakota. Over 250 Sioux were killed.

Today, many Sioux still live on reservations. Others live off the reservation in cities and towns.

Literature Practice

Answer these questions on a separate sheet of paper.

1. Why is the author so embarrassed when Grandpa comes to visit?

2. What is Grandpa's motivation to come to see the family?

3. What is the conflict in the story?

4. Why does Grandpa tell Martin about the vision quest?

Abuela [Grandmother]

by Rosa Elena Yzquierdo

Words to Know

LITERARY TERM

drawing conclusions combining information from a story with information from your own experience to understand the real meaning of what an author has written

SELECTION VOCABULARY

ritual a practice done over and over, often religious

trailing hanging down

rickety weak; about to fall down

profusely many; freely

knead fold, press, and squeeze dough to mix it

heritage family or cultural background

My abuela begins her daily **ritual** with "Santa María, madre de Dios. . . ." She goes outside and waters the **trailing** plants surrounding the **rickety** old fence. Yerbas are growing **profusely** in Folger's coffee cans and an old Motorola. Abuela comes back inside and mixes flour, salt, and shortening to make tortillas for me. One of the tortillas cooking on the comal fills with air.

"That means you're going to get married," she says, then continues to **knead** and cook each tortilla with care, making sure to bless the first one of the stack.

"Abuela, I had a dream about fleas. What does it mean?"

Yerbas are herbs—plants used for cooking and healing. Since Abuela takes such good care of her plants and yerbas, what conclusion can you draw?

A *comal* is a brick or stone oven.

"It means you're going to get some money, mija [my little one]."

"Abuela, my stomach hurts."

"Te doy un tesito mija?" ["Would you like a little tea?"]

She picks the yerbas, prepares them, and makes a tea for me. No smell to it, but it tastes of milk of magnesia—maybe worse.

"Drink this tea every morning for nine days before breakfast, and your stomach-aches will disappear for one year."

She has always said to me, "Remember your dreams because they have special meaning. Remember the yerbas that grow in the wild, how they work, when to use them. Remember the cures for evil eye, fright, and fever.

"Sweep the herbs across the body and repeat three Apostle's Creeds to drive out evil spirits. Crack

Considering Abuela's cures, what conclusion might you draw about her?

Abuela tells her granddaughter to remember the cures she uses. She says that they are a part of her heritage. What does she mean by that?

an egg in a glass of water and say three Hail Marys to take away evil eye and fever. Remember these things. They are all a part of you—a part of your **heritage**."

She said once, "Yo soy mexicana; tu mamá es mexicana pero tú eres americana." ["I am Mexican, your mother is Mexican, but you are American."]

I just try to hold on.

Home Cures

Rosa Yzquierdo's grandmother is not the only one with home cures. People have always used plants to heal wounds and cure diseases. Many home cures are plain common sense. You might drink lemon tea for a cold. Lemons have a lot of Vitamin C. Vitamin C helps people fight colds. If you have a sore throat, you can gargle with salty water. Doctors have found that this kills germs in your throat. Today, scientists say that some home cures really work. So if someone offers you chicken soup, the next time you are sick, maybe you should try it!

Literature Practice

Answer these questions on a separate sheet of paper.

1. Who is telling this story?

2. What conclusion can you draw from Abuela's careful attention to her plants and yerbas?

3. Why does Abuela want the narrator to remember her cures?

4. To what two cultures does the narrator belong?

Chapter Review

Summaries

- **Childtimes**—Eloise Greenfield remembers three members of her family. Her mother sewed clothes for her. Her grandfather told her scary stories and made her laugh. Her great-grandmother, Mama Ridley, died when she was eight. She feels as though she has missed knowing someone special. The narrator also remembers that the family spent its weekends and holidays together.

- **The Medicine Bag**—Martin always bragged about his Native American grandfather. But when Grandpa comes to visit, Martin is embarrassed. He does not want to let his friends meet his grandfather. When Martin finally lets them, Grandpa makes him proud. Martin learns that his grandfather is going to die. Grandpa tells him about his history. Then Grandpa gives Martin the medicine bag that has been passed down from generation to generation.

- **Abuela**—The narrator's grandmother is a wise woman. Abuela seems to have a cure for any problem. She tells her granddaughter to remember her heritage, or background. As an American of Mexican descent, the narrator tries hard to hold on to her heritage.

Chapter Quiz

Choose the letter of the correct answer. Rewrite the sentences on a separate sheet of paper.

1. In "Childtimes," when the narrator's mother sews for her, she feels
   a. grateful.
   b. embarrassed.
   c. impatient.
   d. happy.

2. In "Childtimes," Pa is a
   a. fisherman.
   b. sharecropper.
   c. captain.
   d. teacher.

3. In "The Medicine Bag," Martin is ashamed of Grandpa because
   a. he is Indian.   c. he is very old.
   b. he doesn't look proud and stately.   d. he is sick.

4. Grandpa gives Martin the medicine bag because
   a. it must be passed down.   c. Martin now has money.
   b. Grandpa is afraid to lose it. d. Martin likes it.

5. Grandpa brings money in his boots because he
   a. doesn't need it any more.   c. doesn't trust the banks.
   b. doesn't want to be a burden.   d. wants to buy a new hat.

6. In "Abuela," when the granddaughter's stomach hurts, the grandmother
   a. begins to pray.   c. makes tea.
   b. explains a dream.   d. gets mad.

7. In "Abuela," the grandmother tries to teach her granddaughter
   a. to water yerbas.   c. to make tortillas.
   b. about her heritage.   d. about manners.

Thinking and Writing

Answer the following questions on a separate sheet of paper. Write one or two paragraphs for each one.
1. In "Childtimes," what are some things about Mama that make her memory special for the author?
2. What makes Martin finally understand Grandpa in "The Medicine Bag"?
3. At the end of "Abuela," what might the narrator mean by "I just try to hold on"?

Chapter 15

Families share many things. People in a family may have the same homes or belongings, or the same stories, hopes, and feelings. Memories of our families, and all that belongs to them, are powerful sources of inspiration.

Chapter Learning Objectives

- Learn how poets use images to create pictures
- Learn to recognize the first-person point of view
- Learn about descriptive details that create images and impressions
- Learn how metaphors are used in descriptions
- Learn about lyric poetry
- Learn how repetition can create a mood or feeling
- Learn about descriptive details that show behaviors and actions
- Learn to recognize the third-person point of view
- Learn how poets express emotion through rhyme and rhythm

I Ask My Mother to Sing
by Li-Young Lee

Words to Know

LITERARY TERMS

imagery pictures created by a writer's words to help you see something clearly

first-person point of view in poetry, the author, or poet, is the speaker of the poem

SELECTION VOCABULARY

accordion a musical instrument played by squeezing and pulling it

sway swing or move from side to side

picnickers people who are having picnics; eating outside

overturn turn or tip over

She begins, and my grandmother joins her.
Mother and daughter sing like young girls.
If my father were alive, he would play
his **accordion** and **sway** like a boat.

5 I've never been in Peking, or the Summer Palace,
nor stood on the great Stone Boat to watch
the rain begin on Kuen Ming Lake, the **picnickers**
running away in the grass.

But I love to hear it sung;
10 how the waterlilies fill with rain until
they **overturn**, spilling water into water,
then rock back, and fill with more.

Both women have begun to cry.
But neither stops her song.

This poem is written from the first-person point of view.

These are all places in China. Peking, or Beijing, is a large city. The Summer Palace is where the Chinese emperors lived. Kuen Ming Lake is in a park where people often have picnics. Why do you think the poet tells us about these places?

Literature Practice

Answer these questions on a separate sheet of paper.

1. What is the relationship of the "mother and daughter" in line 2 to the speaker of the poem?
2. What is the song about?
3. What imagery does the poet use to describe China?
4. Why do you think the poet asks her mother to sing?
5. a.) From what point of view is the poem written?
   b.) What details in the poem tell you the point of view?

Mother to Son
by Langston Hughes

Words to Know

LITERARY TERMS

metaphor comparing something to something else to help the reader "see" what the author is writing about

SELECTION VOCABULARY

crystal clear glass or stone that is expensive

splinters thin, sharp pieces of wood that can stick into feet or hands

---

Well, son, I'll tell you:
Life for me ain't been no **crystal** stair.
It's had tacks in it,
And **splinters**,
5 And boards torn up,
And places with no carpet on the floor—
Bare.
But all the time
I'se been a-climbin' on,
10 And reachin' landin's,
And turnin' corners,
And sometimes goin' in the dark
Where there ain't been no light.
So boy, don't you turn back.
15 Don't you set down on the steps
'Cause you finds it's kinder hard.
Don't you fall now—
For I'se still goin', honey,
I'se still climbin',
20 And life for me ain't been no crystal stair.

The poet uses a metaphor here. He compares life to climbing stairs. The mother says that her life was not a crystal stair. This means her life was not easy.

A *landing* (landin') is a place to rest between one set of stairs and the next.

Here the mother teaches her son a lesson. Her life was hard, but she kept going. She tells him not to give up or sit down. He must keep climbing. He must keep trying to succeed, no matter how hard life is.

Literature Practice

Answer these questions on a separate sheet of paper.

1. Who is the speaker in the poem?
2. Why does the mother compare her life to climbing stairs?
3. What might the poet mean by tacks and splinters in the stairs?
4. Why does the mother keep on climbing?
5. What is this mother trying to tell her son about *his* life by using the metaphor of stairs?

My Father's Song
by Simon J. Ortiz

Words to Know

LITERARY TERM

descriptive details details that help you feel, smell, hear, or see an image

SELECTION VOCABULARY

depth deepness; low pitched

tremble shake or shiver

particular separate; special

overturned turned or tipped over

furrow soil cut into a strip

plowshare the blade of a plow, or farm machine, used to cut the soil

unearthed dug up

burrow a hole an animal digs in the ground

scooped picked up

clod a small clump of earth and grass

Wanting to say things,
I miss my father tonight.
His voice, the slight catch,
the **depth** from his thin chest,
5 the **tremble** of emotion
in something he has just said
to his son, his song:

We planted corn one Spring at Acu—
we planted several times
10 but this one **particular** time
I remember the soft damp sand
in my hand.

The poet is remembering how his father looked and sounded when he talked.

Here the poet writes about one memory—planting corn in the Spring. The poet uses the words *soft* and *damp* to explain how the sand felt. As you read on, notice other words that he uses to describe what he felt and saw.

My father had stopped at one point
to show me an **overturned furrow**;
15 the **plowshare** had **unearthed**
the **burrow** nest of a mouse
in the soft moist sand.

Very gently, he **scooped** tiny pink animals
into the palm of his hand
20 and told me to touch them.
We took them to the edge
of the field and put them in the shade
of a sand moist **clod**.

I remember the very softness
25 of cool and warm sand and tiny alive mice
and my father saying things.

The poet describes his father's gentleness. When the father finds the mouse's nest, he teaches his son the value of all living things.

Literature Practice

Answer these questions on a separate sheet of paper.

1. How are the first and last lines of the poem similar?
2. Why does the poet miss his father?
3. What details of touch and feeling does the poet use?
4. What lesson do you think the poet learns from his father "saying things"?

Lineage
by Margaret Walker

Words to Know

LITERARY TERMS

lyric short poem that expresses the writer's personal feelings and thoughts

descriptive details details of how something looks, feels, smells, or tastes

SELECTION VOCABULARY

lineage a direct line of family
members from the past to today

toil work hard; labor

sowing planting

sturdiness strength

My grandmothers were strong,
They followed plows and bent to **toil**.
They moved through fields **sowing** seed.
They touched earth and grain grew.
5　They were full of **sturdiness** and singing.

My grandmothers are full of memories—
Smelling of soap and onions and wet clay
With veins rolling roughly over quick hands
They have many clean words to say.
10　My grandmothers were strong.
Why am I not as they?

Literature Practice

Answer these questions on a separate sheet of paper.

1. What kind of work does the poet remember her grandmothers doing?
2. What smells does the poet remember of her grandmothers?
3. In what way does the poet want to be like her grandmothers?
4. Why might the poet think that she is not as strong as her grandmothers?
5. Why is "Lineage" a lyric poem?

Taking Pride in Your Lineage

Did you know that there are people who get paid to find out more about a person's lineage, or family line? They are called genealogists. Why would someone pay money for this? Knowing your history can help you understand yourself. You might see how values have been passed down to you. You can learn how what happened in the past affects you, or you may come to understand your feelings or habits. You can take pride in how far you have come. You can celebrate your family's successes.

Most people do not need a genealogist. They find out more about their lineage on their own. They ask their parents or grandparents. They find records in government offices. They try to trace their roots, or where they came from.

One person who traced his own roots was Alex Haley. He was an African American writer. He knew that his family had been slaves. But he wanted to learn more. He spent a long time researching his lineage. Haley learned that his family had some horrible experiences. But they also had many successes. He even traced his history back to Africa. Haley wrote about his search. His book is called *Roots*. It became a best-seller. It was even made into a movie. It inspired many others to learn more about their lineage.

Abuela [Grandmother]
by Denise Alcalá

Words to Know

LITERARY TERM

repetition words or sentences used over and over to create a feeling or mood

SELECTION VOCABULARY

crinkling wrinkling
crevices folds; wrinkles

continuous something that keeps happening; constant
sturdy strong; stable
quivering shaking

Sing on
blue eyes, sparkle
in **crinkling crevices**
sing on
5 worn hands, **continuous**
in their motion
sing on
sturdy legs, dancing
against age, time
10 sing on
sing on
with head
thrown back
lips forever **quivering**
15 and heart rolling forth
sing on
to empty
walls
to beds and buses
20 guadalajara
will be nothing
without you

As you read, watch for details that the poet uses to describe her grandmother. Try to picture the woman. (What color were her eyes? How did her hands look? What did her legs look like?)

Guadalajara is a city in west central Mexico.

Literature Practice

Answer these questions on a separate sheet of paper.

1. What words does this poet repeat again and again?

2. What are the grandmother's "crinkling crevices" in line 3?

3. What does the poet remember her grandmother doing?

4. What might the poet mean about her grandmother "dancing/against age, time" in lines 8 and 9?

5. Do you think that the poet's grandmother has died? Explain your answer.

Grandma Ling
by Amy Ling

Words to Know

LITERARY TERM

descriptive details details that show what something or someone looks like

SELECTION VOCABULARY

measure walk across

sturdy strong

image copy; close likeness

tongue language

If you dig that hole deep enough,
you'll reach China, they used to tell me,
a child in a backyard in Pennsylvania.
Not strong enough to dig that hole,
5 I waited twenty years,
then sailed back, half way around the world.

In Taiwan I first met Grandma.
Before she came to view, I heard
her slippered feet softly **measure**
10 the tatami floor with even step;
the aqua paper-covered door slid open
and there I faced
my five foot height, **sturdy** legs and feet,
square forehead, high cheeks and wide-set eyes;
15 my **image** stood before me,
acted on by fifty years.

There is an old saying that if you dig a hole in the ground, you will eventually reach China. This saying probably came about because China is half way around the world. Why would this saying mean something special to a Chinese girl?

Taiwan is an island off the mainland of China.

Tatami is a kind of woven mat used as a floor covering.

Walls and doors are commonly made of paper in China.

She smiled, stretched her arms
to take to heart the eldest daughter
of her youngest son a quarter century away.
20 She spoke a **tongue** I knew no word of,
and I was sad I could not understand,
but I could hug her.

Literature Practice

Answer these questions on a separate sheet of paper.

1. What details does the poet use to describe her grandmother?

2. In what ways does the poet look like her grandma? In what way do the two look different?

3. Since Amy Ling did not speak Chinese, how was she able to tell her grandmother how she felt?

4. What point might this poet be making about family, even family she had never seen?

Aunt Sue's Stories

by Langston Hughes

Words to Know

LITERARY TERMS

third-person point of view someone other than a character is telling the story or poem

descriptive details details that show who someone is or how someone looks

SELECTION VOCABULARY

cuddles holds or hugs with love

bosom chest

dewy air that is full of water drops

mingle mix; join with others

Aunt Sue has a head full of stories.
Aunt Sue has a whole heart full of stories.
Summer nights on the front porch
Aunt Sue **cuddles** a brown-faced child to her **bosom**
5   And tells him stories.

Black slaves
Working in the hot sun,
And black slaves
Walking in the **dewy** night,
10   And black slaves
Singing sorrow songs on the banks of a mighty river
Mingle themselves softly
In the flow of old Aunt Sue's voice,
Mingle themselves softly
15   In the dark shadows that cross and recross
Aunt Sue's stories.

Neither Aunt Sue nor the child is telling the story. The poem is written in the third-person point of view.

The poet repeats the phrase "black slaves" and "and black slaves." What does this repeating tell you about the stories that Aunt Sue tells the boy?

And the dark-faced child, listening,
Knows that Aunt Sue's stories are real stories.
He knows that Aunt Sue never got her stories
20 Out of any book at all,
But that they came
Right out of her own life.

The dark-faced child is quiet
Of a summer night
25 Listening to Aunt Sue's stories.

The child understands
that his Aunt Sue was
once a slave herself. She
did not read about slaves
in any book.

Who might the child be?
Why do you think so?

The Harlem Renaissance

Langston Hughes was a great writer of his time. He was part of the Harlem Renaissance. Harlem is a section of New York City. It has a large African American community. *Renaissance* means rebirth. In European history, it was a time when past ideas were discovered again. The Harlem Renaissance was the rebirth of African American culture. It happened in the 1920s.

African American writers, artists, and musicians came to Harlem. There they met and exchanged ideas. They created many new works. African American culture inspired them. Writers explored how it felt to be African American. Zora Neale Hurston wrote during this time. Aaron Douglas and Augusta Savage created fine art. African American musicians created jazz and blues. These two kinds of music became world famous. Perfomers like Fats Waller and Duke Ellington drew huge crowds. The Harlem Renaissance produced many great works of American culture.

Literature Practice

Answer these questions on a separate sheet of paper.

1. What details does the poet use to describe his aunt?

2. a.) How does Langston Hughes feel about his Aunt Sue?
   b.) How do you know?

3. a.) What are Aunt Sue's stories about?
   b.) Why are they important for the boy to hear?

4. How does the boy know that the stories came out of Aunt Sue's life and not out of books?

5. From what point of view is this story told?

Bailando [Dancing]

by Pat Mora

Words to Know

LITERARY TERMS

descriptive details details that show who someone is or how someone looks

first-person point of view in poetry, the author, or poet, is the speaker of the poem

SELECTION VOCABULARY

swaying swinging or moving from side to side

waltzing dancing a dance for couples

orchid a beautiful flower

tottering rocking back and forth and almost falling

I will remember you dancing,
spinning round and round
a young girl in Mexico,
your long, black hair free in the wind,
5   spinning round and round
a young woman at village dances
your long, blue dress **swaying**
to the beat of *La Varsoviana*,
smiling into the eyes of your partners,
10   years later smiling into my eyes
when I'd reach up to dance with you,
my dear aunt, who years later
danced with my children,
you, white-haired but still young
15   **waltzing** on your ninetieth birthday,
more beautiful than the **orchid**
pinned on your shoulder,
tottering now when you walk
but saying to me, *"Estoy bailando,"*
20   and laughing.

The poet uses the pronoun *I*. The poem is being told from the first-person point of view.

La Varsoviana is a polka, a kind of dance.

The poet first describes her aunt as a young girl. She then shows her aunt at other ages—as a young woman, an aunt, and a 90-year-old woman. How does her aunt change over time? How does she stay the same?

Estoy bailando means "I am dancing."

Literature Practice

Answer these questions on a separate sheet of paper.

1. What words or details does the poet use to describe her aunt?
2. What activity does the poet remember most clearly about her aunt?
3. What does the poet admire most about her aunt?
4. Why do you think the aunt, now more than ninety years old, says, "Estoy bailando"?
5. From what point of view is the poem being told?

To My Dear and Loving Husband
by Anne Bradstreet

Words to Know

LITERARY TERMS

rhyme words with the same sounds, often at the end of a line

rhythm a beat that creates a mood or feeling

SELECTION VOCABULARY

quench stop or put out

nor ought nothing

give recompense can reward

manifold many times over

persevere continue on

In the poem, a woman tells of her love for her husband and his love for her. She says that she and her husband are so in love that they are like one person. His love is worth more than riches to her. He loves her so much that she feels she can never pay him back. She wants the two of them to love each other forever. Even when they die, she says that they will be together.

—∞∞∞—

If ever two were one, then surely we.
If ever man were lov'd by wife, then thee;
If ever wife was happy in a man,
Compare with me ye women if you can.
5 I prize thy love more than whole mines of gold,
Or all the riches that the East doth hold.

Many poems use rhyming words at the end of lines. Find all the words that rhyme.

My love is such that rivers cannot **quench**,
  Nor ought but love from thee, **give recompense**.
  Thy love is such I can no way repay,
10 The heavens reward thee **manifold**, I pray.
  Then while we live, in love let's so **persevere**,
  That when we live no more, we may live ever.

This poem has a rhythm, or beat. Try reading this poem aloud.

How would you pronounce *persevere* to rhyme with *ever* in this last line?

Literature Practice

Answer these questions on a separate sheet of paper.

1. What is the main feeling that this poet is expressing?

2. What is worth all the gold mines or riches in the East?

3. How does the rhyme and rhythm help add to the excitement of the poem?

4. This poet lived at a time when such words of love were valued. Are they valued today?

Chapter Review

Summaries

- **I Ask My Mother to Sing**—A mother and grandmother sing about their homeland in China. The song helps their daughter to imagine it.

- **My Father's Song**—A man misses talking to his father. His father taught him a lesson about gentleness and caring for all living things.

- **Mother to Son**—A mother compares life to climbing stairs. She says that even though her life was hard, she kept climbing. She tells her son that he must also keep trying to succeed.

- **Lineage**—A woman describes how strong her grandmothers are. She wishes that she were as strong as they are.

- **Abuela**—A woman celebrates the life of her grandmother. She remembers how alive her grandmother was.

- **Grandma Ling**—A girl visits her grandmother in Taiwan for the first time. She notices that she looks like her grandmother. The girl hugs her grandmother to show how she feels about her.

- **Aunt Sue's Stories**—A boy's aunt tells him stories. These stories come from his family's history as African Americans. He is glad that she tells him.

- **Bailando**—A woman describes her aunt. All through her life, her aunt danced. Even as an old woman, her aunt still dances. The aunt feels the joy of living by dancing.

- **To My Dear and Loving Husband**—A woman writes about how much she loves her husband. She values his love more than anything else.

Chapter Quiz

Decide whether the statements below are true or false. Use a separate sheet of paper to explain your answers.

1. Li-Young Lee asks her mother to sing because she loves to hear about China where her mother grew up.

2. When Simon Ortiz talks about his father "saying things," he means that he loves his father's voice.

3. Denise Alcalá's grandmother was a singer from Guadalajara.

4. Amy Ling loves her grandmother, even though they did not speak the same language.

5. Langston Hughes's Aunt Sue's stories are about slaves based on stories that Aunt Sue had read in books.

6. Pat Mora danced with her aunt when she was a small child.

Thinking and Writing

Answer the following questions on a separate sheet of paper. Write one or two paragraphs for each one.

1. What are some of the important reasons a poet might write about a family member? Use examples from any of the poems to explain your answer.

2. Compare the advice from the mother in "Mother to Son" with the lesson taught by the father in "My Father's Song." What lesson is learned from each person?

3. How are Pat Mora's memories of her aunt similar to Denise Alcalá's memories of her grandmother?

Unit Six Review

The following questions are about the selections you read in this unit. Write your answers on a separate sheet of paper.

A. Decide if you agree or disagree with each of the following statements. If you disagree, rewrite the statement so that you can agree with it.

1. One reason young Martin in "The Medicine Bag" is ashamed of Grandpa is that his grandfather lives on a reservation.
2. Eloise Greenfield remembers her family laughing often.
3. Rosa Yzquierdo's grandmother doesn't want her to remember Mexican things; she wants her to be American.
4. In "Mother to Son," the mother thinks that her son will not have a hard life.

B. Write one or two sentences for each of these questions about writers. Look back at the selections if you need to.

1. Writers use details (touch, smell, taste, sight) to describe things or people in a way that seems as real as possible. What details in "The Medicine Bag" help you to see Grandpa the way that Martin sees him?
2. Writers use imagery to help readers see pictures as they read. In "I Ask My Mother to Sing," the poet describes a waterlily filling with rain. Find an image in "Grandma Ling" or "Abuela" from Chapter 15 that makes a picture for the reader.
3. What conclusions can you draw about the writer's feelings about her family history in "Lineage"? Can you draw similiar conclusions about Langston Hughes in "Aunt Sue's Stories"?

C. Choose one poem from Chapter 15. Write a paragraph about it. Tell what the poet is saying about the family member. Describe any images, or pictures, the poet uses. Also tell what details the poet uses to show what the person is like. Then tell why you think the poet wrote the poem about the person.

Unit Seven

ADVENTURE

Chapter 16

from Escape: A Slave Narrative
   adapted from the autobiography by
   James W.C. Pennington
At Last I Kill a Buffalo
   adapted from the autobiography by
   Luther Standing Bear

Chapter 17

The Secret Life of Walter Mitty
   an adapted story by James Thurber
The Invalid's Story
   an adapted story by Mark Twain

Chapter 16

Adventures are sometimes full of danger. In these true stories, the narrators are bold and daring. They face great danger. Will they be successful?

Chapter Learning Objectives

- Learn how setting and details create the atmosphere, or mood, of a story
- Learn how an autobiographical essay tells about the author

Escape: A Slave Narrative

adapted from the autobiography by James W. C. Pennington

Words to Know

LITERARY TERMS

setting the place and time in which a story occurs

details pieces of information that help to "paint" a picture for the reader

atmosphere the general mood of a piece of literature; setting, details, and the writer's choice of words create the atmosphere

SELECTION VOCABULARY

narrative a story

quarter area, section

nourishment   food to keep one healthy and alive

desperate frantic; hopeless

tollgate a place where one pays a fee to travel a road or cross a bridge

crisis turning point, climax

blacksmith a person who shapes hot iron into horseshoes, pots, and other metal objects

resistance fighting back

captors people who capture, or catch, someone

fugitive a runaway; a hunted person

It was now two o'clock. I stepped into the **slave quarter**. There was an unusual silence. The house looked poor. The only piece of food I could see was a bit of corn bread. It weighed about a half-pound. I placed it in my pocket. I took a last look at the house and at a few small children who were playing at the door.

I crossed the barnyard and in a few moments reached a small cave. Near the cave's mouth was a

James Pennington grew up as a slave. He wrote this narrative, or story, after he escaped to freedom. This story is just one event that happened to Pennington while he was a slave.

pile of stones into which I had placed my clothes. From here, I had to go through thick and heavy woods to town, where my brother lived.

This town was six miles away. It was now near three o'clock. My goals were not to be seen on the road and to get to the town by daylight. I was well-known in town. If anyone were to have seen me, I would have once again been chased.

The atmosphere in "Escape" is tense. It is full of suspense. As you read, think about how the author creates this atmosphere.

The *North Star* is a very bright star. By looking at its position in the sky, people can tell which way is north. The slave states were in the South. African Americans who were escaping slavery traveled north to freedom. They often looked at the *North Star* to figure out the right direction to travel.

As Pennington travels north, the setting of the story continually changes. He is now hiding from daylight in a field of corn. He describes the setting as being dangerous. This description again adds to the suspense of the story.

The first six miles, I traveled very slowly. During this walk, a difficult question was bothering me: Shall I visit my brother as I pass through town and show him what I've done? My brother was older than me, and we were very close. I always asked him for advice.

I entered the town about dark. I decided not to show myself to my brother. I passed through the town without being seen. Darkness hid me, a lonely wanderer from home and friends. My only guide was the *North Star*. By this star, I knew that I would go north. But at what point I should reach Pennsylvania, or when and where I should find a friend, I did not know. . . .

The night was warm for the time of year. It passed quietly, and I was very tired. Then about three o'clock in the morning, I began to feel cold.

At this moment, I began to feel gloomy. The thought of being completely poor was more than I could bear. My heart began to melt. How will I survive with just a piece of dry corn bread? What **nourishment** is there in it to warm the nerves of one already chilled to the heart?

While these thoughts were on my mind, the day dawned. I was in the middle of an open field. I hid among a pile of corn stalks, a few hundred yards from the road.

Here I spent my first day. The day was an unhappy one. My hiding place was very dangerous. I had to sit in an uncomfortable position the whole day. I had no chance to rest. Besides this, my small piece of bread did not give me the nourishment that I so badly needed.

I was relieved when night came again. By this time, not a crumb of my bread was left. I was hungry and began to feel **desperate**. . . .

At the dawn of the third day, I continued my travel. I had found my way to a public road during the night. Very early in the morning, I came to a **tollgate** where I only saw one person. It was a boy about 12 years old. I asked him where the road led. He said it led to Baltimore. I asked him how far it was. He said it was 18 miles.

That information shocked me. My master lived 80 miles from Baltimore. I was now 62 miles from home. That distance in the right direction would have placed me several miles across the Mason-Dixon line. But I was still in the state of Maryland. . . .

By the time I had walked a mile on this road, it was about nine o'clock. I came upon a young man with a load of hay. He drew up his horses and spoke to me in a very kind tone. The following conversation took place between us:

"Are you traveling far, my friend?"

"I am on my way to Philadelphia."

"Are you free?"

"Yes, sir."

"I suppose, then, you have free papers?"

"No, sir, I have no papers."

"Well, my friend, you should not travel on this road. You will be caught before you have gone three miles. There are men living on this road who are always on the lookout for your people. It is rare that one who tries to pass by day escapes them."

He then very kindly gave me some advice. He told me to turn off the road at a certain point. He said I should find my way to a certain house where I would be met by an old gentleman. That man would tell me whether I should stay until night or go on. . . .

I went on for about a mile more. I had gone about five miles from the tollgate that I mentioned earlier. It was now about ten o'clock in the morning. My strength was nearly gone because I had not eaten very much food. But my mind was greatly excited. I thought very little about my *need* for food.

Normally, I would have been glad to see the

The Mason-Dixon line divided the North from the South. It divided the free states from the slave states. Although Pennington should be across the Mason-Dixon line into the North, he is still in Maryland, a slave state. What went wrong? Why isn't he in the North? The suspense continues to build.

Free slaves had to have documents, or papers, that stated the person was free. If a person was caught without these papers, he or she would be taken back to his or her master, or owner, and severely punished.

Pennington is lying about his being a free man. Why do you think he needs to lie to the man?

Which words does the author use to describe this new setting? How do these words add to the suspense of the story?

tavern I came upon. But as things stood, I thought it was a dangerous place to pass, much less to stop at. I passed it as quietly and quickly as possible. Then from a lot across the road, I heard a serious voice cry, "Halloo!"

I turned my face to the left, from where the voice came. I noticed it was from a man who was digging potatoes. I answered him politely. Then the following conversation took place:

"Who do *you* belong to?"

"I am free, sir."

"Have you got papers?"

"No, sir."

"Well, you must stop here."

By this time, he had made his way into the road and climbed on top of a fence that separated us.

"My business is onward, sir," I said. "I do not wish to stop."

"I will see then if you don't stop, you black rascal."

He was now in the middle of the road. He began to come quickly after me.

I saw that a **crisis** was at hand. I had no weapons of any kind, not even a pocketknife. I asked myself, shall I surrender without a struggle? The answer was, "No."

What will you do? Continue to walk. If he runs after you, run. Get him as far from the house as you can. Then turn suddenly and strike him on the knee with a stone. At least that will keep him from chasing you.

This was a desperate plan. But I could not think of another one. My skill as a **blacksmith** had given me good aim. I felt quite sure that I only needed to get a stone in my hand. If I had time to throw it, I would not miss his knee.

He began to take short breaths. He was mad because I did not stop. And I was angry at being

The narrator was trained as a blacksmith. He was used to accurately hitting metal to make objects. What would happen if Pennington hit the man with a stone? What would happen if he were to miss?

chased by a man to whom I had not done the least harm. I had just begun to look for a stone to grasp. Then he made a tiger-like leap at me. We started running.

At this moment, he yelled out, "Jake Shouster!" At the next moment, the door of a small house to the left was opened. Out jumped a shoemaker with a knife in his hand. He sprang forward and grabbed me by the collar. Then the other man grabbed my arms from behind. I was now in the grasp of two men, both of whom were larger than me. One of them was armed with a dangerous weapon.

Standing in the door of the shoemaker's shop was a third man. In the potato lot I had passed, there was still a fourth man. My heart melted away. I sunk without **resistance** into the hands of my **captors**. They dragged me right away into the tavern that was near.

"Come now, this matter may easily be settled without you going to jail. Who do you belong to, and where did you come from?". . .

I decided to insist that I was free. This was not good enough for them since I could not prove it. They tied my hands. Then we set out to a local official who lived about a half a mile away.

When we got to his house, he was not at home. It was a disappointment to the others, but to me it was a relief. However, I soon learned they planned on going to another official in the neighborhood. About 20 minutes later, we stood before his door. But he was not home, either.

By this time, it had gotten to be one or two o'clock. My captors began to feel restless at the loss of time. We were about a mile and a quarter from the tavern. As we set out on our return, they held a meeting.

They knew it would be difficult for me to climb

Do you think Pennington will escape his captors?

over fences with my hands tied. So they untied me. "Now John," one of the men said. John was the name they had given me. "If you have run away from anyone, it would be much better for you to tell us!"

I continued to say that I was free. However, I knew that my situation was very serious. We were still just a short distance from my home. The knowledge of my being a runaway might catch up with me at any moment. . . .

We got to the tavern at three o'clock. They asked me again to tell the truth. I saw that my attempt to escape only strengthened their feeling that I was a **fugitive**.

I said, "If you don't put me in jail, I will tell you where I am from." They promised.

"Well," I said, "a few weeks ago, I was sold from the eastern shore to a slave-trader. He had a large gang, and he set out for Georgia with us. When he got to a town in Virginia, he became sick. Then he died of smallpox. Several of his gang also died of it. The people in the town became worried. They did not wish the gang to remain among them. No one claimed us or wished to have anything to do with us. I left the rest and thought I would go somewhere and get work."

Smallpox is a disease that can kill. It spreads quickly. Why do you think Pennington leads his captors to believe that he has been exposed to smallpox?

When I said this, they seemed to believe my story. At the same time, however, I noticed that some of the men began to panic. They were frightened by the idea that I was one of a smallpox gang. Several of those who had gathered near me moved away. . . .

I was now left alone with the first man I saw in the morning. In a serious manner, he made this offer to me: "John, I have a brother living in Risterstown, four miles away. He keeps a tavern. I think you had better go and live with him until we see what will turn up. He wants someone to take care of his horses." I agreed to this at once. "Well, take something to eat," he said, "and I will go with you."

I knew it wouldn't do me any good to go into that town. There were prisons, posters, newspapers, and travelers there. My intention was to start with him, but not to enter town alive. . . .

———◇◇◇———

The narrator escapes again before he gets to Risterstown. He keeps going north to freedom.

———◇◇◇———

After several hours, I found my way back to the road. But traveling quickly was not possible. All I could do was keep my legs moving, which I did with great difficulty.

Near the end of the night, I suffered greatly from the cold. There was a heavy frost. I expected at every moment to fall on the road and die. I came to a cornfield covered with Indian corn. I went into this field and ate an ear of corn. I thought I would rest a little in the cornfield before starting out again. But I was so weary that I soon fell asleep.

When I awoke, the sun was shining around. I got up in alarm. But it was too late to think of finding any other shelter. So I settled down and hid myself as best as I could from the daylight.

After I recovered a little from my fright, I began again to eat my corn. Grain by grain, I worked away at it. When my jaws grew tired, I rested. Then I started again fresh. Nearly the whole morning had gone by before I was finished. . . .

I got my strength back. I felt that I was at least safe from starving to death. So, I set out more quickly than I had since Sunday and Monday night. I had a feeling, too, that I must be near free soil. I hadn't the least idea where I should find a home or friend. Still,

How do you think Pennington escaped his captors?

Indian corn is a hard corn with colorful kernels.

my spirits were so high, that I took the whole road to myself. I ran, hopped, skipped, jumped, and talked to myself. . . .

This joyful mood only lasted an hour or two. Then a gloom came over me with these questions: But where are you going? What are you going to do? What will you do with freedom without your father, mother, sisters, and brothers? What will you say when you are asked where you were born? You know nothing of the world.

These questions made me think about the great difficulties I still had to face.

Saturday morning came. My strength still seemed fresh. Yet, I began to feel a hunger that was worse than I had felt before. I decided, at all risk, to continue my travel by daylight. I would ask the first person I met for information. . . .

I continued my flight on the public road. A little after the sun rose, I came in sight of another tollgate. For a moment, all the events that happened at the tollgate on Wednesday morning came back to me. I stopped. But, then I decided that I would try again.

I arrived at the gate. I found it attended by an old woman. I asked her if I was in Pennsylvania. She said I was. Then I asked her if she knew where I could find work. She said she did not. But she told me to go to W. W., a Quaker, who lived about three miles from her. She said he would be interested in me. She gave me directions to get there. I thanked her and wished her a good morning.

In about half an hour, I stood shaking at the door of W. W. I knocked. The door opened upon a well-spread table. The sight of it increased my hunger about seven times. I did not dare to enter. I said that I'd been sent to him to find work.

"Well, come in and take thy breakfast and get warm," he said. "We will talk about it. Thee must be cold without any coat."

At the time this story was written, authors often referred to people by their initials. Initials are the first letters in a person's first and last names. Here, the narrator's savior is called W. W. The author uses initials because he does not want anyone to know who W. W. is because it might be dangerous. It was against the law to help runaway slaves.

"Come in and take thy breakfast and get warm."

The words were spoken by a stranger. But they were spoken with such kindness that they made a great impression on me. They made me believe that I had found a friend and a home. . . .

To this day, those words remind me of what I was at that time. My condition was as terrible as that of any human being could be. I had only four pieces of clothing. I was a starving fugitive, without home or friends. There was a reward offered for me in the public papers. I was being chased by cruel manhunters.

I had no claim upon the man to whose door I went. Had he turned me away, I would surely have died. No, he took me in and gave me his food. He even shared with me his own clothes. I had never before received such treatment at the hands of any white man.

Literature Practice

Answer these questions on a separate sheet of paper.

1. Name three details that help make the atmosphere of this story suspenseful.
2. Where is the narrator trying to go?
3. Why does he have to hide so often?
4. What happens when he tries to pass the tavern?
5. What do you think might have happened to the narrator if the Quaker had not helped him?

At Last I Kill a Buffalo

adapted from the autobiography by Luther Standing Bear

Words to Know

LITERARY TERM

autobiographical essay   writing that focuses on one event in the writer's life

SELECTION VOCABULARY

sufficient as much as is needed; enough

commodity a thing that can be traded or sold; goods

justified showed to be right

gratification something that makes you feel thankful

tackle take hold of; start to do something difficult

gait a way of walking or running

marksmanship aim, accuracy in shooting

temptation something that makes you think about doing something wrong

resolved decided

regretted felt sorry or guilty

customary something that is normally done

exploits heroic or bold actions

At last the day came when my father allowed me to go on a buffalo hunt with him. What a proud boy I was!

Ever since I could remember my father had been teaching me the things that I should know and preparing me to be a good hunter. I had learned to make bows and to string them and to make arrows and tip them with feathers. I knew how to ride my pony no matter how fast he would go, and I felt that I was brave and did not fear danger. All these things I

In this autobiographical essay, Luther Standing Bear describes one event in his life—his first buffalo hunt.

The Sioux are one nation of Native Americans. They live in the Plains—an area that is now North and South Dakota.

Being on the warpath means going out to fight an enemy.

Plains Indians, such as the Sioux, lived in tipis. The tipis were arranged in a circle. To the Sioux, the circle represents the cycle of life and the way in which all living things live peacefully together.

had learned for just this day when father would allow me to go with him on a buffalo hunt. It was the event for which every Sioux boy eagerly waited. To ride side by side with the best hunters of the tribe, to hear the terrible noise of the great herds as they ran, and then to help to bring home the kill was the most thrilling day of any Indian boy's life. The only other event that could equal it would be the day I went for the first time on the warpath to meet the enemy and protect my tribe.

On the following early morning, we were to start, so the evening was spent in preparation. Although the tipis were full of activity, there was no noise nor confusion outside. Always the evening before a buffalo hunt and when everyone was usually in his tipi, an old man went around the circle of tipis calling, "I-ni-la, I-ni-la," not loudly, but so everyone could hear. The old man was saying, "Keep quiet. Keep quiet." We all knew that the scouts had come in and reported buffalo near and that we must all keep the camp in stillness. It was not necessary for the old man to go into each tipi and explain to the men that tomorrow there would be a big hunt, as the buffalo were coming. He did not order the men to prepare their weapons and neither did he order the mothers to keep children from crying. The one word, "I-ni-la," was **sufficient** to bring quiet to the whole camp. That night there would be no calling or shouting from tipi to tipi, and no child would cry aloud. Even the horses and dogs obeyed the command for quiet, and all night not a horse neighed and not a dog barked. The very presence of quiet was everywhere. Such is the orderliness of a Sioux camp that men, women, children, and animals seem to have a common understanding and sympathy. It is no mystery, but natural that the Indian and his animals understand each other very well both with words and without words. There are words, however, that the Indian uses that are understood by both his horses and dogs. When on a hunt, if one of the warriors speaks the word "A-a-ah" rather quickly and sharply, every man, horse, and dog will stop instantly and listen. Not a move will be made by an animal until the men move or speak further. As long as the hunters listen, the animals will listen also.

The night preceding a buffalo hunt was always an exciting night, even though it was quiet in camp. There would be much talk in the tipis around the fires. There would be sharpening of arrows and of knives. New bowstrings would be made and quivers would be filled with arrows.

A quiver is a case for carrying arrows.

It was in the fall of the year and the evenings were cool as father and I sat by the fire and talked over the hunt. I was only eight years of age, and I know that father did not expect me to get a buffalo at all, but only to try perhaps for a small calf should I be able to get close enough to one. Nevertheless, I was greatly excited as I sat and watched father working in his easy, firm way.

I was wearing my buffalo-skin robe, the hair next to my body. Mother had made me a rawhide belt and this, wrapped around my waist, held my blanket on when I threw it off my shoulders. In the early morning I would wear it, for it would be cold. When it came time to shoot, I should not want my blanket, but the belt would hold it in place.

Animal skins are tanned by stretching and drying them in the sun. Tanned hides are used to make shirts, robes, tipis, and blankets. Untanned skin, or rawhide, is used for making belts, whips, and cords.

You can picture me, I think, as I sat in the glow of the campfire, my little brown body bare to the waist watching and listening intently to my father. My hair hung down my back, and I wore moccasins and breechcloth of buckskin. To my belt was fastened a rawhide holster for my knife, for when I was eight years of age we had plenty of knives. I was proud to own a knife, and this night I remember I kept it on all night. Neither did I lay aside my bow, but went to sleep with it in my hand, thinking, I suppose, to be all

Moccasins are leather shoes. A breechcloth is a piece of soft leather tied around the waist. A holster is a case for a knife or gun.

The word *whet* means "to sharpen." A whetstone sharpens metal blades that are rubbed against it.

A quirt is a riding whip. It has a braided leather lash and a short handle. It is used to tell a horse when to run.

the nearer ready in the morning when the start was made.

Father sharpened my steel points for me and also sharpened my knife. The whetstone was a long stone that was kept in a buckskin bag, and sometimes this stone went all over the camp; every tipi did not have one, so we shared this **commodity** with one another. I had as I remember about ten arrows, so when father was through sharpening them I put them in my rawhide quiver. I had a rawhide quirt, too, which I would wear fastened to my waist. As father worked, he knew I was watching him closely and listening whenever he spoke. By the time all preparations had been made, he had told me just how I was to act when I started out in the morning with the hunters.

We went to bed, my father hoping that tomorrow would be successful for him so that he could bring home some nice meat for the family and a hide for my mother to tan. I went to bed, but could not go to sleep at once, so filled was I with the wonderment and excitement of it all. The next day was to be a test for me. I was to prove to my father whether he was or was not **justified** in his pride in me. What would be the result of my training? Would I be brave if I faced danger and would father be proud of me? I did not know it that night that I was to be tried for the strength of my manhood and my honesty in this hunt. Something happened that day which I remember above all things. It was a test of my real character, and I am proud to say that I did not find myself weak, but made a decision that has been all these years a **gratification** to me.

The next morning the hunters were catching their horses about daybreak. I arose with my father and went out and caught my pony. I wanted to do whatever he did and show him that he did not have to tell me what to do. We brought our animals to the tipi and got our bows and arrows and mounted. From all

over the village came the hunters. Most of them were leading their running horses. These running horses were eager for the hunt and came prancing, their ears straight up and their tails waving in the air. We were joined with perhaps a hundred or more riders, some of whom carried bows and arrows and some armed with guns.

The buffalo were reported to be about five or six miles away as we should count distance now. At that time, we did not measure distance in miles. One camping distance was about ten miles, and these buffalo were said to be about one–half camping distance away.

Some of the horses were to be left at a stopping place just before the herd was reached. These horses were pack animals that were taken along to carry extra blankets or weapons. They were trained to remain there until the hunters came for them.

Some of the Sioux have guns. This fact means that this story is taking place after white people began moving west. Native Americans did not have guns before contact with whites.

Often the Sioux had to travel great distances to find a herd of buffalo. So they had to carry supplies with them.

Though they were neither hobbled nor tied, they stood still during the shooting and noise of the chase.

My pony was a black one and a good runner. I felt very important as I rode along with the hunters and my father, the chief. I kept as close to him as I could.

Two men had been chosen to scout or to lead the party. These two men were, in a sense, policemen whose work it was to keep order. They carried large sticks of ash wood, something like a policeman's billy, though longer. They rode ahead of the party while the rest of us kept in a group close together. The leaders went ahead until they sighted the herd of grazing buffalo. Then they stopped and waited for the rest of us to ride up. We all rode slowly toward the herd, which on sight of us had come together, although they had been scattered here and there over the plain. When they saw us, they all ran close together as if at the command of a leader. We continued riding slowly toward the herd until one of the leaders shouted, "Ho-ka-he!" which means "Ready, Go!" At that command, every man started for the herd. I had been listening, too, and the minute the hunters started, I started also.

Away I went, my little pony putting all he had into the race. It was not long before I lost sight of father, but I kept going just the same. I threw my blanket back and the chill of the autumn morning struck my body, but I did not mind. On I went. It was wonderful to race over the ground with all these horsemen about me. There was no shouting, no noise of any kind except the pounding of the horses' hooves. The herd was now running and had raised a cloud of dust. I felt no fear until we had entered this cloud of dust, and I could see nothing about me—only hear the sound of hooves. Where was father? Where was I going? On I rode through the cloud, for I knew I must keep going.

Then all at once I realized that I was in the midst

A billy is a short, wooden club.

of the buffalo, their dark bodies rushing all about me and their great heads moving up and down to the sound of their hooves beating upon the earth. Then it was that fear overcame me, and I leaned close down upon my little pony's body and clutched him tightly. I can never tell you how I felt toward my pony at that moment. All thought of shooting had left my mind. I was seized by blank fear. In a moment or so, however, my senses became clearer, and I could distinguish other sounds beside the clatter of hooves. I could hear a shot now and then, and I could see the buffalo beginning to break up into small bunches. I could not see my father nor any of my companions yet, but my fear was vanishing and I was safe. I let my pony run. The buffalo looked too large for me to **tackle**, anyway, so I just kept going. The buffalo became more and more scattered. Pretty soon I saw a young calf that looked about my size. I remembered now what father had told me the night before as we sat about the fire. Those instructions were important for me now to follow.

I was still back of the calf, being unable to get alongside of him. I was eager to get a shot, yet afraid to try, as I was still very nervous. While my pony was making all speed to come alongside, I chanced a shot and to my surprise my arrow landed. My second arrow glanced along the back of the animal and sped on between the horns, making only a slight wound. My third arrow hit a spot that made the running beast slow up in his **gait**. I shot a fourth arrow, and though it, too, landed, it was not a fatal wound. It seemed to me that it was taking a lot of shots, and I was not proud of my **marksmanship**. I was glad, however, to see the animal going slower, and I knew that one more shot would make me a hunter. My horse seemed to know his own importance. His two ears stood straight forward, and it was not necessary for me to urge him to get closer to the buffalo. I was soon by the side of the buffalo and one more shot brought the chase to a close. I jumped from my pony, and as I stood by my fallen game, I looked all around wishing that the world could see. But I was alone. In my determination to stay by until I had won my buffalo, I had not noticed that I was far from everyone else. No admiring friends were about, and as far as I could see I was on the plain alone. The herd of buffalo had completely disappeared. As for Father, much as I wished for him, he was out of sight, and I had no idea where he was.

I stood and looked at the animal on the ground. I was happy. Everyone must know that I, Ota K'te, had killed a buffalo. But it looked as if no one knew where I was, so no one was coming my way. I must then take something from this animal to show that I had killed it. I took all the arrows one by one from the body. As I took them out, it occurred to me that I had used five arrows. If I had been a skillful hunter, one arrow would have been sufficient, but I had used five. Here it was that **temptation** came to me. Why could I not take out two of the arrows and throw them away? No one would know, and then I should be more greatly admired and praised as a hunter. As it was, I knew that I should be praised by my father and mother, but I wanted more. And so I was tempted to lie.

I was planning this as I took out my skinning knife that father had sharpened for me the night before. I skinned one side of the animal, but when it came to turning it over, I was too small. I was wondering what to do when I heard my father's voice calling, "To-ki-i-la-la-hu-wo. Where are you?" I quickly jumped on my pony and rode to the top of a little hill nearby. Father saw me and came to me at once. He was so pleased to see me and glad to know that I was safe. I knew that I could never lie to my father. He was too fond of me, and I too proud of him. He had always told me to tell the truth. He wanted me to be an honest man, so I

resolved then to tell the truth even if it took from me a little glory. He rode up to me with a glad expression on his face, expecting me to go back with him to his kill. As he came up, I said as calmly as I could, "Father, I have killed a buffalo." His smile changed to surprise, and he asked me where my buffalo was. I pointed to it, and we rode over to where it lay, partly skinned.

Father set to work to skin it for me. I had watched him do this many times and knew perfectly well how to do it myself, but I could not turn the animal over. There was a way to turn the head of the animal so that the body would be balanced on the back while being skinned. Father did this for me, while I helped all I could. When the hide was off, father put it on the pony's back with the hair side next to the pony. On this, he arranged the meat so it would balance. Then

he covered the meat carefully with the rest of the hide, so no dust would reach it while we traveled home. I rode home on top of the load.

I showed my father the arrows that I had used and just where the animal had been hit. He was very pleased and praised me over and over again. I felt more glad than ever that I had told the truth, and I have never **regretted** it. I am more proud now that I told the truth than I am of killing the buffalo.

We rode to where my father had killed a buffalo. There we stopped and prepared it for taking home. It was late afternoon when we got back to camp. No king ever rode in state who was more proud than I that day as I came into the village sitting high up on my load of buffalo meat. Mother had now two hunters in the family, and I knew how she was going to make a fuss over me. It is not **customary** for Indian men to brag about their **exploits,** and I had been taught that bragging was not nice. So I was very quiet, although I was bursting with pride. Always when arriving home I would run out to play for I loved to be with the other boys, but this day I lingered about close to the tipi so I could hear the nice things that were said about me. It was soon all over camp that Ota K'te had killed a buffalo.

My father was so proud that he gave away a fine horse. He called an old man to our tipi to cry out the news to the rest of the people in camp. The old man stood at the door of our tipi and sang a song of praise to my father. The horse had been led up, and I stood holding it by a rope. The old man who was singing called the other old man who was to receive the horse as a present. He accepted the horse by coming up to me, holding out his hands to me, and saying, "Ha-ye," which means "Thank you." The old man went away very grateful for the horse.

That ended my first and last buffalo hunt. It lives only in my memory, for the days of the buffalo are over.

Here, the author is referring to feeling as proud as a king.

The End of the Buffalo

Luther Standing Bear says his first buffalo hunt was also his last hunt. What did he mean that the days of the buffalo are over?

There used to be millions of buffalo. Herds of buffalo covered the Plains area of what is now the midwest part of the United States. Buffalo were (and still are) very important to the Plains Indians. These Native Americans depended on the buffalo for food, supplies, and clothing.

Then, in the 1860s, white people began to hunt buffalo in greater numbers than before. Many of them hunted the buffalo just for fun. Others killed them for their hides, or fur, and for their tongues, which they traded for money. Many white hunters killed more buffalo than they could ever use. Soon, there were fewer and fewer buffalo. Millions of buffalo were killed by whites. Only a few hundred survived.

By the 1880s, the Plains Indians had nothing to eat. The way of life that Luther Standing Bear describes was changed forever.

Literature Practice

Answer these questions on a separate sheet of paper.

1. What is the event for which every Sioux boy eagerly waits?

2. What is special about the evening before a buffalo hunt?

3. What is Luther Standing Bear tempted to lie about?

4. Why does he decide to tell the truth?

5. Why do you think Luther Standing Bear is more proud of himself for telling the truth than killing his first buffalo?

6. How does the father show how proud he is of Luther Standing Bear?

Chapter Review

Summaries

- **Escape: A Slave Narrative**—In this excerpt, we follow the narrator's frightening and dangerous flight from a slave state to a free state. With only a piece of corn bread to eat, he flees to the North, using the North Star as his guide. The atmosphere is full of suspense and fear as the young man again and again escapes capture and starvation. Finally, he finds food, safety, and freedom in the home of a Pennsylvania Quaker.

- **At Last I Kill a Buffalo**—Luther Standing Bear describes his first and last buffalo hunt. The reader is given a picture of the Sioux's preparations for the hunt and an understanding of its importance to the boy and his tribe. Luther Standing Bear's autobiographical essay also tells how his honesty as well as his skill as a hunter were tested. When he realizes that it has taken him many arrows to bring down the young buffalo he kills, Luther Standing Bear is tempted to lie about the number to his father. Instead, he tells the truth. In the end, his decision to be honest proves more important to him than his success in the hunt.

Chapter Quiz

Choose the letter of the correct answer. Rewrite the sentences on a separate sheet of paper.

1. In "Escape: A Slave Narrative," where is the narrator going?
   a. North to freedom
   b. to his brother's house
   c. further south
   d. to visit a friend

2. Why do the men near the tavern try to catch the narrator?
   a. They think he is a criminal.
   b. They want to help him.
   c. They think he is a runaway slave.
   d. They want to catch smallpox.

Chapter Review

3. Why do the Quaker's words make such an impression on the narrator?
   a. He is treated kindly by a white man.   c. He hears them in a dream.
   b. He does not understand the words.   d. He gives up hope.

4. In "At Last I Kill a Buffalo," Luther Standing Bear is very excited in the beginning of the story because he
   a. is going to protect his tribe.   c. has to stay home during the hunt.
   b. is too loud before the hunt.   d. is allowed to go on the buffalo hunt.

5. The buffalo that Luther Standing Bear kills is
   a. a calf.   c very big.
   b. sick.   d. too old.

6. What is Luther Standing Bear more proud of than killing the buffalo?
   a. He brags about killing the buffalo.   c. He tells his father the truth.
   b. His father gives away a fine horse.   d. He brings home a lot of meat.

Thinking and Writing

Answer the following questions on a separate sheet of paper. Write one or two paragraphs for each one.

1. In "Escape: A Slave Narrative," the narrator has many different feelings during his journey. Make a list of the feelings the narrator has. Then choose one feeling that best summarizes the journey. Explain why your choice is the best one.

2. Why is it so important to Luther Standing Bear that he tells his father the truth?

3. To a Sioux boy, killing his first buffalo is a great adventure. Write about an adventure you had or would like to have.

Chapter 17

Here are two funny adventure stories. But the adventure takes place in the main characters' minds. The events are the result of a wild imagination.

Chapter Learning Objectives

- Learn how malapropisms make us laugh
- Learn how metaphors and similes make comparisons
- Learn how dialogue makes characters seem more real
- Learn the "tricks" a fiction writer uses to make us feel that a story is true

The Secret Life of Walter Mitty
an adapted story by James Thurber

Words to Know

LITERARY TERMS

malapropism a humorous misuse of a word

metaphor a comparison of two things without using *like* or *as*

simile a comparison of two things using *like* or *as*

SELECTION VOCABULARY

auxiliary back up; supporting

turret part of an airplane

hydroplane an airplane that can land on water

aimlessly without a goal or place to go

intern a doctor in-training

objection in a court of law: a complaint against something said

defendant a person on trial for a crime

sergeant an officer in the armed forces

undefeated never having lost or been beaten

"WE'RE GOING THROUGH!" The Commander's voice was like thin ice breaking. He wore his full-dress uniform. He had his white cap pulled down over one cold, gray eye.

"We can't make it, sir. A hurricane is coming, if you ask me."

"I'm not asking you, Lieutenant Berg," said the Commander. "Throw on the power lights! Rev her up to 8500! We're going through!"

Look at the wonderful beginning of this story. Thurber grabs your attention with the Commander's order. Then he describes the Commander's voice in a simile. To what is his voice being compared?

The pounding of the engines increased: ta-pocketa-pocketa-pocketa-*pocketa-pocketa*. The Commander stared at the ice forming on the pilot's window. He walked over and twisted a row of dials.

"Switch on Number 8 **auxiliary**!" he shouted. "Switch on Number 8 auxiliary!" Lieutenant Berg repeated.

"Full strength in Number 3 **turret**!" shouted the Commander. "Full strength in Number 3 turret!" Berg repeated.

The crew went at their various tasks inside the huge, eight-engine navy **hydroplane**. The men looked at each other and grinned. "The Old Man will

The setting of the story has changed.

get us through," they said to one another. "The Old Man ain't afraid of nothing!" . . .

"Not so fast! You're driving too fast!" said Mrs. Mitty. "What are you driving so fast for?"

"Hmm?" said Walter Mitty. He looked at his wife with shock. She was sitting in the car beside him. She seemed very unfamiliar. She was like a strange woman who had yelled at him in a crowd.

"You were up to fifty-five," she said. "You know I don't like to go more than forty. You were up to fifty-five."

Walter Mitty drove on toward Waterbury in silence. The roaring of the SN202 hydroplane through the worst storm in twenty years of navy flying faded in his mind.

Now it becomes clear that Walter Mitty was daydreaming about the hydroplane.

"You're tensed up again," Mrs. Mitty said. "It's one of your days. I wish you'd let Dr. Renshaw look you over."

Walter Mitty stopped the car. They were in front of the building where his wife went to have her hair done. "Remember to get those overshoes while I'm having my hair done," she said.

"I don't need overshoes," Mitty said.

"We've been all through that," she said, getting out of the car. "You're not a young man any longer." He raced the engine a little. "Why don't you wear your gloves? Have you lost your gloves?"

Walter Mitty reached in a pocket and brought out the gloves. He put them on. After she'd gone into the building, and he'd driven off to a red light, he took them off.

"Hurry up, brother!" a cop snapped as the light changed. Mitty quickly put his gloves back on and drove off. He drove around the streets **aimlessly** for a time. Then he drove past the hospital on his way to the parking lot.

This is another one of Mitty's daydreams. The gloves he is removing here are surgical gloves.

There is no such thing as "obstreosis of the ducal tract." It is a made-up term. It is supposed to sound like something a doctor would say. It is a malaprop. *Ducal*, by the way, refers to a *duke*, not to any part of the body.

Coreopsis is another malapropism. A coreopsis is actually a kind of flower, not a medical term.

. . . "It's the millionaire banker, Wellington McMillan," said the pretty nurse.

"Yes?" said Walter Mitty. He removed his gloves slowly. "Who has the case?"

"Dr. Renshaw and Dr. Benbow. But there are two specialists here. Dr. Remington came in from New York. Mr. Pritchard-Mitford flew over from London."

A door opened down a long, cool hallway. Dr. Renshaw came out. He looked upset and tired. "Hello, Mitty," he said. "We're having a terrible time with McMillan. He is the millionaire banker and a close friend of President Roosevelt. Obstreosis of the ducal tract. I wish you'd take a look at him."

"Glad to," Mitty said.

In the operating room, everyone was introduced to each other in whispers. "I've read one of your books," said Pritchard-Mitford, shaking hands with Mitty. "A brilliant performance, sir."

"Thank you," said Walter Mitty.

A huge machine, with many tubes and wires, was connected to the operating table. At this moment, it began to go *pocketa-pocketa-pocketa*.

"The new anesthetizer is giving way," an **intern** shouted. "There is no one in the East who knows how to fix it!"

"Quiet, man," Mitty said, in a low, cool voice. He went over to the machine. It was now going *pocketa-pocketa-queep-pocketa-queep*. He began softly touching a row of dials. "Give me a fountain pen!" he snapped.

Someone handed him a fountain pen. He pulled a broken part out of the machine. Then he put the fountain pen in its place. "That will hold for ten minutes," he said. "Get on with the operation."

A nurse hurried over and whispered to Renshaw. Mitty saw the man turn pale. "Coreopsis has set in," Renshaw said nervously. "If you would take over, Mitty?"

Mitty looked at him and at the cowardly figure of

Benbow. The two great specialists looked grave and uncertain. "If you wish," Mitty said. They slipped a white gown on him. He adjusted a mask and put on thin gloves. Nurses handed him . . .

"Back it up, Mac! Look out for that Buick!" Walter Mitty jammed on the brakes. "Wrong lane, Mac," said the parking-lot attendant, looking at Mitty closely.

"Gee. Yeah," Mitty muttered. He began to carefully back out of the lane marked "Exit Only."

"Leave it there," said the attendant. "I'll put it away." Mitty got out of the car. "Hey, better leave the key."

"Oh," Mitty said, handing the man the car key. The attendant jumped into the car, backed it up, and put it where it belonged.

They're so high on themselves, Walter Mitty thought, as he walked along Main Street. They think they know everything. He kicked at the slush on the sidewalk. "Overshoes," he said to himself. He began looking for a shoe store.

A little while later, Walter Mitty came out onto the street again. He had the overshoes in a box under his arm. He began to wonder what the other thing was his wife told him to get. She had told him twice, before they left their house for Waterbury.

In a way, he hated these weekly trips to town. He was always getting something wrong. Tissues, he thought, razor blades? No. Toothpaste, toothbrush, medicine? He gave it up. But she would remember it. "Where's the what's-its-name?" she would ask. "Don't tell me you forgot the what's-its-name?" A newsboy went by shouting something about the Waterbury trial.

. . . "Perhaps this will refresh your memory." The District Attorney suddenly shoved a heavy automatic gun at the person on the witness stand. "Have you ever seen this gun before?"

Walter Mitty took the gun and examined it like an expert. "This is my Webley-Vickers 50.80," he said calmly. An excited buzz spread through the courtroom. The judge called for order.

"You are an expert with any sort of gun, I believe?" said the District Attorney.

"**Objection**!" Mitty's attorney shouted. "We have shown that the **defendant** could not have fired the shot. We have shown that he wore his right arm in a sling on the night of July 14th."

Walter Mitty raised his hand briefly. The arguing attorneys stopped talking. "With any gun, I could have killed Gregory Fitzhurst at 300 feet *with my left hand*," he said evenly.

A near riot broke loose in the courtroom. A

Notice how things that Mitty is doing, seeing, or hearing trigger, or start, another daydream. Here, he hears a boy shouting something about a trial. He then starts daydreaming that he is on trial for murder. Why does he connect the name Waterbury to this daydream?

woman's scream rose above the noise. Suddenly, a lovely dark-haired girl was in Walter Mitty's arms. The District Attorney hit her. Without rising from his chair, Mitty punched the man right on the chin. "You miserable dog!" . . .

"Puppy biscuit," Walter Mitty said. He stopped walking. The buildings of Waterbury rose up out of the imaginary courtroom and surrounded him again.

A woman who was passing laughed. "He said 'Puppy biscuit,'" she said to her friend. "That man said 'Puppy biscuit' to himself."

Walter Mitty hurried on. He went into a supermarket. "I want some dog biscuits for small, young dogs," he said to the clerk.

"Any special brand, sir?"

The greatest pistol shot in the world thought for a moment. "It says 'Puppies Bark for It' on the box," Walter Mitty said.

The description "the greatest pistol shot in the world," refers to what Mitty was in his last daydream.

Mitty looked at his watch. His wife would be finished at the hairdresser's in fifteen minutes. She'd be done unless they had trouble drying her hair. Sometimes they had trouble drying it. She didn't like to get to the hotel first. She would want him to be there waiting for her as usual.

He found a big leather chair in the lobby of the hotel, facing a window. He put the overshoes and the puppy biscuits on the floor beside the chair. He picked up an old copy of *Liberty* magazine and sank down into the chair. He read, "Can Germany Conquer the World Through the Air?" Walter Mitty looked at the pictures of bombing planes and ruined streets.

. . . "Young Raleigh is too frightened by the enemy firing on us. He doesn't want to go, sir," said the **sergeant**.

What triggers this daydream?

Captain Mitty looked up at him. "Get him to bed," he said wearily, "with the others. I'll fly alone."

"But you can't, sir," said the sergeant anxiously. "It

In this metaphor, war is
compared to a storm. It
thunders and it batters at
the door the way hail or
rain does.

takes two men to handle that bomber."

"Somebody has got to get the weapons factory,"
Mitty said. "I'm going over." War thundered around the
dugout and battered at the door. Then there was a
shattering of wood, and splinters flew through the room.

"That was a bit close," Captain Mitty said carelessly.

"They're closing in," said the sergeant.

"We only live once, Sergeant," Mitty said with a
slight smile. "Or do we?"

Captain Mitty stood up. He strapped on his huge
Webley-Vickers automatic gun.

"It's twenty-five miles through hell, sir," the sergeant
said.

"After all, what isn't?" Mitty said softly.

The pounding of the cannon increased. There was the *rat-tat-tatting* of the machine guns. From somewhere came the threatening *pocketa-pocketa-pocketa* of the new flame throwers. Walter Mitty walked to the door of the dugout humming a tune. He turned and waved to the sergeant. "Cheerio!" he said. . . .

Something struck his shoulder. "I've been looking all over this hotel for you," Mrs. Mitty said. "Why do you have to hide in this old chair? How did you expect me to find you?"

"Things close in," said Walter Mitty.

"What?" Mrs. Mitty said. "Did you get the what's-its-name? The puppy biscuits? What's in that box?"

"Overshoes," Mitty said.

"Couldn't you have put them on in the store?"

"I was thinking," Walter Mitty said. "Does it ever occur to you that I am sometimes thinking?"

She looked at him. "I'm going to take your temperature when I get you home," she said.

They went out through the revolving doors. It was two blocks to the parking lot. At the drugstore on the corner, she said, "Wait here for me. I forgot something. I won't be a minute."

She was more than a minute. Walter Mitty waited. It began to rain, rain with sleet in it. He stood up against the wall of the drugstore . . .

He put his shoulders back and his heels together. Then, with a slight, fleeting smile, he faced the firing squad. He stood straight, still, and proud. He was Walter Mitty the **Undefeated**, mysterious to the last.

Mrs. Malaprop's Famous Quotations

Have you ever used the wrong word when you were talking to someone? It has happened to all of us.

In 1775, Richard Brinsley Sheridan wrote a play. It was a comedy called *The Rivals*. One character in the play was named Mrs. Malaprop. Mrs. Malaprop often used the wrong words in very funny ways. Sheridan's audiences loved her. They laughed at everything she said.

Mrs. Malaprop became very popular. We still use her name today, over two hundred years later. When we refer to a funny misuse of a word, we call it a malapropism.

Following are two examples of malaprops:

- It was a piece of pie. (Of course, the saying is, "It was a piece of cake.")

- It was as easy as cake. (The real saying is, "It was as easy as pie.")

- I am so hungry, I could eat a house. (This saying is, of course, "I am so hungry, I could eat a horse.")

Can you think of another example of a malaprop?

Literature Practice

Answer these questions on a separate sheet of paper.

1. What personality traits do all of Mitty's fantasy characters have in common?

2. How do people treat the real Mitty? How do people treat Mitty in his fantasies?

3. Thurber uses similes and metaphors in Mitty's fantasies but not when describing his real life. Why do you think Thurber does this?

4. Why do you think Mitty daydreams the way he does?

The Invalid's Story
an adapted story by Mark Twain

Words to Know

LITERARY TERMS

dialogue conversation between characters in literature

fiction literature that tells about events and people that are not real

SELECTION VOCABULARY

invalid a sick, weak person

athlete a person trained in sports who has great physical strength

actual real

driving strong, vigorous

express nonstop, high speed

departed dead

trance a coma, state of being unconscious

suffocating unable to breathe

aimless pointless, purposeless

hoarsely gruffly, harshly

I look like I am sixty years old and married. But that is because of my condition and my sufferings. I am really unmarried and only forty-one years old. It will be hard for you to believe that I was a healthy, strong man two short years ago. I used to be a man of iron, an **athlete**! Now I am only a shadow. This is the simple truth.

The way in which I lost my health is a strange story. I lost it when I was helping to take care of a box full of guns on a 200-mile train ride one winter's night. This is the **actual** truth, and I will tell you about it.

I live in Cleveland, Ohio. One winter's night, two years ago, I came home just after dark. I had arrived

Though this tale is fiction, Twain uses many fiction writer's "tricks" to make us think that the story really happened. For example, the narrator tells us twice in the first two paragraphs that his story is the truth.

in a **driving** snowstorm. When I entered the house, I found out that my dearest boyhood friend, John B. Hackett, had died the day before. I also found out that in his last words he asked that I take his body home to his poor, old father and mother in Wisconsin.

I was very surprised and very saddened. But there was no time to waste in emotions. I had to start right away. I picked up the card marked "Deacon Levi Hackett, Bethlehem, Wisconsin." Then I hurried off through the whistling storm to the train station.

When I arrived there, I found the long, wooden box that had been described to me. I fastened the card to it with some nails. Then I watched a man put it safely aboard the **express** car. After that, I ran into the dining room in the train station to buy a sandwich.

When I returned in a little while, there was a box that looked just like my coffin-box *back again*! A young fellow was looking all around it. He had a card in his hands and some nails and a hammer! I was surprised and puzzled. He began to nail on his card. I rushed out to the express car, in a terrible state of mind, to ask for an explanation. But no! There was my box in the express car. It hadn't been moved.

I didn't know it, but a huge mistake had been made. In my box was a load of *guns*. That young fellow owned them and had come to the station to ship them to a rifle company in Peoria, Illinois. But *he* had got in his box the body of my dead friend!]

Just then the conductor sang out, "All aboard." I jumped into the express car and got a comfortable seat on a pile of buckets. The expressman was there hard at work. He was a plain man of fifty. He had an honest, happy face and a friendly way about him.

As the train moved off, a stranger skipped through the car. He set a package of very old and very stinky Limburger cheese on one end of my coffin box. I mean my box of guns. That is to say, *now* I know that it was Limburger cheese. But at that time, I had never

Have you ever noticed that some cheeses have very strong smells? Perhaps the worst smelling cheese of all is Limburger.

heard of this cheese in my life. So, of course, I had no idea what it was like.

Well, we sped through the wild night with a terrible storm outside. Soon I became sad and miserable. My heart went down, down! The old expressman made a remark about the freezing weather. Then he slammed his sliding doors shut, locked them, and closed his window tight. He continued to busy himself here and there around the car. All the time, he happily hummed "Sweet By and By" in a low voice.

Soon I began to notice a terrible, stinking odor in the frozen air. This odor made me even more miserable. Of course, I thought the smell was the dead body of my dear **departed** friend. I was upset, too, because I thought the old expressman might notice it. However, he went humming happily on and gave no sign. For this I was grateful.

I may have been grateful, but I was still uneasy. Soon I began to feel more and more uneasy every minute. For every minute that went by, the smell thickened up more and more. It became more and more difficult to stand.

Soon the expressman got some wood and built a huge fire in his stove. This fire upset me more than I can tell, for I believed that it was a mistake. I was sure that the heat would harm the body of my poor departed friend.

Thompson—that was the expressman's name—now went poking around his car. He stopped up whatever stray cracks he could find in the walls. He said that it didn't make any difference what type of a night it was outside. He was going to make us comfortable, anyway.

I said nothing. But I believed he was not choosing the right way. Meanwhile he was humming to himself just as before. Meanwhile, too, the stove was getting hotter and hotter, and the place stuffier and stuffier. I

The small details that Twain includes are another trick to make this story seem like it really happened. Here, Twain tells us which song the expressman hums. As you continue to read, look for other details, or "tricks," that make this story seem like it really happened.

felt myself growing pale and slightly ill. But I was silent and said nothing.

Soon I noticed that the "Sweet By and By" was gradually fading out. Next, it stopped altogether. Then there was an uneasy stillness. After a few moments, Thompson spoke up.

"Pfew! It ain't no cinnamon I've loaded up this-here stove with!"

He gasped once or twice. Then he moved toward the cof—gun-box. He stood over the Limburger cheese for a moment. Then he came back and sat down near me. He looked a good deal changed.

After a pause, he pointed to the box. "Friend of yours?" he asked.

"Yes," I said with a sigh.

"He's pretty ripe, *ain't* he!"

Nothing further was said for perhaps a couple of minutes. Each of us was busy with his own thoughts. Then Thompson spoke up again in a low voice.

"Sometimes it's uncertain whether they're really gone or not. They *seem* gone, you know—body warm and limp. So, although you *think* they're gone, you don't really know. I've had cases in my car. It's perfectly awful, because *you* don't know what minute they'll sit up and look at you!" Then after a pause, he slightly lifted his elbow toward the box. "But *he* ain't in any **trance**!" he said. "No, sir."

We sat for some time, thinking. We listened to the wind and the roar of the train. Then Thompson spoke again with a good deal of feeling.

"Well-a-well, we've all got to go. There's no getting around it. Man that is born of woman is of few days and far between, as the Bible says. Yes, you look at it any way you want to. There isn't anybody can get around it. *All's* got to go—just *everybody*, as you may say. One day you're healthy and strong."

Here he got to his feet and broke a window pane and stretched his nose out for a moment or two. Then

he sat down again while I got up and thrust my nose out at the same place. We kept on doing this every now and then.

"The next day he's cut down like the grass. Yes'n deedy, we've all got to go, one time or another. There's no getting around it."

There was another long pause. Then he said, "What did he die of?"

I said I didn't know.

"How long has he been dead?"

It seemed wise not to tell him it was only yesterday. So I said, "Two or three days."

However, it did no good. For Thompson received it with a hurt look. It was a look that plainly said, "Two or three *years*, you mean." Then he went right along, like he hadn't heard my statement. He gave his views at great length upon the foolishness of putting off burials too long. Then he walked off toward the box. After a moment, he came back at a sharp trot and visited the broken window pane.

"It would have been a darn sight better if they'd started him along last summer," he said.

Thompson sat down and buried his face in his red silk handkerchief. He began to slowly rock his body. He looked like someone suffering to put up with something impossible.

By this time, the smell was just about **suffocating**. Thompson's face was turning gray. I knew mine didn't have any color left in it. Soon Thompson rested his forehead in his left hand, with his elbow on his knee. He sort of waved his red handkerchief toward the box with his other hand.

"I've carried a many a one of 'em," he said. "Some of them were really ripe, too. But, lordy, he just lays over 'em all!—and does it *easy*. Cap, they were sweet roses compared to *him*!"

Thompson began to mumble in an **aimless** and low-spirited way. He started calling my poor friend by different titles. Sometimes he gave him military titles, sometimes civil ones. I noticed that as my friend's odor grew, Thompson gave him a bigger title.

Finally, he said, "I've got an idea. Suppose we give the Colonel a shove toward the other end of the car? Say about ten feet. We wouldn't smell him so much then, don't you think?"

I said it was a good plan. We took in a good fresh breath at the broken window pane and held it. Then we went there and bent over that deadly cheese. We grabbed onto the box. Thompson nodded, "All ready." Then we threw ourselves forward with all our might.

Thompson slipped, however. He fell down with his nose on the cheese and his breath got loose. He choked and gasped and made a break for the door. "Don't stop me," he said **hoarsely**. "Gimme the road! I'm dying, gimme the road!"

Notice how Twain uses dialogue to tell what is going on in the story. It also tells what his characters are thinking. In good dialogue like this, the dialogue even *describes* the characters. Readers can almost see their facial expressions by listening to what they say and how they say it. They become real people.

Out on the cold platform, I sat down and held his head awhile. In a moment, he felt better. Presently he said, "Do you think we moved the General any?"

I said no, we hadn't moved him a bit.

"Well, then, that idea's up in smoke. We got to think up something else. He likes it where he is, I guess. He's made up his mind he don't wish to be troubled. If that's so, you bet he's going to have his own way. Yes, better leave him right where he is. Because he holds all the cards. It stands to reason that the man that lays out to change his plans for him is going to get left."

However, we couldn't stay out there in that mad storm. We would have frozen to death. So we went in again and shut the door. We began to suffer once more and took turns at the break in the window. Soon, we began to move away from a station where we had stopped for a moment.

Thompson danced in happily and shouted, "We're all right, now! I think we've got the Commodore this time. I judge I've got the stuff here that will take the smell out of him."

It was acid. He had a large glass bottle filled with it. He sprayed it all around everywhere. In fact, he soaked everything with it—rifle box, cheese, and all. Then we sat down feeling pretty hopeful. But it wasn't for long. You see, the two smells began to mix—and then. Well, pretty soon we made a break for the door. Out there, Thompson wiped his face with his handkerchief. Then he spoke up in an unhappy way.

"It's no use. We can't fight against *him*. He just uses everything we use to change him. He gives it his own flavor and plays it back on us. Why, Cap, it's 100 times worse in there now than it was when he first got going. I never *did* see one of 'em start to smell so. No sir, not as long as I've been on the road. And I've carried a many of one of 'em, as I was telling you."

We went in again after we were frozen pretty stiff. But my, we couldn't *stay* in now. So we just walked back and forth, freezing and warming up, and choking by turns. In about an hour, we stopped at another station. Thompson came in with a bag.

"Cap, I'm going to give him one more chance," he said. "Just this once, and if we don't get him this time—. Well, the thing for us to do then is to just throw in the towel."

He had a lot of chicken feathers, and dried apples, and leaf tobacco, and rags. He also had some old shoes and some leaves from a plant. He piled everything on some sheet iron in the middle of the floor. Then he set fire to them.

When they got going, I couldn't see how anything could stand it. All that went before was nothing compared to that new smell. But mind you, the original smell stood up out of it just as strong as ever.

The fact is, these other smells just seemed to give it a better hold. And my, how rich it was!

I didn't have these thoughts right there. There wasn't time. I had them on the platform. Breaking for the platform, Thompson suffocated and fell. Before I got him dragged out, I was almost gone myself. When we came to, Thompson spoke up again.

"We got to stay out here, Cap. We got to do it. There isn't any other way. The Governor wants us to leave him alone. He's fixed so he can make us do it."

Then soon, he added, "And don't you know, we're *poisoned*. It's *our* last trip. You can make up your mind to it. Typhoid fever is what's going to come of this. I feel it coming right now. Yes, sir, we're sick with the fever. Just as sure as you're born."

We were taken from the platform an hour later at the next station. We were frozen and senseless. I went

Typhoid fever is a deadly disease. It can easily spread from person to person. It was a very common disease in Mark Twain's time.

straight off into a terrible fever and never knew anything again for three weeks.

I found out then that I had spent the night with a harmless box of rifles and a lot of smelly cheese. But the news was too late to save *me*. Imagination had done its work. My health was gone for good. Neither Bermuda nor any other land can ever bring it back to me. This is my last trip. I am on my way home to die.

Literature Practice

Answer these questions on a separate sheet of paper.

1. Why is the narrator taking a coffin on the train?

2. What is really in the box?

3. What do you think would have been the reaction of the person who opened the box sent to Peoria?

4. What would you have done if you were in the boxcar with the coffin and the cheese?

5. Twain writes, "Imagination had done its work." What do you think Twain means by this statement?

6. What lesson do you think Twain wants readers to learn from this story?

Chapter Review

Summaries

- **The Secret Life of Walter Mitty**—This is a funny story about a man who likes to daydream. The story begins in the middle of a daydream. Walter Mitty imagines that he is a Navy Commander aboard a hydroplane. He is bravely taking his men through a hurricane. But Mitty is then brought back to reality. He is in a car, taking his nagging wife to town. While he is in town, Mitty keeps imagining that he is different people. He imagines that he is a famous doctor. He then imagines being an expert gunman. Next, he imagines that he is a fighter pilot. At the end, he imagines that he is facing death before a firing squad.

- **The Invalid's Story**—The narrator's friend dies. He agrees to take the dead body home to be buried. On the train, the box with the body in it is switched with a box of guns. But the narrator does not know that the boxes have been switched. Someone leaves a package of smelly cheese in the box of guns. The narrator thinks that the smell is from the dead body. The expressman on the train also thinks the smell is the body. The two men try to cover up the smell, but they cannot. To get away from the smell, they ride outside the boxcar. It is snowing and is very cold. The narrator gets sick. He later finds out that the smell came from Limburger cheese. But it is too late. The narrator is so sick that he is going home to die.

Chapter Quiz

Choose the letter of the correct answer. Rewrite the sentences on a separate sheet of paper.

1. In "The Secret Life of Walter Mitty," what does Mitty imagine himself to be like?
   a. weak
   b. a great hero
   c. funny
   d. a boring, old man

2. How does Mitty's wife treat him?
   a. She treats him like an important man.
   c. She acts like he is a hero.
   b. She nags him.
   d. She makes him happy.

3. In "The Invalid's Story," what is the narrator supposed to take on the train?
   a. a box of guns
   c. his friend's body in a coffin
   b. a bag of cinnamon
   d. some cheese

4. The narrator does not know about the cheese. What does he think is causing the smell?
   a. the rotting dead body
   c. the guns
   b. the wood from the fire
   d. some roses

5. Why does the narrator become so sick at the end of the story?
   a. He stays outside in the snowstorm.
   c. He catches typhoid fever.
   b. He faints from the heat of the car.
   d. He is allergic to cheese.

Thinking and Writing

Answer the following questions on a separate sheet of paper. Write one or two paragraphs for each one.

1. In "The Secret Life of Walter Mitty," Mitty imagines that he has great adventures. If you were writing this story about your life, what adventure would you have? How would other people treat you? Explain.

2. Write a newspaper article about what happens in "The Invalid's Story." Include lots of funny details.

3. In "The Invalid's Story," the narrator says that he will die because of his imagination. Why do you think he says this?

Unit Seven Review

A. Decide whether each statement below is true or false. If it is false, rewrite the statement on a separate sheet of paper so that it is true.

1. In "The Secret Life of Walter Mitty," Mitty imagines that he lives an ordinary life.
2. In "At Last I Kill a Buffalo," Luther Standing Bear regrets telling his father the truth.
3. In "The Invalid's Story," the narrator gets sick because of his imagination.
4. In "Escape: A Slave Narrative," the Quaker does not invite the narrator in.

B. The following questions are about the selections you read in this unit. Write one or two sentence answers on a separate sheet of paper.

1. "Escape: A Slave Narrative" is part of James Pennington's autobiography. What other selection in this unit is part of an autobiography?
2. "The Commander's voice is like thin ice breaking." What literary term is this sentence an example of?
3. What is the definition of dialogue?

C. Answer the essay questions below on a separate sheet of paper. Write one or two paragraphs for each one.

1. Which selection in this unit do you think is the best adventure story? Why?
2. Choose one of the selections in this unit. Write another ending to the story. Then explain how your ending changes the story.

Appendix

Glossary

Handbook of Literary Terms

Index of Authors and Titles

Acknowledgments

Art and Photo Credits

Index of Fine Art

GLOSSARY

abandoned   left alone, deserted

accept   admit, give in to

accordion   a musical instrument played by squeezing and pulling it

ached   hurt

actual   real

affrighted   afraid of; frightened

aflame   very warm and alive

aimless   pointless, purposeless

aimlessly   without a goal or place to go

amid   among, surrounded by

amigo   a friend; an amigo brother is a best friend

ancestors   people in your family who came before you, such as your parents and grandparents

appliances   household machines, such as dishwashers and refrigerators

appreciate   value, cherish

assurance   confidence

assure   make a person sure of something; comfort

athlete   a person trained in sports who has great physical strength

authentic   genuine; real

auxiliary   back up; supporting

awl   a sharp pointed tool for making holes in leather

balance   steadiness; being stable

balm   something that makes someone or something feel better

barracks   a group of buildings used for temporary housing

barren   empty, dull, not interesting

bayonets   rifles with steel knives attached to the end of the barrel

beseeching   begging

betrayed   broke someone's trust; disappointed

blacksmith   a person who shapes hot iron into horseshoes, pots, and other metal objects

bleak   cheerless, unhappy

blurry   when something cannot be seen clearly

boast   brag

bold   without fear or shame

bond   money paid as bail so the accused can be freed from jail

bosom   chest

boutique   a small, fashionable shop

bouts   fights or matches

brawn   strength

brute   beast, animal

buffalo   a large furry animal from the oxen family

burial   bury the dead

burrow   a hole an animal digs in the ground

captors   people who capture, or catch, someone

casks   kegs or barrels

cavern   a large cave

centuries   periods of a hundred years time

ceremonies   special events, such as weddings and graduations

challenger   in boxing, the one who fights the champion

challenging   daring someone to a contest

champion   the winner of a match or series of matches

channeled   made into passageways

chariot   a two-wheeled, horse-drawn cart used in battles, races or parades during ancient times

choir   a singing group

choke   to block or clog

citizens   people living in a city or country who have rights under the law

civil rights   rights which are guaranteed to an individual by the U.S. Constitution

civilization   an area where people live and do business

clawed   to have dug with nails

clefted   split; divided

clerk   an official in charge of records and accounts

clod   a small clump of earth and grass

clumsy   awkward

commence   start; begin

commodity   a thing that can be traded or sold; goods

communicate   talk; express thoughts and feelings

contact   two things or people coming together

continuous   something that keeps happening; constant

convinced   made to feel sure

corpse   a dead body

courteously   politely; with manners

courtesy   good manners, kindness

cranes large birds with very long legs and necks and long, straight bills

craze drive

cremated burned a dead body

crevices folds; wrinkles

crinkling wrinkling

crisis turning point, climax

cruel very mean, unfeeling

crystal clear glass or stone that is expensive

cuddles holds or hugs with love

curious eager to learn or know

curry groom, brush

customary something that is normally done

customs special habits, traditions, things that people do regularly

cylinder a long, round tube

dashing very stylish

debates thinks about; tries to decide

decayed rotten; plants which are slowly broken down

defendant a person on trial for a crime

defiance not doing something you're told to do

degrading insulting, embarrassing

densely thickly, close together

departed dead

depth deepness; low pitched

derelict something thrown away

descendants people in your family who came after you, such as your children and grandchildren

desperate frantic; hopeless

destiny the future, fate

determination firmness of purpose or mind

dewy air which is full of water drops

diadem a crown

discerned understood

discipline punishment, correction

disputed argued, quarreled

distinguished seen, identified, recognized

division in boxing, a group or class of boxers

draw a tie; the fighters have equal points at the end of the match

dread great worry or fear

dreary gloomy and dull

drive to force a piece of metal, or a chisel, into rock with a hammer

driving strong, vigorous

ecstasy great feeling of joy

encircled made a circle around; surrounded

engaged planning to get married

entreating asking

evoke bring out

exaggerated made something seem better than it really is

exile forced away from one's country or home

explode blow up, go off

exploits heroic or bold actions

explosion blast from a bomb bursting

express nonstop, high speed

faded dull; no longer bright

farewell a way of saying "good-bye"

fast held tight, fastened

fathomless not understood

felled cut down

fierce violent, cruel

film a thin coat of something

flail a farm tool used to cut seed from a plant

flourishing growing well

forge a blacksmith's fire where metal is heated and shaped

foul play dishonest behavior, murder

frail weak, thin

fugitive runaway; hunted person

furious very angry

furrow the strip that a plow makes as it goes through the soil

gait a way of walking or running

gasped the sound heard when a person very loudly and quickly draws in a breath after being shocked or surprised

generosity willingness to give; unselfishness

ghastly awfully

gigantic very large

give recompense can reward

glaciers huge layers of ice

glimpse a peek; a quick look

gnarled knotty; twisted

gratification something that makes you feel thankful

greed wanting too much

grenadiers soldiers who carried small bombs in their hands

grisly terrible

grounds area of land around a building

grove a small group of trees

grub food

grunt   a deep, unpleasant sound

guilty   did something against the law; proven to have committed a crime

harbors   places where ships can land

hardship   trouble; pain and suffering

harpoon   a spear used for whaling

harsh   cruel, unpleasant

haughty   proud acting, stuck up

hauled   pulled

haunted   reappeared, often in a scary way

harkened   answered

heed   pay attention to

helm   a ship's steering wheel

heritage   family or cultural background

hist   hush, silence

hoarse   grating, harsh

hoarsely   gruffly, harshly

hopper   grain bin

humble   not proud

humblest   most simple

hydroplane   an airplane that can land on water

hymn   a song of praise to God

ignored   did not pay attention to

image   copy, close likeness

impetuous   to act in a sudden way

implore   to beg for

impressed   made someone think highly of something

impulse   a force that pushes forward or a sudden desire to act

increased   became greater in degree

insulting   disrespectful; hurting someone's feelings

intense   something that is very strong

intern   a doctor in-training

invalid   a sick, weak person

invisible   cannot be seen

jerked   gave a quick pull or twist

joint   a section of a finger

justified   showed to be right

knead   fold, press, and squeeze dough to mix it

knots   a measurement of a ship's speed

lack   need

lairs   animals' homes; dens

lantern   a lamp or light with a cover that can be carried

latching   holding tightly

latitude   the distance north and south from the Earth's equator

leathery   like leather

lightweight   a weight class for boxers from 127 to 135 pounds

lineage   a direct line of family members from the past to today

loathed   hated

locomotive   an engine used to push or pull railroad cars

logging   cutting trees down for wood

longitude   the distance east and west from Greenwich, England

lopsided   uneven

manifold   many times over

mantel   a shelf over a fireplace

marge   edge

mark   a written line or check used in a book to show where a person should begin reading

marksmanship   aim, accuracy in shooting

measure   walk across

memoir   a record of events

mighty   very; extremely

mingle   mix; join with others

mischievousness   playfulness or naughtiness

moil   work hard for

molding   the trim on a wall or ceiling

moorings   a place where a boat is tied up; anchors, weights to hold down ships

mortals   humans

mount   rise; go up

muffled   made less loud or less clear; deadened the sound

mushing   traveling on a sled pulled by dogs

muttered   said softly

narrative   a story

neglected   ignored; failed to care for

nor ought   nothing

notch   a V-shape mark cut into a material, such as wood or cloth

nourishment   food to keep one healthy and alive

numbed   deadened; unable to feel as a result of the cold

obeisance   a bow or another sign of respect

objection   in a court of law: a complaint against something said

oration   a speech

orbit   area stayed in

orchid   a beautiful flower

outlive   last longer than someone or something else

overcome   defeat or beat; master

overturn   turn or tip over

paced   walked back and forth

parings   shavings, scraps

pallid   pale

pampered   treated with a great deal of attention; spoiled

paradise   a heaven on earth

particular   separate; special

passion   a strong or deep feeling

patiently   calmly putting up with something

pause   to stop or wait a short time

paved   put a road surface on

peril   danger

permit   allow

persevere   continue on

phony   fake, not truthful or real

pickaxe   tool with a sharp point

picnickers   people who are having picnics; eating outside

pier   a landing or walkway extending out into a body of water

pierced   made a hole; stabbed; broke through

pioneers   early settlers

pitifully   very sadly

plain   flat land, as in a valley, without trees

plantation   a large piece of property on which crops are grown

platform   where one waits for a train

plough   a farm tool used to cut and turn over soil

plowshare   the blade of a plow, or farm machine, used to cut the soil

possessed   took hold of; owned

pout   make a face to show you are unhappy; frown; sulk

powwow   a meeting or gathering of the tribe

prairie   a large area of land with rich soil, grass, and very few trees

prefer   to choose one over another

prejudiced   intolerant, closed-minded, racist

preserved   food prepared in a special way, such as dryingor canning, so it can be saved for a long time

procession   people moving forward one after another

profusely   many; freely

protection   defense against harm or danger

protest   to speak out against something that seems unfair

prowling   sneaking, hiding out

pulpit   a raised platform where a person stands to give a worship service

pyramid   a structure with a square base and four triangular sides that meet at the top

quaint   old-fashioned, out of date

quarter   area, section

quench   stop or put out

quest   a search

quiver   shaking just a little bit

quivering   shaking

racism   the belief that some people are superior to others, bigotry

rail   railroad, train

rallied   came together

ravines   valleys

recalled   remembered

referee   the person who judges the match

reflection   an image given back, like from a mirror

refresh   make fresh again; renew

refugee   a person who leaves their country to seek safety in another country

regiment   group of soldiers

regret   to feel sorry for something that happened

reluctantly   not wanting to do something; unwillingly

reputation   what people generally think about a person; fame

requirements   what is needed

resistance   fighting back

resolved   decided

rickety   weak; about to fall down

ritual   a practice done over and over, often religious

roaring   making a huge, loud sound

roomers   people who pay money to live in a room or building

rut   a track made in the ground by wheels

sacred   holy; belonging to or God

sacredness   being worthy of deep respect

salvation   rescue, deliverance from harm

scab   the crust that forms on the skin where a sore or cut is healing

scooped   picked up

scuttling   running or moving quickly

seized   grabbed suddenly

seldom   not often; rarely

sentinel   a guard

serenade   sing below someone's window to get his or her attention

sergeant   an officer in the armed forces

shade   color

sharecropper   someone who works a farm for part of the crop

shroud   a cloth used to wrap a dead body

shutters   attached window covers

silhouette   a dark shape or outline seen against a light background

skulk   sneak away, slink

slaughter   killing, slaying

slugger   hitter

sod   earth, soil, dirt

sowing   planting

sparring   boxing

spectacular   unusual, an exciting show

spiritual   a religious song, first created by African Americans living in the South during the 18th and 19th centuries, which combined elements of European and African music

splinters   thin, sharp pieces of wood that can stick into feet or hands

startled   surprised

stately   appearing important and worthy of respect

steam drill   a machine that uses steam power and a sharp tool to cut a hole through rock

steed   war horse

steel-drivin'   using a hammer to pound a pointed piece of metal, or chisel, into rock

steep   a very high hill

steward   a person who takes care of the food and people on a ship

store   keep; collect

stroke   a sudden attack of illness

sturdiness   strength

sturdy   strong; stable

subway   a train that runs underground

suede   soft leather

sufficient   as much as is needed; enough

suffocating   unable to breathe

surcease   stop

sway   swing or move from side to side

tackle   take hold of; start to do something difficult

temptation something that makes you think about doing something wrong

tenement apartment building

terror great fear

texture surface; the way a certain surface feels

thrashing whipping, tossing about

threatened in danger

toil work hard; labor

token sign

tolerably fairly good

tollgate a place where one pays a fee to travel a road or cross a bridge

tongue language

tornado a fierce, twisting wind

tottering rocking back and forth and almost falling

touched made to feel deeply

trailing hanging down

trance a coma, state of being unconscious

tremble shake or shiver

trenches ditches, gullies

trice a very short time, a moment

triumph an important success

turret part of an airplane

tweeds wool cloth with a rough surface

undefeated never having lost or been beaten

unearthed dug up

unsung haven't been praised or spoken well of

untamed wild

untapped not used

utter speak

vaults safes where money or jewels are kept

vigor power, strength, energy

vinyl a material made of strong plastic

virtue goodness, uprightness, excellence

visions things that are seen, especially in a dream or while praying

void empty

waltzing dancing a dance for couples

weary tiresome

whereupon after which

whimper whine or cry

whist hush, silence

HANDBOOK OF LITERARY TERMS

alliteration   the repeating of consonant sounds

analogy   a comparison between two different things

apostrophe   in this figure of speech, the poet talks to, or addresses, a person or thing that is not present

assonance   the repeating of vowel sounds

atmosphere   the general mood of a piece of literature; setting, details, and the writer's choice of words create the atmosphere.

autobiographical essay   writing that focuses on one event in the writer's life

autobiography   a true story about a person, told by that person

ballad   a song or poem that tells a story

biography   account of a person's life told by another person

cause and effect   any event or action that leads to a certain result

character   a person in a story

character's motivation   the reason a character does what he or she does in a story

character clues   thoughts, actions, and words in a story that help the reader find out what a character is like

coin words   make up words

colloquial language   the everyday language people use when talking to friends

comparison and contrast   writing that tells how things are alike and how they are different

conflict   a fight or a battle between two or more characters; the problem that needs to be solved in a story

connotation   an idea or feeling suggested by a word

couplet   two lines of poetry—one right after the other—that rhyme

denotation   the plain meaning of a word

description   writing that uses details and the senses to give the reader a feeling of "being there"

descriptive details   details of how something looks, feels, smells, or tastes

details   pieces of information that help to "paint" a picture for the reader

dialogue   conversation between characters in literature

drawing conclusions   forming an opinion based on information

exaggeration   making something seem more than it really is

external conflict   a character's struggle against something outside himself or herself, such as society, nature, or another person

fable   a short story that teaches a lesson

fiction   literature that tells about events and people that are not real

figurative language   words that describe something by making comparisons

first-person point of view   the story or poem is told by a narrator, using the pronouns *I, me,* and *mine*

foreshadowing   clues in a story about what is going to happen next

genre   a type of literary work, such as a novel, short story, poem, drama, biography, or autobiography

idiom   a group of words with a special meaning

imagery   vivid words that help the reader to "see" how something looks, sounds, feels, or tastes

internal conflict   conflict within a person; the character struggles to make a difficult decision

irony   the difference between what seems to be real and what is real

lyric poem   a short poem that expresses the writer's personal feelings and thoughts

making predictions   using what you know and what you have read to tell what might happen next in a story

malapropism   a humorous misuse of a word

metaphor   comparing something to something else to help the reader "see" what the author is writing about; a comparison without *like* or *as*

meter   the rhythm, or beat, in poetry

mood   the feeling one gets from reading a story

myths ancient stories that try to explain the mysteries of the world

narrative hook the point in a story in which the author grabs the reader's attention

narrative poem a poem that tells a story

narrator a person who tells a story

nonfiction literature that tells about things that are real

omniscient point of view the author tells the thoughts and feelings of all the characters; the omniscient narrator uses the third person, *he, she,* and *they*, and stays outside the story

paradox a statement that at first seems impossible but that may actually be or feel true

personification giving human characteristics to nonliving things

quatrain a four-line stanza

quote the words that someone says, written with quotation marks (" ") around the statement

refrain lines repeated in a poem or song

repetition words or sentences used over and over to create a feeling or mood

rhyme words that have the same end sounds

rhyme scheme the pattern of rhyme in a poem

rhythm   a special sound pattern of stressed and unstressed syllables, or beats, in a poem

sensory details   details of how something looks, feels, smells, or tastes

setting   the place and time in which a story occurs

simile   a comparison of two things using *like* or *as*

stanza   a group of lines in a poem or song

symbolism   using something to stand for an idea

tall tale   a story in which facts and details are exaggerated

theme   the main idea of a story, novel, play, or poem

third-person point of view   someone other than a character is telling the story or poem

tone   the feeling the writer shows toward the subject of the poem or story

topic sentence   the sentence that tells the main idea of a paragraph

verbal irony   what is meant may be the opposite of what is said

Index of Authors and Titles

A Chant of Darkness, p. 110
A Taste of Snow, p. 204
A Visit to the Clerk of the Weather, p. 169
Abuela, (Yzquierdo) p. 326
Abuela, (Alcalá) p. 344
Alcalá, Denise, p. 433
Amigo Brothers, p. 276
At Last I Kill a Buffalo, p. 375
Aunt Sue's Stories, p. 350
Avila, Alfred, p. 16
Bailando, p. 353
The Ballad of Birmingham, p. 287
The Ballad of John Henry, p. 103
Behind the Waterfall, p. 127
Big Yellow Taxi, p. 231
Birdfoot's Grampa, p. 218
Bradstreet, Anne, p. 356
Bruchac, Joseph, p. 218
Chase, Owen, p. 194
Chief Seattle's Oration, p. 253
from *Childtimes*, p. 304
The Circuit, p. 80
Colon, Jesus, p. 249
Crane, Stephen, p. 296
The Cremation of Sam McGee, p. 36
Cummings, e.e., p. 43
Dickinson, Emily, p. 215
Douglass, Frederick, p. 239
Dunbar, Paul Laurence, p. 114
Dust Tracks on a Road, p. 51
Escape: A Slave Narrative, p. 364
Fire, John/Lame Deer and Richard Erdoes, p. 60
The First Tornado, p. 177

Frost, Robert, p. 221
Giovanni, Nikki, p. 212
Grandma Ling, p. 347
Greenfield, Eloise and Lessie Jones Little, p. 304
Greenfield, Eloise, p. 107, 148
Harriet Tubman, p. 107
Hawthorne, Nathaniel, p. 169
Hayes, Joe, p. 3
Hist, Whist, p. 43
Houston, Jeanne Wakatsuki, p. 204
Hughes, Langston, p. 139, 335, 350
Hunt, Evelyn Tooley, p. 290
Hurston, Zora Neale, p. 51
I Ask My Mother to Sing, p. 332
In Hardwood Groves, p. 221
The Invalid's Story, p. 399
Izenberg, Jerry, p. 156
The Jacket, p. 91
Jiménez, Francisco, p. 80
Keller, Helen, p. 110
La Llorona: The Weeping Woman, p. 3
Lame Deer Remembers His Childhood, p. 60
Lee, Li-Young, p. 333
Lineage, p. 341
Ling, Amy, p. 347
Little Things Are Big, p. 249
Longfellow, Henry Wadsworth, p. 117
The Medicine Bag, p. 312
Mitchell, Joni, p. 231
Mora, Pat, p. 353
Mother to Son, p. 335
My Father's Song, p. 338

Narrative of the Life of Frederick Douglass, p. 239

Oritz, Simon, p. 338

Osborne, Mary Pope, p. 133

Paul Bunyan, The Mightiest Logger of Them All, p. 133

Paul Revere's Ride, p. 117

Pennington, James W. C., p. 364

The Pepper Tree, p. 16

Piercy, Marge, p. 293

Pijoan de Van Etten, Teresa, p. 181

Poe, Edgar Allan, p. 8, 25

Prisoner of My Country, p. 68

Randall, Dudley, p. 287

The Raven, p. 25

Ribbons, p. 263

River Man, p. 181

Roberto Clemente: A Bittersweet Memoir, p. 156

Rosa Parks, p. 148

Seattle, Chief, p. 253

The Secret Life of Walter Mitty, p. 389

Service, Robert W., p. 36

Shipwreck of the Whaleship Essex, p. 194

Siebert, Diane, p. 224

Sierra, p. 224

Simple-song, p. 293

The Sky Is Low, p. 215

Sneve, Virginia Driving Hawk, p. 312

Soto, Gary, p. 91

Standing Bear, Luther, p. 375

Taught Me Purple, p. 290

Taylor, C. J., p. 177

The Tell-Tale Heart, p. 8

Thank You, M'am, p. 139

Thomas, Piri, p. 276

Thoreau, Henry David, p. 190

Thurber, James, p. 389

To My Dear and Loving Husband, p. 356

Twain, Mark, p. 399

Uchida, Yoshiko, p. 68

The Unsung Heroes, p. 114

Walker, Margaret, p. 341

War Is Kind, p. 296

Winter Animals, p. 190

Winter, p. 212

Wood, Marion, p. 127

Yep, Laurence, p. 263

Yzquierdo, Rosa Elena, p. 326

Acknowledgments

Unit 1

Joe Hayes. *La Llorona/The Weeping Woman: A Hispanic Legend.* Reprinted by permission of Cinco Puntos Press, El Paso, Texas.

"The Pepper Tree" by Alfred Avila, compiled by Kat Avila is reprinted with permission from the publisher of *Mexican Ghost Tales of the Southwest* (Houston: Arte Publico Press–University of Houston, 1994).

E. E. Cummings. "Hist, Whist," Reprinted from *Tulips and Chimneys* by E.E. Cummings, Copyright © 1973, 1976 by Nancy T. Andrews. Copyright © 1973, 1976 by George James Firmage; Gerald Duckworth & Co.

Unit 2

Zora Neale Hurston. Adaptation of excerpt from *Dust Tracks on a Road* by Zora Neale Hurston. Copyright © 1942 by Zora Neale Hurston; Copyright renewed © 1970 by John C. Hurston. Reprinted by permission of HarperCollins publishers, Inc.

Lame Deer Remembers His Childhood. Copyright © 1972 by John Fire/Lame Deer and Richard Erdoes. Reprinted by permission of Simon & Schuster, Inc.

"Prisoner of My Country," from the book: *The Invisible Thread.* By: Yoshiko Uchida, Copyright © 1991.

Francisco Jiménez. Adaptation of "The Circuit." First published by *The Arizona Quarterly* (Autumn, 1973). Copyright © 1973 by Francisco Jiménez.

"The Jacket," from *Small Faces* by Gary Soto. Copyright © 1986 by Gary Soto. Used by permission of Delacorte Press, a division of Bantam Doubleday Dell Publishing Group, Inc.

Unit 3

Unabridged Text of "Harriet Tubman" *Honey, I Love* by Eloise Greenfield. Text: Copyright © 1978 by Eloise Greenfield.

From Dennis Wepman, *Helen Keller: Humanitarian,* Copyright © 1987 by Chelsea House Publishers, a division of Main Line Book Co.

"Behind the Waterfall," from *Spirits, Heroes and Hunters from North American Indian Mythology* by Marion Wood. Copyright © 1981 by Eurobook Limited.

Adaptation of "Paul Bunyan, the Mightiest Logger of Them All," from *American Tall Tales* by Mary Pope Osborne. Copyright © 1991 by Mary Pope Osborne. Reprinted by permission of Alfred A. Knopf, Inc.

"Thank You Ma'am" reprinted by permission of Harold Ober Associates Incorporated. Copyright © 1958 by Langston Hughes. Renewed 1986 by George Houston Bass.

"Rosa Parks" by Eloise Greenfield. Copyright © 1973 By Eloise Greenfield.

Adaptation of "Roberto Clemente: A Bittersweet Memoir," from *Great Latin Sport Figures* by Jerry Izenberg. Reprinted by permission of Jerry Izenberg.

Unit 4

"The First Tornado" taken from *How We Saw the World.* Copyright © 1993 By C. J. Taylor, published by Tundra Books.

Unit 7

Art and Photo Credits

p. 2:   Art Resource, NY

p. 4-6:   Illustrations by Andre Maroc

p. 10-14:   Illustrations by Sam Vaughn

p. 19:   National Museum of American Art, Washington, DC /Art Resource

p. 20:   Art Resource

p. 24-32:   The Bettmann Archive

p. 37-39:   UPI /Bettmann

p. 45:   The Bettmann Archive

p. 50:   Courtesy of the Corcoran Gallery of Art

p. 55-65:   Illustrations by Laurie Harden

p. 69:   Security Pacific National Bank Photograph Collection / Los Angeles
               Public Library

p. 72:   National Archives # 210-GC-324

p. 79:   The Bettmann Archive

p. 83-86:   Giraudon /Art Resource, NY

p. 92-95:   Illustrations by P. M. Blanchard

p. 102:   National Museum of American Art, Washington DC /Art Resource, NY

p. 104:   The Granger Collection

p. 108:   Courtesy of The Library of Congress

p. 111:   Library of Congress

p. 115-120:   The Granger Collection

p. 126:   National Museum of American Art, Art Resource

p. 128-130:   Illustrations by Steven Cavallo

p. 135:   The Granger Collection

p. 140-143:   Illustrations by David Tamara

p. 147:   UPI /Bettmann

p. 149:   The Bettmann Archive

p. 153:   UPI /Bettmann

p. 157:   National Museum of American Art, Washington DC /Art
               Resource, NY

p. 161:   UPI /Bettmann

p. 168:	National Museum of American Art, Washington, DC /Art Resource, NY
p. 170-173:	The Bettmann Archive
p. 178:	National Museum of American Art, Washington, DC /Art Resource, NY
p. 179:	The Bettmann Archive
p. 185:	National Museum of American Art, Washington, DC /Art Resource, NY
p. 189:	Art Resource
p. 191:	National Museum of American Art / Hemphill Collection /Art Resource, NY
p. 196:	The Granger Collection
p. 198-200:	The Bettmann Archive
p. 205:	Geoffrey Gove
p. 211:	The Bettmann Archive
p. 213:	National Museum of American Art, Washington, DC /Art Resource, NY
p. 216:	The Bettmann Archive
p. 219:	The Bettmann Archive
p. 222:	Art Resource, NY
p. 225:	The Bettmann Archive
p. 226:	National Museum of American Art, Washington, DC /Art Resource, NY
p. 228:	Grant Heilman Photography
p. 233:	Art Resource, NY
p. 238:	National Museum of American Art, Washington, DC /Art Resource, NY
p. 242:	Illustration by Laurie Harden
p. 245:	National Museum of American Art, Washington, DC /Art Resource, NY
p. 246:	Courtesy of the Sophia Smith Collection
p. 250:	National Museum of Art, Washington, DC /Art Resource, NY
p. 254:	The Granger Collection

p. 257:	The Bettmann Archive
p. 262:	The Bettmann Archive
p. 264-275:	Illustrations by Donna Nettis
p. 278-280:	Illustrations by Laura Lou Pollock
p. 286:	The Bettmann Archive
p. 288:	Anton Cobb
p. 291:	National Museum of American Art, Washington, DC /Art Resource, NY
p. 294:	Tate Gallery, London /Art Resource, NY
p. 297:	Bettmann
p. 303:	National Museum of American Art, Washington, DC /Art Resource, NY
p. 306-310:	Illustrations by Jan Spivey Gilchrist
p. 314-321:	Illustrations by Eileen Sandeen
p. 327:	The Bettmann Archive
p. 331-336:	National Museum of American Art, Wahington, DC /Art Resource NY
p. 339:	UPI /Bettmann
p. 342:	Ariel Skelley /The Stock Market
p. 345:	Courtesy of Carmen Lomas Garza
p. 348:	UPI /Bettmann
p. 351:	Cincinnati Art Museum
p. 354:	Courtesy of Tony Ortega
p. 357-363:	National Museum of American Art, Washington DC /Art Resource, NY
p. 365:	Illustrations by Steve Mc Daniel
p. 373:	Steve Mc Daniel
p. 379-383:	The Granger Collection
p. 388:	The Bettmann Archive
p. 390-396:	Illustrations by Sam Vaughn
p. 403-407:	Illustrations by Steve Cavallo
p. 412:	National Museum of American Art, Washington, DC /Art Resource NY

Index of Fine Art

p. 2:   *Night Shadows*, Edward Hopper

p. 19:   *Georgia Landscape*, Hale Aspacio Woodruff

p. 20:   *Apocalypse of St. Jean,* Rufino Tamayo

p. 27:   *The Girl I Left Behind Me,* Eastman Johnson

p. 29:   *Moon Mad Crow*, Morris Graves

p. 32:   *Captive Bird*, Karl Zerbe

p. 50:   *A Pastoral Visit in Virginia*, Richard Norris Brooke

p. 79:*   *Girl Jumping Rope*, Ben Shahn

p. 83:   *The Flower Vendor*, Diego Rivera

p. 84:   *The Rural Schoolteacher* (detail of mural), Diego Rivera

p. 86:   *Fruits of Labor,* Diego Rivera

p. 102:   *Underground Railroad*, William H. Johnson

p. 104:   *Ballad of John Henry*, William Gropper

p. 126:   *The Library*, Jacob Lawrence

p. 157:   *Baseball at Night*, Morris Kantor

p. 168:   *Day,* Paul Manship

p. 178:   *Enchanted Rider*, Bob Thompson

p. 179:   *Listen to the Living*, Matta Echaurren

p. 185:   *Swing Low, Sweet Chariot*, William H. Johnson

p. 189:   *Horse Running Before the Storm*, Anonymous

p. 191:   *Stag at Echo Rock*, M.A. Hall

p. 211:   *April Showers*, Abraham Rattner

p. 213:   *Orion in December*, Charles E. Burchfield

p. 216:   *Landscape*, Georgia O'Keefe

p. 219:   *Sunday Painting,* Ben Shahn

p. 222:   *Greenwood Lake*, detail Jasper Francis Cropsey

p. 225:   *Yosemite,* Albert Bierstadt

p. 226: *Rainbow Over Grand Canyon of the Yellowstone*, Thomas Moran

p. 233: *Telegraph Poles with Buildings*, Joseph Stella

p. 238: *Civilization is a method of living, an attitude of equal respect*, George Giusti

p. 245: *Three Great Abolitionists*, William H. Johnson

p. 250: *Subway*, Lily Furedi

p. 262: *The Fisherman's Last Supper*, Marsden Hartley

p. 286: *The Resurrection*, Jose Clemente Orozco

p. 291: *Gwendolyn*, John Sloan

p. 294: *Man and Woman*, Rufino Tamayo

p. 303: *Shadow and Sunlight*, Allan Rowan Crite

p. 327: *Pulpit Flowers*, Robert Gwathmey

p. 331: *Story Teller*, Velino Shije Herra

p. 332: *Water Lily*, John La Farge

p. 336: *Berthelia*, Doris Rosenthal

p. 345: *Tamalada*, Carmen Lomas Garza

p. 351: *The Underground Railway*, Charles T. Webber

p. 354: *Four Couples Dancing*, Tony Ortega

p. 357: *In The Garden*, Childe Hassan

p. 363: *Going West*, Jackson Pollock

p. 388: *The Chase*, Ralph Blakelock

p. 412: *The Unveiling of the Statue of Liberty*, Katherine Westphal Rossbach